The Football Thesaurus

THE FOOTBALL THESAURUS

Jesse Goldberg-Strassler

With warmest wishes,

Jesse Goldberg-Strassler

 **August Publications**

Middleton, WI

To my mother

CONTENTS

COPYRIGHT

The Football Thesaurus

Lineup Books / August Publications
3543 John Muir Dr.
Middleton, WI 53562
608.836.3730
augustpublications.com

Print ISBN: 978-1-938532-25-2
eBook ISBN: 978-1-938532-18-4

9 8 7 6 5 4 3 2 1

Designer (cover): Natalie Nowytski. Original design: Funnel Incorporated, Lin Wilson.

FOREWORD

I'm fortunate enough to get the chance to earn a living on the fields, and in the arenas of sport. It's a dream job, having the opportunity to be in some of the best seats in the house for some of the best games each week. In those seats, I've witnessed tremendous moments, from the Final Four to the AFC and NFC Championship games. But I've always been puzzled by a characterization of some of the athletes that play these games.

For example, there's somehow been painted a picture of the typical football player that has become the stereotype for generations. The football player is a bit of a Neanderthal. He's slow-witted. He's, for lack of a better word, a dullard. I've always wondered how that could be. For you see, football is among the more complicated of games.

Basketball? There are five players on the floor. See the basket? Put the ball in there, or keep the other team from putting the ball in there.

How about baseball? Not a complicated game. See ball, hit ball. And if you're on the other side, see runner? Keep him from crossing home plate! Now, obviously that's easier said than done, but still, there's a gentle simplicity to the game of baseball that has been welcoming for generations of sports fans. But football? Oh, that can be very complicated indeed.

What's the difference between a press corner, a shutdown corner, a strong-side corner, a zone corner? How about one-gap technique versus two gap technique? And where does the 0-tech and 1-tech come into play? How do I know what Cover 1 or Cover 2 even means when I hear it said by an analyst? And all these pass routes? A corner route? Is that different from a flag route? The curl? The fade? The cross? A flat route?

And what about the history of these terms? I've always found the history of any of our games fascinating, and I appreciate knowing where they came from. Who was first to use this term? And why? You'll find in here great stories from the people who were involved in the games…and from the very folks who created the terms you're looking up in this thesaurus.

Those kinds of questions and stories are why I think you'll find Jesse's work so helpful. Whether you're a seasoned veteran of the game of football, or just a casual fan, you'll find something you can use and enjoy in the work he's put together here. He's gone to painstaking lengths to simplify a very complicated game and give you some perspective on where this has come from in the history of the game.

One thing you'll find, though, as you parse through this thesaurus: You'll find something you didn't know. You'll discover the history of a term. You'll find out who created this phrase to describe this specific coverage. You'll even find terms that are considered archaic and aren't even used anymore, but Jesse's made sure it's in there anyway!

What you **won't** find is confusion. Too many times, you'll read a work like this and walk away more confused than you were before about the term or feel like you've learned nothing. That's not going to happen here. Jesse's done an excellent job in putting some complicated topics and football tenets into very easy to under-stand form.

One of the things I always tell a new analyst I'm working with is that the best analysts not only describe what happened to the foot-ball savant, but can describe what happened to my mom, who is **not** a football savant. She's a wonderful mom, but not a football expert by any means. Jesse's book will appeal to both the expert analyst and the most casual of fans, like my mom, who might just want to learn something more about the game of football.

This season, when you watch a football game, keep Jesse's work handy. It's fun to have this thesaurus by your side as you watch. There's a better than average chance you'll catch one of us broad-casters using a term incorrectly!

On second thought, scratch that. Put this book aside during the game. In fact, forget you have it while watching or listening to us do our work. We don't need that kind of pressure. Thanks a lot, Jesse. You've exposed some of us with your work here! We might have to get **real** jobs!

—Kevin Kugler
June 2015

Kevin Kugler is the Sunday Night Football broadcaster for Westwood One and college-football broadcaster for the Big Ten Network.

ACKNOWLEDGEMENTS

This book would not have been written without Kevin Reichard. The idea of a sports thesaurus was born from generic verb lists in 2005. From this, it evolved into a baseball thesaurus that was thrillingly published in 2012, with a second expanded edition released in 2014. What about a football version? Kevin asked. Well, that's reaching a bit too far, I thought (but didn't say aloud)—think of all that football's vocabulary encompasses! Yet here it is, in your hands, and that's because of Kevin. Heartfelt gratitude also to my friends/readers/editors Owen Serey, Jared Sandler, Jason Benetti, Al Yellon, Jay Burnham, and Andy Potter of Football Outsiders, who cast their expert eye upon the manuscript, polishing the rough ends and offering additional nuts and bolts. The book's inception came with Erik (Doc) Love, Ronnie Burton, Jr., Chris Kluwe, and Dan Daly offering advice and assistance, and it ended with greatly appreciated support from Adam Amin, Joe Davis, Jon Chelesnik, Jason Schwartz, and Ian Eagle, who really is as terrific a person as I'd always heard. Full credit to John T. Reed's exhaustive online American Football Terminology Dictionary, an excellent resource. Spence Siegel and Kate Bruce, I'm thinking of you and your strength. Here's to Ari, incomparable and unstoppable; Dina, with all of the new initials after her name; Christie, pushing me onward; Drew Stein, Howie Strassler, and the Boxwood Village P.R. agency.

INTRODUCTION

My earliest football memory is of John Elway hooking up with Ricky Nattiel for a 56-yard bomb of a touchdown two plays into Super Bowl XXII, poor Barry Wilburn hanging onto Nattiel's jersey on the way into the end zone. In order to tell you about this, I admit, I had to look up Nattiel and Wilburn's names. My memory is of the pass, the catch, the touchdown, and the instant emotion it caused, even though I barely knew what I was watching. Three years later, my heartbeat was pushed to the limit by Super Bowl XXV, with Jim Kelly scrambling for crucial yard after yard in a last-minute drive. It ended in a difficult field-goal attempt from Scott Norwood. The kick faded. I was hooked.

This book is about football. It's about the ball, the plays, the players, the coaches, and the fans. It's about the blitz, whether a red dog, a jailbreak, or a wildcat. It's about stickum, pancakes, horse collars, and Omaha. It's about why a football field is called a gridiron, whether a football is oblate or prolate, when football officials started to wear black and white stripes, and how the Gatorade bath got started. It's about Spider 2 Y Banana; Georgia Tech 222, Cumberland College 0; the Fearsome Foursome, the Cyclodrome.

There's a lot to process here. Football may be violent, but it is not simple. Plays are meticulously designed, players are heavily drilled, and an inordinate amount of significance is placed on every outcome. Besides this, football language is difficult to catalog. Each team's offense and defense has its own terminology, swiftly adapting and changing to combat the opposition. In one city, the linebacker is the Mike, Leo, or Sam. In another, he's the Cat, Star, Whip, or Joker. We cannot know all of the names thus far devised without studying every playbook, but we most certainly can gain insight from the terms players and coaches use.

To this end, this Football Thesaurus cannot simply be a list of terms by itself. A compilation of 50 different types of blocks, for instance, is darn intimidating without context. So it is that we'll hear Jerry Kramer's explanation of the Green Bay Packers' audible system, Jim Ricca's definition of the panic-stricken "Look out!" block, and John Madden's recollection of the time quarterback Bob Griese forgot the snap count in the Super Bowl.

The game has come a long way from its rugby origins, with interesting steps along the journey: Walter Camp created the down system. St. Louis University showcased the newfangled forward pass, to the initial elation of Bradbury Robinson and later Benny Friedman and Sammy Baugh. The football started round, slimmed down, and—for a time—was painted white at night. Place-kickers toed it up, went barefoot, and learned to boot soccer-style. The World Football League experimented with 1-, 2-, and 3-point field goals, introduced the post-touchdown action point, and (very briefly) tried out garishly colorful position-coded pants. The Colgate Red Raiders finished the season undefeated and unscored upon, yet were left out of the championship scene. The New York Giants invented "The Golden Stairs" to give running back Eddie Price an easy leg up into the end zone, only to discover the Cleveland Browns' defense had built an imposing response. And David Rosenbaum, a high-school standout from D.C., took a kickoff back for a touchdown before booting a 62-yard extra point.

We'll find Rosenbaum's name herein beside such legends as Fielding (Hurry Up) Yost, (Automatic) Otto Graham, (Slingin') Sammy Baugh, and (Wrong Way) Roy Riegels. Coaches Pop Warner, John Heisman, Tom Nugent, and Urban Meyer receive their time to shine, as do their innovations, ranging from the single wing to the center snap, the I-formation to the spread offense. And we'll delight in the plenitude of gadget plays that have been dreamed up through the decades: the bounce-rooski, the flea-flicker, the Statue of Liberty, the swinging gate, and more.

Football is America's great spectator sport, but we are not content to simply watch it. We breathe it, feel it, live it, and—above all else—talk it.

Here is the language of the game.

—**Jesse Goldberg-Strassler**
June 27, 2015

A

Green Bay Packers QB Bart Starr calling an an audible.

audible

n. automatic, change-up, check, check-off, check-signal; SPECIFIC
dummy audible, live audible
v. audibilize, call an audible, change the play at the line, check,
check down, check off, go to a hot read

*"Modern football has been marked by shifting defenses, in which the
offense is often faced with the possibility that the play it called in the
huddle will run into a stone wall. Therefore, the signal caller tries to
counter the defense and to come up with a better play. Thus, he goes to an
audible. When they automatic, most of the teams will pass or go to quick
hitting runs or trap-type plays. The quarterback should be positive that*

he has a good idea and that it is going to work. He shouldn't be guessing."—George Allen, "Inside Football"

Terms and Lingo

- An *audible* sees the quarterback switch the play called in the huddle to a different play at the line of scrimmage, based upon the defense shown. The idea of the audible has crossed the boundary from football into everyday usage. If someone makes a change on the fly, perhaps in a meeting or a presentation, he/she "calls an audible."
- If the quarterback changes the play call at the line, the audible is *live*. If he doesn't, and is merely barking out insignificant words, numbers, and phrases in order to deceive the defense, the audible is a *dummy*.
- "There is one column of plays which demand that a lineman be able to run against every defense," wrote Chris Schenkel in *How to Watch Football on Television*. "A second column of plays is designed for certain defenses. The 'automatics,' of course, are chosen from that list of plays which can be run against any defense....Y.A. Tittle had a favorite trick of calling the same 'automatic' three times during the first three quarters of a ball game, each play executed exactly the same way. Then, in the fourth quarter, he would call the same 'automatic' number, this time with a new meaning altogether."
- Not every team approaches the line of scrimmage with a particular play in mind. From Pat Kirwin in *Take Your Eye Off the Ball*:

  There are times when teams won't actually call a specific play and will instead call one of three "check" principles: a check-with-me run (a run to one side or the other), a check-with-me pass (one of two possible pass plays), or a check-with-me-at-the-line (could be either a run or a pass).

  When everyone's lined up and the quarterback has had a chance to survey the defense, he'll call the play that he thinks provides the best matchup against what he's seeing.

- In a *hot read*, the quarterback notices which defenders will be pass-rushing and diagnoses which areas of the field will be open for a quick pass. He then signals the local receiver verbally or nonverbally to let him know that a quick pass is coming at the snap—or he trusts that the hot receiver will be aware that his defender will be blitzing and has adjusted his route accordingly, making him ready to take advantage of the quick toss.

It Sounds Complicated....

- In *Instant Replay*, Jerry Kramer explained the 1967 Green Bay Packers' system:

  If [quarterback] Bart [Starr] comes up to the line of scrimmage and sees the defense set up to stop a 49 [a specific running play], he'll call an "automatic"—also known as an "audible"—a signal to change the play. Before he says "hut," he always calls out two numbers, first a single-digit number, then a double-digit number. If the single-digit number is the same as the snap signal—"two," in this case—that means he's calling an automatic; the double-digit number that follows is the new play. In this case, if he comes up to the line of scrimmage and says, "Two-46-hut-hut," I know that 49 is off, that the new play is a 46....

  I realize it sounds complicated—it even looks complicated on paper—but after a while it all comes very easily, very naturally.

B

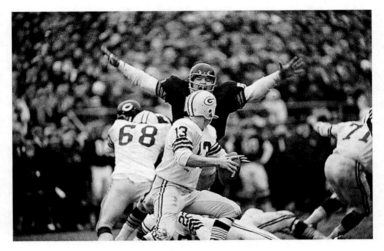

Chicago Bear Dick Butkus blitzing Green Bay Packers QB Don Horn.

back

n. see **cornerback, defensive back; fullback, quarterback, running back**

v. cheer for, patronize, root for, support, wear their colors; see **fan**

- A back refers to any player who lines up behind the *line of scrimmage*. Offensively, seven players are required on the line for every play, leaving a maximum of four players in the backfield. The defense is merely required to remain on its side of the line of scrimmage before the snap. (See **formation**)

blitz

n. SPECIFIC A-gap blitz, all-out blitz, B-gap blitz, blitz off the edge, C-gap blitz, corner blitz, Cover 0, dawg, designer blitz, D-gap blitz, dog, double-backer blitz, double-corner blitz, 11-up blitz, fire zone, five-man pressure (or six-man pressure, etc.), green dog, inside-backer blitz, inside blitz, jailbreak blitz, outside-backer blitz, overload blitz, read blitz, red-dog, red dog, safety blitz, shooting linebackers, slot blitz, snatch blitz, wildcat, zero-man, zone blitz

v. attack, bring the heat, charge, come, dial up the pressure; SPECIFIC bring the house, come off the corner, come off the edge, come up the middle

Blitz Basics

- The typical offensive line features five blockers. The typical pass rush features four rushers. With a blitz, short for *blitzkrieg*, adding additional rushers (bringing "heat"), the offensive line's burden grows heavier—although the secondary now must make do with fewer players in coverage.
- According to David L. Porter, in his *Biographical Dictionary of American Sports: Football*, it was Heartley "Hunk" Anderson who "initiated the practice of blitzing linebackers to disrupt an opponent's offense."
- A *blitz* in its original meaning referred to a charging defensive back. If a linebacker fired in with the rush, it was termed a *dog*. (The variant *dawg* comes from modern slang and accent.) Dog is a shortened form of the initial term, *red dog*. It was the nickname of Don "Red Dog" Ettinger, a linebacker for the New York Giants from 1948-1950, who was notable in pioneering the practice.
- *Football Lingo* (1967) gives *Jumbo* as a name for a Detroit Lions linebacker of the 1960s. George Plimpton offers more specificity in *Paper Lion*:

  The middle linebacker had the following responsibilities: "If rushing the passer, 'red-dogging,' call 'Jumbo!'

to your tackles to let them know you are gone, and they will drive and pinch the middle."

The reading, what little of it I could understand, made me feel somewhat uncomfortable—the knowledge that in a few days the linebackers would be jumping around behind their linemen trying to look into my eyes to see if I was going to tip my plays. I was not at ease about such phrases as "pinch the middle" and about the linebacker's cry "Jumbo!—to signify, apparently, that the red-dog was on—the linebackers' bulling rush toward the quarterback."

- The *corner blitz*: Wrote Dan Holmes on the Detroit Athletic Co. blog, January 8, 2012, about Dick "Night Train" Lane, "At various times during the game, Night Train would bolt from his defensive position and run past the receiver he was assigned to defend, taking a direct route toward the quarterback. It had never been seen before, because no other player had shown the nerve and speed to pull it off. 'The Corner Blitz' was born."
- A *wildcat* is a safety blitz, and it gave its name to the fearless Larry "Wildcat" Wilson, a Hall of Fame safety for the St. Louis Cardinals from 1960-1972. (A different definition for *wildcat* emerged in 2008 with the Miami Dolphins' wildcat offense, featuring running back Ronnie Brown in the shotgun and quarterback Chad Pennington spread wide to one side as a receiver.)

Blitzing Jargon

- A defense utilizing a blitz *dials it up*.
- An unblocked blitzer *comes free*; a blocked blitzer is *picked up*. (See **block** for more.)
- A defense's *blitz packages* are its blitz play-calls and schemes.
- A defender *showing blitz* begins his approach to the line before the ball is snapped, giving the impression that a blitz is coming.

- Before the snap, the quarterback *diagnoses a blitz* by figuring out which defenders will be attacking, adjusting the offensive line's blocking accordingly. If the blitzing defenders approach too soon, giving away their intentions to the quarterback, they *tip their hand* (a reference to playing cards and showing off what one is holding). The defense counters by *disguising* the blitz, hiding its intentions from the quarterback and offensive line until the snap.
- When a blitz is properly combatted/blocked by the offense, it is *cured*.

Types of Blitzes

- The *11-up* sees all 11 defenders arranged along the line of scrimmage.
- An *A-gap blitz* is directed in the gaps between the center and guards (with a *double A-gap* blitz sending defenders through both A-gaps); correspondingly, a *B-gap blitz* is between the guards and tackles, a *C-gap blitz* is between tackle and tight end, and a *D-gap blitz* is outside the tight end.
- When the defense "brings the house," virtually everyone's coming. This is the *all-out blitz*, sometimes called the *jailbreak blitz* if multiple players find free lanes to the quarterback. (When this occurs, the defensive players "hold a meeting in the backfield.")
- Another form of the all-out blitz is the *Cover Zero* (Cover 0 or zero-man), which leaves zero safeties back deep and puts all defensive backs in single coverage.
- The *designer blitz* is a Jon Grudenism: "[B]litzes that are dialed up just for a particular game or a particular situation," as defined for Tim Layden.
- The *overload blitz* brings more rushers at the same gap/blocker/part of the line than the offense is able to block, outnumbering the blocking scheme and ensuring a free rusher or two.
- The *read blitz*, or *green dog*, puts the onus on a defender to read his assignment. Let's say that a linebacker is tasked to cover a running back. If the running back

leaves the backfield (releasing/leaking out), looking for a pass, the linebacker is assigned to cover him. If the back remains to block for the quarterback, however, the linebacker is given the green light to blitz.

- Similar to this is the *snatch blitz*, as defined by Pat Kirwan: "When a blitzer has the back or tight end in coverage and bull rushes the player at the line." In other words, the offensive player might very well be going out in a pass pattern, but the defender jams them with a blitz, snatching them out of their route and muddying the offense.

- The *zone blitz*, also called the *zone dog* and *zone pressure*, was popularized by defensive gurus Dick LeBeau and Dom Capers with the Pittsburgh Steelers in the 1990s. In its simplest sense, a zone blitz combines a blitz at the same time that the defense plays zone, presenting the aggressiveness of a blitz look while tricking the quarterback and the offensive line into miscounting the true amount of pass-rushers and misreading the coverage. The success of the zone blitz caused the Steelers defense to be nicknamed "Blitzburgh," also written as "Blitz-burgh." Dick LeBeau's favorite zone blitz was the *fire zone*. As defined by Chris B. Brown: "three defenders in deep pass coverage, three in underneath zones for the receivers who run intermediate and short routes, and five defenders who rush the passer and look to stop the run." As defined by Pat Kirwan: "one of the rushers jumps at a tackle as if he was a blitzer. Simultaneously, another linebacker or a defensive back blitzes from somewhere else. Then, that first rusher suddenly stops his forward progress and drops back into coverage. As a result, the tackle—often the left tackle and the team's best pass blocker—is left with no one to block. The man he was assigned to block one-on-one is no longer rushing, and it's too late for him to pick up the man who is."

Furthermore

- The 1977 Atlanta Falcons' fearsome defense, directed by

defensive coordinator Jerry Glanville, was nicknamed the "Grits Blitz" (or "sticky blitz"). Wrote researcher Mark Speck in a piece for *The Coffin Corner* in 1998 (Vol. 20), "The Falcons' scheme included a play called the 'Sticky Sam' in which no less than nine players blitzed." (More accurately, three linebackers and two safeties joined four down linemen in rushing the passer.)

- The Philadelphia Eagles' blitz-happy defense of 1999-2004, headed by defensive coordinator Jim Johnson, was known as "Blitz, Inc."

- If a blitz is well-disguised, creative, and rarely seen/utilized, it's *exotic*. This term caught the attention of writer Chris White, who penned a marvelous piece of fiction for *McSweeney's* titled "On Third and Long, Philadelphia Eagles Defensive Coordinator Jim Johnson Dials Up 'Exotic' Blitz Packages." It opened with this passage:

Exotic Zone LB Stunt

Facing a three-wide-receiver set, the defense sets up in a nickel package with cornerbacks slightly off the line and safety Brian Dawkins deep. Linebacker Omar Gaither feints toward the line of scrimmage during the snap count, then backpedals into zone coverage, anticipating a crossing pattern to the slot receiver near the first-down marker. Tackles Darwin Walker and Mike Patterson run a twist, while left defensive end Trent Cole pushes his man toward the sideline. Nickelback Shawn Barber retreats five yards, slides into the lane created by Cole, and begins the sensuous Dance of the Seven Veils. The quarterback, stunned by the surreal balance between indomitable control and pulsating chaos evident in Barber's satiny motion, suddenly questions how civilized we really are; how man is, in his basest impulses, no more than a frenzied animal lusting for survival. As waves of sobriety and panic wash alternately across the quarterback's mind, Roderick Hood rushes off the corner and hits him in the sternum with his helmet.

block

n. interference; SPECIFIC alley block, angle block, arc block, area block, ax block, base block, body block, brush block, chip, chop block, cockroach block, combination block, combo, crab block, crackback block, cross block, cross-body block, cut block, cut-off block, dominator block, double-team (or single- or triple-team), down block, downfield block, drive block, fill block, finesse block, fold block, grisly block, high-low block, hook block, horn block, isolation, key block, kickout block, knockdown block, lead block, log block, look-out block, man-on-man block, mousetrap, pancake, pass block, position step block, power block, pull block, radar block, reach block, reverse cross-body block, reverse shoulder block, rodeo block, roll block, rolling block, rub, run block, sandwich, scoop block, scramble block, screen block, seal block, shoulder block, single leg block, slide block, stalk block, straight ahead block, straight shoulder block, tandem block, trap block (short trap or long trap), wait block, wedge block, wham, zone block; ILLEGAL block in the back, chop block, clip, peel-back block, pick, roll up block
v. blaze a trail, block down, brush, carve out, cancel out, chip, clear out, contain, crack, cut, drive, escort, execute a blocking assignment, finesse, guard, handle, hedge, hook, impede, maul, negate, nullify, occupy, obstruct, pass-block, pick, pick up, pin, pinch, pin inside, pin outside, pop, protect, rub, run-block, run interference, screen, screen off, seal, seal off, shade, shadow, shield, spill, take, throw a block, trap, wall off, ward off, wedge, wipe out

"Football is blocking and tackling. Everything else is mythology."—*Vince Lombardi*

Terms and Jargon

- A fine run-block *seals* the defender off the play (blocking him either to the inside or the outside) and *springs* the ball carrier, opening up a *hole*. This hole might be so wide, the cliché goes, that a *truck could have driven through it*. A large hole is an *alley*, *avenue*, or *lane*. A medium-sized hole is a *crease*. A small hole is a *crack*.

- In pass blocking, the offensive linemen wish to create a *pocket* around the quarterback. (see **pocket**)
- A blocker seeks to *engage* a defender, but he faces resistance:

  The defensive player seeks to *disengage, fight off, shed, shake off,* or *slip a block* in order to make the play. (This is not always true. In certain schemes, defensive tackles are asked to occupy two offensive linemen, thereby freeing up linebackers to stop the ball carrier.)

- A *blocking assignment* gives the blocker his responsibility for each specific play.
- A *pass-blocking lineman* is taught to stay upright and may move backward upon the snap, while a *run-blocking lineman* seeks to get low and drive forward. Since the *hat* in football refers to a player's helmet, a *high-hat* is an upright pass-blocker while a *low-hat* is a head-down run-blocker. If a lineman shows *high-hat* too early, it could betray a quarterback's play-action and telegraph the coming pass play to the defense. The *fit* position is the proscribed stance for a pass-blocker. As described by former scout Chris Landry, "Head up, butt down, knees bent, legs spaced, back flat."

  George Allen's two types of pass blockers: (1) "Riders," who let the defenders come to them and ride them away from the quarterback, and (2) "Fire and Recoil, " blockers who fire off the ball and hit the defender first before backing away.

- The call of "bob" or "BOB," described by John Madden in *One Knee Equals Two Feet*, assigns a running back to block a linebacker. The term is an acronym: *b*ack *o*n *'b*acker. John T. Reed offers a wider definition, with the letters standing for "big-on-big," offering an equivalence in size in justifying putting an offensive lineman on a defensive lineman and a running back on a defensive back. It is related to "FOF," standing for "*fast-on-fast.*"
- The *first level* for an offensive line to block is the

defensive line, also known as the "level one defenders." The *second level* is beyond the defensive line, with linebackers referred to as the "level two defenders." The separation between the first and second levels is the *bubble*.

- A blocked blitz is *picked up*. (see **blitz**)
- *Scat protection* sees a running back sneak (or *leak*) out of the backfield rather than pick up a pass rusher, allowing the quarterback the opportunity for a short, unexpected pass to an uncovered receiver.
- According to football lingo, what's the plural of "blocker"? When moving forward, a *convoy* of blockers, leading the way downfield. When set up ahead of time, a *wall* of blockers, making sure defenders are unable to reach the accelerating ball carrier.
- A missed block is a *whiff* or an *olé!*
- An unblocked defender, resulting either due to a calculated risk or a miscommunication by the offense, is left to "play against air."
- A ball carrier can *set up his blocks* by pushing toward one side, either inside or outside, forcing a defender to commit to an angle around an offensive lineman. With the block now set up, the ball carrier skirts around to the other side, placing his lineman in the way of the defender.
- Before the snap, a lineman may set up in the *two-point stance* ("up"), with neither hand touching the ground; the *three-point stance* ("down"), with one hand touching the ground; or the *four-point stance*, with both hands on the ground.

Types of Blocks

- Many blocks wait for the defender to approach before engaging. Not so the *angle block*. "[A]ngle blocking," wrote Pat Kirwan, "is all about throwing that first punch. Angle blocking lineman don't take a read stop [like zone blocking linemen]; instead, they get to do what they like to do best—'go big on big' against the guy in front of them. It's a power scheme that also removes the need for the running back to read the defense at the point of attack. The linemen lead him to the gap they want him to run through with a pulling lineman, usually the guard."

- An *arc block*, as defined by John T. Reed in his online football dictionary, refers to a running back's "inward block on a defensive contain man or linebacker….he initially moves outward, then comes back in to make the block; the running back's path to the block is roughly a half circle."

- An *ax block*, from *The Encyclopedia of Sports Talk*: "A block a defensive man executes on a wide receiver to nullify him from the play as he tries to run downfield."

- The *body block*, also called the *cross body block* and originally known as the *rolling block*, is attributed to Pop Warner's Carlisle Indians. The Indians' blockers left their feet and threw themselves bodily at the opposition to clear pathways for ball carriers, leading to the technique being nicknamed the "Indian block." The invention is specifically credited to William "Lone Star" Dietz by Bernie McCarty in *The Coffin Corner*, Vol. 1, No. 8 (1979), "introduc[ing] the block against heavily-favored Harvard in 1911. Prior to that time no blocker left his feet."

- A *brush block* sees the blocker subtly get in the defender's way, if only even for a moment, keeping him out of the way.

- Pass rushers beware: The *chip* sees a back or tight end assist an engaged offensive lineman by delivering a blow to the blocked defender before continuing into his pass pattern.

- The *combination block* (or *combo*) is the same as a double-team or a tandem, with two offensive lineman combining to handle a solo defender.

- The *cockroach block* and *rodeo block* were each invented by Auburn University offensive line coach Hugh Nall, who told *ESPN.com*'s Ivan Maisel in 2005, "When we cut block and somebody goes down, that's a cockroach block. The guy is either crawling on the ground or laying on his back. A rodeo block is when you're in pass protection. You want them to be a perfect fit on a defender. If he stays on that defender until the pass is thrown, like riding a bull for the eight count, that's a rodeo block. If everybody does it, all five blockers, that's rodeo protection."

- The *crab block*, explained George Allen in 1970, "also known as the single leg block, is effective against a strong opponent who knows how to use his hands, particularly the big defensive ends and linebackers in our league. The blocker tries to drive his knee up between the legs of the defensive man. He immediately 'crabs' around his opponent, digging with his outside leg but keeping his inside foot stationary. He goes down on all fours and keeps after his man on all fours."
- The *crackback block* is used by a receiver, slanting in toward the line and blindsiding a linebacker/defensive back to the inside, thereby opening up the outside for the ball carrier.
- The *cut block* is aimed beneath the defender's knees.
- The *down block* comes from an angle (in contrast to straight on) and blocks the defender's feet, keeping him from pursuing a play.
- The *fill block* sees a lineman help out a pulling teammate, filling in the hole in the line that his fellow lineman vacated.
- The term *grisly block* was coined by former Utah State Aggies and Washington Redskins tight end Chris Cooley in 2012, according to Cooley himself on his ESPN-980 WTEM radio show in Fall 2014, as a way of describing the "grisly thoughts" necessary to motivate a lead-blocking fullback or tight end in front of ball-carrying quarterback Robert Griffin III.
- The *high-low block*, often illegal, sees one offensive lineman go low, cutting the defender, while another offensive lineman finishes him off up high.
- The *hook block*, often utilized by the tight end, shields an outside linebacker and keeps him inside, freeing up the outside for the ball-carrier.

- The *kickout block* is the opposite of a crackback block, taking an outside rusher (end or linebacker) and pushing him outside of the ball carrier.
- The *lead block* is delivered by the blocker leading the way for the running back. An offensive lineman *pulling* leaves his position and heads down to the other side of the line to lead the way for the ball carrier.
- In a *look-out block*, the offensive lineman misses the block entirely, allowing the defender a free rush. With his task failed, there's nothing left for the lineman to do but turn around and holler, "Look out!"

> Old lineman Jim Ricca knew all about the look-out block. "When Sam [Baugh] was the quarterback," he told Stuart Leuthner, "it was great because as soon as he got the ball, it was gone. He was like Dan Marino. Later on we had Eddie LeBaron and Jack Scarbath and they'd be back there doing all sorts of tricky stuff with the ball and we'd be yelling, 'Look out!' as the guy went by. When we were playing the Colts, they had Gino Marchetti, Artie Donovan, Don Joyce—they just brought them in one right after another. You'd think, 'Which one of these guys am I supposed to hit?' You'd take one and the other one was gone. We'd be yelling, 'Coming right! Coming left!' "

- The *pancake block* sees an offensive lineman block a defensive player so hard that he knocks the other player off his feet and onto his back. When Orlando Pace starred at Ohio State University in 1996, the Buckeyes distributed promotional pancake magnets featuring Pace's name. A more recent name for the pancake is the *dominator block*.
- Banned entering the 2013 season, the *peel-back block* (also written as the *peel back block*) is related to the crackback block—a dangerous blindside block at or below the waist.
- A *pinch* sees a double-team by the tackle and the tight end on a defensive end, thereby helping the ball carrier to *gain the corner*.

- A *reach block* is applied not to the defender directly across from the blocker, but to a nearby defender whom the blocker is able to reach.
- In setting up a *screen block*, the lineman decoys the defender into slipping past him with a brush before getting out in front of the designated receiver and thundering down the field as his bodyguard.
- In a *slide block*, the offensive line slides either to its left or right, moving the pocket or setting up a stretch run. An offensive lineman *slide-protects* with quick, lateral movement, shutting off a rusher's angle.
- The *stalk block* sees a wide receiver blocking a defensive back, looking to free up the corner on an outside rush.
- The *trap block*, also called the *mousetrap*, brings a defender through the initial wash of the line of scrimmage before surprising him with a block in the backfield, putting him behind and out of the play.
- The *wait block* sees the blocker wait for a beat before blocking his man.
- The *wham block*, writes Andy Potter of *FootballOutsiders.com*, "similar to the trap block, uses a skill player to block a penetrating defensive lineman from an unexpected angle."
- The *zone block*, as defined by the website, is "an offensive line scheme that requires linemen to block specific gaps, not specific defenders. Zone blockers often double team a defensive linemen at the snap, with one of the blockers peeling off to engage the linebacker once he commits to a certain gap. Linemen who do a lot of zone blocking use the 'four hands, four eyes' rule: keep both sets of hands on the defender in front of you, but keep your eyes on the second level." Greg Cosell, writing in a Q&A on April 23, 2013, for *NFLFilms.com*, adds colorfully, "zone-running schemes really require offensive linemen to be as close to dancing bears as they can possibly be.... Zone-running schemes require tremendous synchronization. All five offensive linemen need to have the same footwork. They have to look like, as we say, elephants on parade."

Jack, Boom, Pitch, Switch, and Change

- The terms for blocking techniques laid out by Steve Belichick in *Football Scouting Methods*:

  Jack Blocking. Both guards pull on a play off tackle or around end.
  Boom Blocking. Only the far guard pulls on a play off tackle or around end.
  Pitch Blocking. The near guard pulls on a play off tackle or around end.
  Switch Blocking. The guard and tackle cross block at the point of attack.
  Change Blocking. The tackle and end cross block at the point of attack.

blocker

n. bodyguard, chaperone, escort, guard, interferer, protection, protector, road grader, shielder; see **center, fullback, offensive guard, offensive line, offensive lineman, offensive tackle, tight end**

"Being an offensive lineman is about the most boring job in football. It's just a head-butting contest.... [T]he only satisfaction comes from knocking someone on his rear end. And if it helps score a touchdown, it is all the more satisfying."—Ron Yary

- A *road grader* is defined by Pat Kirwan in *Take Your Eye Off the Ball* as a "very wide-bodied and powerful blocker."
- A lynchpin moment for blockers in football history, from Michael Lewis: "In 1978, NFL linemen were permitted, for the first time in history, to use their hands when they blocked. Overnight the image of the lineman with his elbows stuck out in imitation of a coat hanger became charmingly antiquated."

C

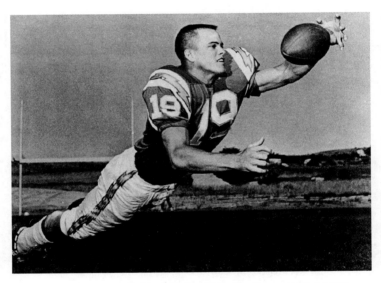

The sure-handed Lance Alworth, diving for a ball in a 1963 San Diego Chargers publicity shot. (AP.)

catch

n. caught ball, collection, completed ball, completion, connection, grab, haul, pick, pluck, pass reception, reception, snag, snare, snatch, squeeze; SPECIFIC acrobatic catch, basket catch, casual catch, circus catch, diving catch, double catch, fair catch, first down reception, helmet catch, interception, juggling catch, over-the-head catch, over-the-shoulder catch, pick, running catch, scoop, shoestring catch, sliding catch, touchdown reception, trap

v. accept, bag, bring in, capture, chase down, clasp, clutch, collar, collect, come down with, come up with, corral, dig, eat up, fetch, field, flag down, gain, gather, get, glove, gobble, grab, grasp, handle, hang on, haul in, high-point, hug, intercept, latch hold of, nab, obtain, pick, pluck, pounce on, procure, put away, rake in, receive, reel in, rob, secure, seize, snag, snare, snatch, spear, squeeze, stab, steal, swallow, take, track down

Terms and Jargon

- An *acrobatic catch*, also called a *circus catch*, is so gracefully and astonishingly executed as if the receiver was a member of a circus troupe.
- A *double catch* is juggled initially before the receiver secures the ball on a second attempt.
- A *fair catch* may be called for on any kick—free kick (following a safety), kickoff, or punt. The receiver must wave one hand high, alerting the officials and the defense to his choice of a fair catch. The positive: He does not take a hit from the defense. The negative: The play is over the second he catches the ball, with his offense taking over from that spot. If a fair catch is *muffed* (not caught cleanly), the ball is loose and able to be recovered by either team.
- Following a fair catch, the offensive team may choose to attempt the rare *fair-catch kick* from that spot, a kick without defense, equaling the three points of a field goal if successfully converted. The kick may be attempted even if the fair catch occurred with zero seconds left on the clock; the fair-catch kick would then be a single untimed play.
- A *high-point catch* requires the receiver to grab the ball at the highest point he can manage, perhaps with a leap. A receiver who can high-point the ball adeptly receives high points from scouts.
- An *interception*, also called a *pick*, is a pass legally caught by the defensive team. (see **interception**)
- A receiver playing *patty-cake* drops a pass that hits him in the hands. (He played patty-cake with it, à la the old children's hand-slapping rhyme.)

- A *shoestring catch* is secured, yes, at the same height as the receiver's cleats.
- A *trap* sees the player snag the football either against the field or following a short-hop off the field. If the officials spot that a player has trapped the ball, his potential catch is negated.
- The letters YAC, pronounced "yak," stands for "yards after the catch." A play in which a receiver snags a short pass and turns it into a long touchdown might go down as a straightforward 80-yard touchdown in the box score. With the inclusion of YAC, fans can see just how much of the play was supplied by the receiver on his own. Researcher Dan Daly found the statistic was kept as early as 1927 by a *Syracuse Herald* writer.

Those Last Six Inches

- "Many receivers do not follow the ball the last six inches into their hands with their eyes," wrote George Allen in *Inside Football*. "They follow the ball to a point about 6 to 8 inches from their body. Then, there comes a place on every catch, where he has to move his head in order to keep the eyes on the ball. This is the place where many receivers will not turn their head. The head remains in the position where they were looking back at the passer, and, consequently, they do not follow the last six inches into their hands with their eyes….We have a little drill where we watch the head '*pop down.*' If the head snaps right down and looks into the hands, we know they are watching the ball. That's one reason why they drop a pass—the head hasn't snapped down right into the fingers."

Completing the Process of a Catch

- In order to make an official catch, as the Detroit Lions' Calvin Johnson learned to his detriment on September 12, 2010, a receiver must complete the process. In that fateful game, Johnson made what looked to be the go-ahead touchdown reception with a leap, but in going softly to the ground afterward, put his hand out and had the ball squeeze out of his grip. He thought nothing of it; the officials thought otherwise, ruled the pass incomplete upon review, and the Lions lost. The official wording from the rule book: "A player who goes to the ground in the process of attempting to secure possession of a loose ball (with or without contact by an opponent) must maintain control of the ball throughout the process of contacting the ground, whether in the field of play or the end zone. If he loses control of the ball, and the ball touches the ground before he regains control, there is no possession. If he regains control prior to the ball touching the ground, it is a catch, interception, or recovery." In *Take Your Eyes Off the Ball*, Pat Kirwan delivers a straightforward list of the receiver's process to completing a catch: (1) extending [one's hands toward the football], (2) catching, (3) tucking [the ball in], (4) turning [one's vision and focus away from the ball and toward the field]. This fourth step is also termed "making a football move."

- On January 11, 2015, countless incensed Dallas Cowboys fans became all too familiar with the rule. Down 26-21 with under five minutes remaining in their NFC playoff game against the Packers, the Cowboys appeared to seize control of the game in a spectacular way. On fourth down, receiver Dez Bryant made a superb grab inside the Packers' 5-yard line—but he lost control of the ball upon taking several steps in lunging forward as he went to the ground. The play was declared an incomplete pass upon review, and Green Bay went on to eliminate Dallas and advance to the NFC Championship.

Notable Catches

- *The Immaculate Reception*, December 23, 1972. Terry Bradshaw's fourth-down pass struck someone—but did it strike Oakland Raiders safety Jack Tatum and/or Pittsburgh Steelers back French Fuqua? A ricochet off of Fuqua would have rendered the loose ball illegal for another Steeler to return. Ah, but the officials ruled that the pass bounced off of Tatum and not Fuqua. The Raiders safety completed his brutal hit and the ball caromed up into the air and serendipitously found Steelers running back Franco Harris, who brought it in and then raced down the sideline for a game-winning touchdown, eliminating the Raiders from the AFC playoffs.

- *The Catch*, January 10, 1982. "The play was nothing special. It's a play we practice from Day 1 in camp," dismissed San Francisco 49ers head coach Bill Walsh. With 58 seconds remaining in the NFC Championship Game, Walsh's 49ers trailing the Dallas Cowboys 27-21. San Francisco quarterback Joe Montana faced a third-and-3 from the Cowboys' 6-yard line. Looking back on the moment for the *San Francisco Chronicle*, December 15, 1997, Tim Keown wrote:

> The six most important yards in 49er history were gained in a way that was awfully close to poetic. Even a cynic would have to admit that much.
>
> Joe Montana rolled right, holding the ball, tapping it once or twice. You've seen it, over and over and over. Dallas Cowboys linemen in pursuit, the fans in the orange Candlestick background standing with their mouths open and their hearts firing like a Briggs and Stratton.
>
> It was called Sprint Right Option....
>
> He threw it, finally, off his back foot and slightly across his body. His flamingo legs scissored a little from the torque, and it looked for all the world like a throwaway, with everybody walking back to the huddle to confront fourth down.
>
> But Dwight Clark caught it. He reached above the unfortunate immortality of Everson Walls and

caught the ball in the back of the end zone. Those faces in the stands thawed into a delirium of incredulity and joy.

The 49ers' 28-27 victory clinched their first NFC Championship. They would soon have their first Super Bowl rings.

- *Catch-42 / The Helmet Catch*, February 3, 2008. The New York Giants popped the New England Patriots' dream of an undefeated season with a 17-14 triumph in Super Bowl XLII, and David Tyree's helmet figured mightily in the result. On a 3rd and 5 with 1:15 remaining, down 14-10, Giants quarterback Eli Manning pulled away from a fierce rush and hurled a pass upfield. Tyree, battling against safety Rodney Harrison, jumped up and tried to pull the ball in with both hands. Harrison, in perfect position, locked his right arm around Tyree's right arm and attempted to wrestle the ball away. Tyree fought back. Unable to bring his arms down, he clutched the ball with his right hand against the crown of his helmet and went down to the ground, rolling over, the nose of the ball passing achingly close to the grass. It was a 32-yard play, and it led—four plays later—to a 13-yard touchdown from Manning to Plaxico Burress, cinching the upset.

center

n. pivot man, snapper; SPECIFIC long snapper (LS)
v. deliver, hike, snap; see also "get the snap from center" under **quarterback**

"We're the only family I know of that plays catch without facing each other."—center Jay Hilgenberg, whose brother, father, and uncle were also centers

Terms

- The *center* starts each play by delivering the ball to the quarterback or another player in the backfield (if the team is in a *wildcat* set), termed a *snap* or a *center-quarterback exchange*.

- The *long snapper* delivers the ball on the longer snaps, whether to the punter (for a punt) or to the holder (for a field goal or extra point). On many a team, the long snapper is a different player than the center, entering in for his teammate on special teams plays.

clock

n. SPECIFIC delay of game timer, electric clock, 40-second clock, game clock, play clock, running clock, stadium clock, 25-second clock

v. dirt, grass, ground, spike, throw the ball at the dirt, turf; see "spike" under **pass**

The Clocks

- The *game clock* keeps the official time of the game. In the NFL and college football, there are 15 minutes in each quarter, equaling 60 minutes in a game. At the varsity high school ranks, quarters last 12 minutes (with a running clock depending on the state and the size of the lead in the second half).

- The *play clock*, otherwise known as the 40-second clock or the 25-second clock, times the duration between plays. At the end of a play with the clock rolling, the offense has 40 seconds to get the next play off or otherwise suffer a *delay of game penalty*. Following a clock stoppage, the offense is given 25 seconds to start the next play. The play clock is the field judge's responsibility, though the clocks are personally set/run/stopped by the *clock operator*. (see **official**)

Reasons for a Clock Stoppage

ball carrier out of bounds, coach's challenge, end of a quarter, inadvertent official's whistle, incomplete pass, injury, official measurement, official's timeout, penalty, possession change (due to turnover on downs, fumble, interception; kickoff; or punt), replay review, scoring play (field goal, safety, or touchdown), two-minute warning; first down (college)

- A different form of "killing the clock": stopping time entirely, thanks to the quarterback racing to the line, receiving the snap, and spiking the ball.

Terms and Jargon

- A team with the lead has the *clock on its side*; a trailing squad finds that the *clock is against them*.
- Seconds on the clock are *ticks*.
- A spare few seconds over a minute mark leaves *change*; if there 3:06 remains in a quarter, for instance, you may hear, "Three minutes and change remaining."
- When the offense keeps the clock rolling with a long, time-consuming drive, thanks mostly to rushing plays, this is known as *bleeding the clock*, *eating the clock*, *killing the clock*, *milking the clock*, *sitting on the ball*, and *taking the air out of the ball*.
- The end of the game is *crunch time*.
- There is an official stoppage at the professional ranks at the two-minute mark of each half for the *two-minute warning*. (The space of time leading up to the two-minute warning is the *front side* of the two-minute warning.) After the two-minute warning, the team on offense goes into its practiced *two-minute drill*, pushing its pace, perhaps completing sideline pass routes (making it easier for receivers to stop the clock), and hustling to the line to prepare for the next play, all in an effort to score points in the fleeting time remaining.

coach

n. ball coach, boss, braintrust, coordinator, director, head man, pilot, play-caller, staff man; ROLE architect (of the offense/defense), assistant, assistant coach, assistant head coach, backfield coach, booth coach, control freak, cornerbacks coach, defensive assistant, defensive backs coach, defensive coordinator, defensive line coach, defensive passing game coordinator, director of the defense, director of the offense, fullbacks coach, graduate assistant coach, head coach, (outside/inside) linebackers coach, line coach, offensive assistant, offensive coordinator, offensive line, passing game coordinator, (offensive/defensive) quality control coach, quarterbacks coach, running backs coach, running game coordinator, safeties coach, special teams coordinator, strength coach, strength and conditioning coach, tight ends coach, wide receivers coach; SPECIFIC conservative coach, defensive-minded coach, dictator, disciplinarian, fundamentalist, (riverboat) gambler, genius, guru, innovator, lame-duck coach, miracle man, offensive-minded coach, passing coach, player's coach, running coach, throwing coach, wizard, yell-your-head-off coach

"They call it coaching, but it is teaching. You don't just tell them it is so. You show them the reasons why it is so, and then you repeat and repeat it until they are convinced, until they know."—Vince Lombardi

History, Terms, and Jargon

- Words of wisdom, from the prologue to Tim Layden's *Blood, Sweat and Chalk*, detailing what the author had learned during his research and observation: "Almost no coach will lay claim to inventing anything. Early in my reporting I had a long conversation with Joe Gibbs, who guided the Washington Redskins to three Super Bowl titles and is regarded as one of the most gifted strategists of modern football. During the interview I twice tried to credit Gibbs with being the 'first coach' to run a particular scheme. Both times Gibbs stopped me in my tracks. 'You'll never hear me say I was the first to do anything,' he said, 'because there's a pretty good chance somebody did it before me, but nobody knows about it.' "
- 1944 was the first year that the NFL allowed coaches to communicate with the players from the sideline; before this, they had to remain mum during games, forcing the players to coach (and decide on their plays) themselves. The next year, 1945, Purdue's Cecil Isbell became the

first coach to work from the press box during a game, offering him a better vantage point to see the full field.

- How influential was Paul Brown, the first coach of the Cleveland Browns? "Many of the techniques that are accepted procedure today," wrote Dave Anderson, "were unknown until Paul Brown introduced them: year-round coaching staffs, notebooks and classrooms, film scouting, grading players from film study, lodging the team at a hotel before home games, specific pass patterns, face bars on helmets, intelligence tests for players to determine learning potential, switching college offensive players to defense, using messenger guards to bring in the next play from the sideline."

- A *coaching tree* traces and connects coaches' backgrounds in the same style as a family tree. The Marty Schottenheimer coaching tree, for instance, branches out into Schottenheimer's assistant coaches who have since become head coaches—Cam Cameron, Bill Cowher, Tony Dungy, Herm Edwards, and Wade Phillips—and then branches out further from these secondary coaches, with Cowher's staff begetting future head coaches Chan Gailey, Marvin Lewis, and Ken Wisenhunt, and Dungy's staff including such future head coaches as Jim Caldwell, Lovie Smith, Rod Marinelli, and Mike Tomlin. The granddaddy of all coaching trees is that of Bill Walsh, whose legacy is now stretching four generations of assistants-turned-head-coaches.

Types and Terms

- A football coach is a *ball coach.* Steve Spurrier, who made his name coaching Duke, Florida, and South Carolina, is nicknamed the "Head Ball Coach" ("the HBC") or the "Ol' Ball Coach" ("the OBC").
- An awful coach "can't coach his way out of a paper bag."
- His superb counterpart, in contrast, is able to *coach up* his players ("coach 'em up"), getting the most of their abilities.
- Any coach who complains, for whatever

reason—disputed calls, media coverage—is accused of getting out the *crying towel.*

- A *disciplinarian* is strict and implacable, keeping a tight ship. From *Pro Football: The Early Years*: "[Washington] Owner George Marshall decided that his team needed discipline, so he hired John Whelchel, a retired admiral and ex-coach at Navy, as his new head coach. As things turned out, Whelchel got along fine with the players but couldn't stomach interference from the owner. Marshall figured that Whelchel was using his players all wrong, so he came to a practice and told the coach where to play his men. Whelchel looked Marshall in the eye, pulled an about-face, and marched off the field. Marshall turned a dark shade of purple, gathered a few of the players together, and yelled, 'How could you let that man ruin the ball club?' When the players answered that Whelchel, after all, was the coach, the owner replied, 'Hell, I hired him for a disciplinarian, not for a g.d. coach.' "
- A *fundamentalist* emphasizes fundamentals of the game above all else: blocking, tackling, and the like.
- A coach with diminishing job security is "on the hot seat."
- The opposite of a disciplinarian is a *player's coach*, who is well-liked and lenient.
- The *upstairs coach* is an advance scout, as in this description of Steve Belichick in Shirley Povich's foreword for Belichick's *Football Scouting Methods*: "[Navy head coach Eddie] Erdelatz had another name for Belichick. 'My Upstairs Coach,' he called him. It is from the scouting coops high above the stadium that Belichick works, with his charts, his field glasses, his bundle of pencils and his pipe. He has been one of football's best-known figures for more than a decade, traversing the continent in espionage against Navy's future opponents."

Game Film

- Every play in every NFL game is filmed in "All-22" and

"High End Zone" camera angles. What are these angles? From *NFL.com*: "The 'All 22' camera is positioned high above the NFL playing field and shows a view of the field that includes all 22 players (11 on offense, 11 on defense) at the same time…. The High End Zone camera is positioned on either side of a field, high above the goal posts and behind the end zone." When coaches, players, and pundits break down footage following a week of games, they generally work with the All-22 game film (and refer to it specifically as "the All-22").

- Leading up to the next game, the coaches and players dedicate themselves to film study, with the opposition's performances edited and organized for easy viewing in "cut-ups." After each game, they go through film review, grading their execution of the plays.
- The All-22 film is open to everyone to break down, making life easier for analysts in the media. Before this, Fred Russell bemoaned the lot: "The way football is played, college and pro, an offensive guard or center can go through an entire season and never be mentioned. To some extent television, with its replays, has helped show what the linemen do but I think the only way you could cover a game fairly would be if you assigned twenty-two reporters, one for each defensive and offensive position."

cornerback

n. back, C, CB, corner, cornerman; SPECIFIC boundary cornerback (BC), closed-side corner (CC), cover corner, drop corner, Eagle corner (EC), field cornerback (FC), left corner (C), left cornerback (LCB), lockdown corner, man corner, physical corner, press corner, quick corner (QC), right corner (RC), right cornerback (RCB), shutdown corner, strong-side corner (SC), wide-side corner (WC), zone corner; see **defensive back**

"I try to see through the receiver and anticipate him. I play him as close as possible, but when the quarterback releases the ball, I figure it belongs as much to me as to anyone else."—Johnny Sample

Specific Positions and Terms

- Certain teams designate their cornerbacks by side (left and right); others choose to vary by situation. The *boundary cornerback* spends the game on the short side of the field, playing the side that is nearest to the sideline.
- His counterpart, the *field cornerback*, is entrusted to cover far more territory. If the ball is placed on the far side hashmark, for instance, the field corner covers to the near side.
- One of the main differences between the *man corner*, who works in man-to-man coverage, and the *zone corner*, who covers in zone coverage, is that the man corner plays *inside technique*, shading inside the receiver at the snap, preventing an inside route, and using the sideline as a second defender, while the zone corner plays *outside technique*, guarding against an outside route and funneling receivers toward help on the inside. Because of this, the man corner keeps his eyes on the receiver, while the zone corner is able to look directly into the backfield and read the quarterback's eyes.
- A *physical corner*, like a *press corner*, covers the receiver as tightly as possible, jamming at the line of scrimmage, engaging in hand-fighting, and keeping in close contact as they advance downfield together.

defend a receiver

v. contest, cover, cover up, D up, mark, match up with, play, stick on, stick with, take, watch; DEFEND WELL blanket, bottle up, clamp down on, contain, cork up, deny, frustrate, harness, limit, lock down, muffle, muzzle, negate, neutralize, nullify, plaster to, quiet, silence, smother, stifle, stymie, suppress, swallow up, take away, take out of the game

Terms

- A "pass-defense" is a specific stat, quantifying the amount of times a defensive back breaks up a pass, separating the receiver from the ball, or batting, deflecting, knocking, poking, slapping, swatting, tapping, tipping, or whacking it aside.

- A defensive back covering a receiver closely "blankets" him—but if he's covering a little *too* closely, he's "on top of" or "draped all over" the receiver.
- A defensive back is only allowed to initiate contact with a receiver in the first five yards; after that, any contact comes with an illegal contact penalty, costing five yards and a first down.
- A *cover corner* is respected for his above-average pass-defense, though his tackling ability is likely considered substandard. At his best, he's a *lockdown* or *shutdown* corner, blessed with the ability to tightly defend the production of the opposition's top wide receiver. Howie Long preferred the term "black hole," defining it with Mike Haynes in mind: "any player he covered seemed to go into a black hole, disappearing from the field."
- A cornerback placed *out on an island* is put in man coverage against a receiver with no one to help him. In certain matchups, this leaves the defender in great trouble—but if the corner is worth his salt, he relishes the opportunity. Hall of Famer Deion Sanders was noted for his ability to take away half of the field from the offense. From 2008-2011, the New York Jets' Darrelle Revis developed such a reputation around the NY/New Jersey metropolitan region, he (and the area he covered) received the nickname "Revis Island."
- When a defensive back *sits down in coverage*, he anticipates an underneath route, stops backpedaling, and holds his ground.
- A safety who helps a cornerback out in coverage, rolling over to cover against the long pass, offers *deep help.*

Negative Outcomes

- In trying to get open, receivers will give defensive backs different jukes, whether a head-and-shoulder fake or a double move (seeming to delay or staggering steps before suddenly taking off with the real route). A defensive back who "bites" on a fake is fooled by the receiver. (If he's badly fooled, he "bites hard.")

- A defensive back beaten cleanly by a receiver gets *burned, torched*, or *undressed*. If the receiver uses pure speed to burn the defensive back, he *blows by* him.
- A defensive back who "gets lost" has misplaced his assigned receiver, giving him a feeling of panic and his coach a feeling of anguish. Worse, if the receiver "gets behind him," only an inaccurate pass or a drop will stop that receiver from scoring a touchdown.
- If the offense finds a *mismatch* with a receiver/ cornerback matchup, the quarterback will *pick on* or *prey on* that corner, targeting the receiver over and over to the misery and frustration of the helpless defender.

Positive Outcomes

- The defensive back who isn't fooled can *bait* the quarterback into making a throw he thinks is open, only to see the defender *jump the coverage*, cutting in front of the receiver ("breaking" on the pass) and making the play.

D

The Los Angeles Rams' Fearsome Foursome in 1966: Lamar Lundy, Rosey Grier, Merlin Olsen, and Deacon Jones. (AP.)

defeat

n. blemish, bump in the road, collapse, debacle, disaster, downfall, failure, fall, gut-punch, heartbreaker, hiccup, L, loss, meltdown, moral victory, setback, slip, slip-up, stomach-punch, stumble, trip-up, undoing

v. ace, ambush, annex, annihilate, arrest, assail, assault, attend to, avenge, awe, axe, baffle, bag, barrel over, bash, batter, beat, beat down, beat the daylights out of, beat the tar out of, beat up, bedevil, belt, best, better, blank, blanket, blast, blindside, blister, block, blot out, blow away, blow out, bludgeon, bog down, bomb, bombard, boost over, boot, bottle up, bounce, bowl over, brain, breeze past, brush off, buck, bulldoze, bully, bump, bumrush, burn, bury, bust, butcher, buzzsaw, cage, can, cancel, cap, carve up, catch, check, chop down, chop up, circumvent, clamp down on, claw past, clean their clocks, clean up, clear, clip, clobber, clock, close out, clout, clown, club, coast, come from behind, confound, confuse, conk, conquer, contain, cook, counterpunch, cream, crown, crunch, cruise, crush, curb, cut down, cut off, cut through, D up, dart past, dash past, daunt, daze, dazzle, deal a loss, debilitate, decimate, deck, deep six, defend, deflate, demolish, dent, deny, depose, derail, desecrate, destroy, detain, deter, detonate, devastate, devour, dice, disappoint, dish, dismantle, dismiss, discard, dispatch, dispense with, dispose of, disrupt, dodge, do in, dominate, double up, douse, down, drill, drop, drown, drub, drum, dump, dust, ease past, eclipse, edge, eke out, eliminate, embarrass, escape, eviscerate, exceed, expose, fell, fend off, fight off, flatten, finish off, flabbergast, flog, flummox, fluster, fly past, foil, frazzle, frustrate, gag, gang up on, gash, get by, get past, get to, give the boot, grind out a win, guide past, gun down, gut, halt, hammer, hand a loss, handcuff, handle, harness, harpoon, haunt, head off, hem in, hogtie, hold at bay, hold down, hold off, hold on, hold scoreless, hose, house, humble, humiliate, hurdle, hush, impose will against, jackknife, jar, jolt, jump, jump on, kill, knock around, knock off, knock out, K-O (or K.O.), lambaste, lasso, lather, lay waste to, leap, leap on, leapfrog, level, lick, light up, manhandle, maneuver past, march past, maroon, mash, massacre, master, maul, mesmerize, mop the floor with, mow down, muffle, mug, murder, muzzle, mystify, navigate past, negate, nettle, neutralize, nick, nip, nonplus, nose out, notch, nullify, obliterate, oust, outbattle, outclass, outgun, outhit, outlast, outmaneuver, outmuscle, outpace, outplay, outrun, outscore, outslug, outstrip, overcome, overpower, overrun, overstep, overtake, overwhelm, paddle, parade, past, pass, paste, pepper, pen in, perplex, pick apart, pick off, pick on, pin, pin down, pitch a shutout, plant, plaster, plow under, plug, poleax, polish off, pop, post (a win), pounce on, pound, power past, prevail against, prevail over, pull away from, pull out a win, pulverize, pummel, punk, punish, push around, put away, put in their place, put it on (the other team), puzzle, quash, quell, quiet, race past, rack, rally past, rattle, ram, rap, rattle, ravage, raze, rebuff, reel in, reject, repel, repulse, resist, riddle, rip, rise above, rock, roll, roll over, roll past, romp past, rough up, rout, ruin, rule, rumble past, run away from, run out of town, run over, run roughshod over, ruffle, sack, sail, salvage a win, savage, scale, school, scorch, score a win, scrape by, scuttle, sear, send packing, shackle, shade, shake, shake off, shame, shatter, shave, shed, shell, shellack, shock, shoot down, short-circuit, shove, shred, shut down, shut out, silence, sink, skewer, skunk, slam, slaughter, slay, slip, slip by, slip past, slow down, soar past, solve, smack, smack down, smash, smear, smite, smoke, smother, sneak by, sneak past, snuff, spank, spike, spill, spoil, squash, squeak out a win, squeak past, squeeze, squelch, squish, stagger, stampede, startle, stave off, steal a win, steamroll, stifle, sting, stop, stomp, stop, storm past, streak past, strum, stuff, stump, stun, stupefy, stymie, subdue, submarine, suffocate, suppress, surge past, surmount, surpass, surprise, survive, swallow, swamp, swarm, swat, sweep past, swindle, swipe, tag, take, take apart, take care of, take down, take to the cleaners, take their lunch money, tame, tan, tattoo, teach a lesson to, tear apart, tear down, tear into, thrash, throttle, thump, thunder past, thwart, tie up, tip, tiptoe past, toast, top, topple, torch, total, toy with, trample, trap, trash, trim, trip, trip up, triumph over, trounce, trump, turn aside, turn back, undo, unhinge, unnerve, unplug, upend, upset, vault past, vanquish, veto, victimize, waffle, wallop, ward off, waste, wax, waylay, wear down, whack, whale on, whip, whip up on, whitewash, whomp, whop, win against, wing, wipe out, work over, wreck, wring, zap, zip, zip past

"If you can accept losing, you can't win."—Vince Lombardi

defense

n. Big D, D, defensive unit, eleven, platoon; SPECIFIC 3–4 defense, 4-3 defense, dime defense, multiple 4-3 defense, 4-4 defense, 46 defense, Eagle defense, end-but-don't-break defense,(Arkansas) Monster 50, multiple, nickel defense, Notre Dame 4-4,

Oklahoma 5-2, Oklahoma 5-4, prevent defense, Pro 4-5, psycho defense, radar defense, split-6, stack defense, zone defense

"All the height, strength, and speed in the world can be neutralized if the guy across from you gets a jump on the ball."—George Perles, while assistant head coach of the Pittsburgh Steelers

Schemes and Terms

- See "Defensive Formation" under **formation**
- A defense is made up three levels: the *defensive line* (the *defensive ends* and *defensive tackles*); the *linebackers*; and the *defensive backfield* (also called the *secondary*, featuring the *cornerbacks*, the *free safety*, and the *strong safety*).
- The *bend-but-don't-break* defense allows the opposition to move the ball from one 20-yard line to the other, bending, before tightening up near its own goal line and refusing to allow a touchdown.
- The *front four* of the defense refers to a four-man defensive line. The *front seven* counts a defensive line and linebacking corps equaling seven (whether in the 4-3 or the 3-4). The back seven counts a linebacking corps and a secondary equaling seven, with three linebackers, two cornerbacks, and two safeties. These numbers may all be adjusted based upon the amount of players used in each level of the defense.
- In the *Gap-8 defense* and Tom Landry's *Flex defense*, the hallmark of the Dallas Cowboys' "Doomsday Defense," eight defenders are assigned to fill the eight gaps in the offensive line, one to each gap. Those eight gaps: two between the center and guards (A), two between the guards and tackles (B), two between the tackles and tight ends (C), and two outside the tight ends (D). Cowboys linebacker Chuck Howley explained Tom Landry's Flex to Bob Carroll:

> "Basically the flex is a reading defense. Read and react. Every man on the defense has certain keys he looks for in the opponent's offense. When he sees one of those keys, he reacts immediately. Normally, the offense has

all the advantage because they know where the play is going to go. If you wait and let it happen, you're going to get buried. The flex takes some of that advantage away by cueing the defense as to what's happening. Then, if you're fast enough, you can stop it. For example, I would be at linebacker and I'd see the guard on the other side pulling. He'd be coming to get me. But, if I react immediately, I can beat him to the point of attack. And by being there before he expects me to be, I have the advantage."

- The *prevent defense* is used with the lead late in the game, utilizing seven or eight defensive backs. In its ideal, the prevent stops receivers from getting to the side line and prevents long touchdown passes. Critics invariably add that the prevent only "prevents you—the defense—from winning," allowing the offense to march down the field without danger of blitz or pass rush.
- A defense *sells out* when it entirely gambles on one type of play occurring. A defense selling out on the run, for instance, crashes everyone down on the line and becomes vulnerable to a play-action pass.
- A defense that is *stemming around* has defenders milling about before the snap, not allowing the offense to gauge its alignment. Specifically, the *radar defense* (created by Hofstra coach Howard "Howdy" Myers in the 1960s), used at least nine stemming defenders. Dom Capers converted the same look into Green Bay's *Psycho defense* in 2009, using only one down lineman with five linebackers and five defensive backs in a 1-5-5 look.
- It is the responsibility for the defenders on the edge (defensive end, outside linebackers, and cornerbacks) to *force / funnel* everything toward the middle. The reason: there are far more players in the middle of the field than near the sidelines. If the ball carrier reaches the corner, there could be trouble—but if the ball carrier is forced back toward the middle of the field, he'll find a grinning group of defenders waiting for him.
- A *defensive stand* sees the defense "rise up" and stop the

opposition offense on fourth down and short yardage. A
goal-line stand takes place at the doorstep of the end
zone.

- A defense that gathers itself and stops the offense cold
  may be said to *bear down, dig in, rise up, stiffen,* or *tighten
  up.*

Reading Keys

- Let's expand on Chuck Howley's words from earlier. A
  key, John T. Reed wrote, "is the use of an opposing
  player's movement to make a decision." The notion of
  reading keys relates both to offensive and defensive
  players; reading the opposition's keys provided the basis
  of Tom Landry's defensive schemes, first with the New
  York Giants as defensive coordinator, and then heading
  the Dallas Cowboys' defense as a head coach. Mark
  Ribowsky goes into greater detail:

  > Peter Halas, a scout for uncle George's Chicago Bears,
  > discovered how to read Greasy Neale's Philadelphia
  > Eagle defense in the late 1940s. Seems Neale's middle
  > linebacker Alex Wojciechowicz would use his fingers
  > to signal the number of linemen. One hand across his
  > chest meant a five-man line. Two hands meant a six-
  > man line, the only other option....

  > [Giants All-Pro linebacker Brad] Van Pelt's favorites
  > include a back who jiggles his face mask before taking
  > his stance if he's getting the ball and another who
  > "looks me in the eye if he's coming out of the backfield,
  > checking to see where I am. If he's not coming out, he
  > looks at the ground."...

  > "Take the backs," said [linebacker Bob] Matheson. "If
  > the fullback is up a bit—maybe only a foot, so you
  > really have to see the field in little sections—you know
  > he's not going anywhere outside. Geometrically, he
  > can't get the angle. he'd have to back up. And he can't
  > get a block from the halfback. So it's probably a quick

trap [a lineman won't block his man, who'll then be hit from the blind side by a pulling guard or a back], with him running or blocking the target lineman."

Nickel, Dime, and Prevent

- The base personnel for the defensive backfield sees two corners, usually with one on each side of the field, and two safeties, a free safety, and a strong safety.
- The *nickel defense* features five defensive backs, one more than usual (the *nickel back*), helping out against offenses featuring receiver. A nickel is equal to five cents; hence, the reference to five defensive backs. The *big nickel* refers to a nickel defense, which features an extra safety (bigger and stronger) instead of the usual nickel cornerback. The *speed nickel* uses a quick, small corner as its fifth player in coverage.
- The *dime defense*, also called the "nickel plus one," utilizes six defensive backs, featuring four corners—including a *dime back*—and two safeties. Why is it called a "dime" defense? Because it features two added nickels. Adding a third safety, rather than a third corner, has been termed the *Giant/giant dime* as a credit to the New York Giants' use of three-safety sets. The dime is similar to the pressure-oriented *Nickel 40*, which also drops six players in coverage while making sure to rush the quarterback with four top linemen.
- Defenses with more than six defensive backs proceed accordingly through the currency ranks: the *quarter defense* features seven defensive backs, and the *half-dollar defense* features eight DBs.
- Both the quarter and half-dollar alignments are utilized in the *prevent defense*, used by teams looking to protect a late lead, aiming to keep the clock moving until it runs out on the opposition. Because of this, the prevent is designed to keep the offense away from the sideline and from hitting a deep pass, though it opens up the middle of the field. Note that if the prevent defense is unsuccessful at stopping a game-tying or game-winning

touchdown, you'll invariably hear the old complaint: "All the prevent defense does is prevent you from winning."

Buddy Ryan's 46 Defense

- The Chicago Bears' intimidating 46 defense was not named for a 4-6 alignment. The unit was named by defensive coordinator Buddy Ryan after safety-turned-linebacker Doug Plank, who wore #46. "Buddy was very creative," Plank told Tim Layden. "Every week he would come up with some sort of new defense. He was always trying new things. Most of them didn't last very long. So this one day [in 1979] he puts this defense up on the board where I move from free safety to middle linebacker, along with some other shifts and changes. We're getting ready to leave the room, and one of the guys says, 'What are we going to call this one?' Well, Buddy was always drawing up packages but never drew them up with peoples' names or with X's and O's. He would always just write numbers." Here, Layden takes over the story: "Ryan circled Plank's number 46 several times, over and over, and then said, 'We'll call it 46.' " The 46 locked down the interior of the offensive line with man-on-man matchups, stopping double-teams from the offensive guards, and then doubled the offense's difficulties with aggressive blitzing. By the mid-1980s, Ryan had added linebacker Mike Singletary and unstoppable defensive end Richard Dent. Each week was unfair: the Bears roared to 15-1 record in the regular season, and then stomped on the Giants (21-0), Rams (24-0), and Patriots (46-10) in the playoffs, bringing Chicago its first championship of the Super Bowl era.

"Tighten the loose ends and loosen the tight ends."—Mike Singletary on the Bears' defensive philosophy

Other Notable Defenses

- *The Doomsday Defense*, Dallas Cowboys, 1966-1974, 1975-1983. Who spelled doom for the opposition? Big

Jethro Pugh and Hall-of-Famer Bob Lilly on the line, Chuck Howley and Lee Roy Jordan in the linebacking corps, Cornell Green and Hall-of-Famer Mel Renfro at the corners. There were others, too, like George Andrie and Dave Edwards, Herb Adderly and Charlie Waters, D.D. Lewis and Cliff Harris. When these players faded away, new doom arrived in the personages of Ed "Too Tall" Jones, Harvey Martin, and Hall-of-Famer Randy White. With such a defensive backbone in place, Tom Landry's Cowboys posted records above .500 from 1966 through 1985, making the playoffs in every year but two, winning Super Bowls VI and XII and losing Super Bowls V, IX, and XIII.

- *The 11 Angry Men*, Oakland Raiders, 1967. The Raiders mauled the AFL to the tune of a 13-1 record, blowing out Houston 40-7 in the AFL Championship before losing Super Bowl II to the Green Bay Packers. There were Pro Bowlers aplenty, led by corners Willie Brown and Kent McCloughan and middle linebacker Dan Conners. Sacks were not yet kept as an official statistic, but interceptions were, and the Raiders picked off 30 passes in 14 regular-season games, seven by Pro Football Hall-of-Famer Brown.

- *The No-Name Defense*, Miami Dolphins, 1971-1972. Madcap Hall of Fame middle linebacker Nick Buoniconti was the force behind a crew of Miami Dolphins who, fired up by their perceived anonymity ("I can't recall the names of the players on Miami's defensive unit," said Dallas head coach Tom Landry), reached three straight Super Bowls, won the last two, and put their names in the record books with 17 consecutive wins in the NFL's first Super Bowl-era undefeated season. The No-Namers pitched three shutouts during the '72 campaign, and they would have blanked the Washington Redskins in Super Bowl VII, too, if kicker Garo Yepremian had not attempted to grab a blocked field goal. Instead, he batted the ball up in the air, Washington's Mike Bass snatched it and raced away, and Washington had its only points in a 14-7 Miami win, completing the perfect No-Name D's perfect campaign.

- *Orange Crush*, Denver Broncos, 1977. Named for their bright uniforms, the Broncs' defense helped the team win 14 of its 17 games. Two of the three losses came against the Dallas Cowboys—including a defeat to Dallas in Super Bowl XII. Denver gave up more than 14 points only once during the regular season, limiting the opposition to single-digits in seven separate contests. The team leaders were defensive end Lyle Alzado, linebackers Randy Gradishar and Tom Jackson, strong safety Bill Thompson, and corner Louis Wright.

- *The Magic Defense*, Penn State, 1982-1983. It was called the Magic Defense, explained John Papanek in *Sports Illustrated*, January 10, 1983, " 'as in, now you see it, now you don't.' Linemen and linebackers shifted into various configurations, sometimes showing an eight-man front, sometimes a five or a six. They switched from nose to gap alignments, and at times as few as two defenders got down into a four-point stance." The Nittany Lions brought out their "Magic Defense" for big games. In the 1982 Fiesta Bowl, it frustrated Heisman Trophy-winner Marcus Allen, who entered averaging over 200 yards rushing per game, helping Penn State triumph, 26-10. In the 1983 Sugar Bowl, it came face to face with the force of nature that was Georgia's Herschel Walker. Walker finished the game with 28 carries, leading to 107 yards. It was a fine total—but it was also far lower than the Bulldogs were used to receiving from their great back. #2 Penn State upended #1 Georgia, 27-23, winning the national title.

- *The Wrecking Crew*, Texas A&M, 1989-1993. Headed up by new coach R.C. Slocum, the Wrecking Crew brought the Aggies to the top of the Southwest Conference, not losing a game in the SWC from 1991-1994. The last gasp for the Wrecking Crew came from 1995 to 1998, with Dat Nguyen stepping in at middle linebacker and recording a school-record 517 tackles during a decorated career.

- Baltimore Ravens, 2000. Yes, it's far more fun to detail the best monikers compiled over the years, but a compilation of the NFL's top defenses must mention the Super Bowl XXXV champions. The Ravens' offense was much maligned, managing only field goals from Week 5 through Week 9—but after suffering defeat in Week 9, 9-6 to Pittsburgh, they did not lose again. The defense was anchored by fearsome middle linebacker Ray Lewis and featured the beefy Sam Adams and Tony Siragusa up front, corners Chris McAlister and Duane Starks playing the tightest of press coverage, and difference-makers Rob Burnett, Jamie Sharper, Peter Boulware, and the iconic Rod Woodson at the tail end of his career. Baltimore posted four shutouts during the regular season, limiting the opposition to seven points or fewer in four other games. In the playoffs, they stopped the Broncos (21-3), Titans (24-10), Raiders (16-3), and, in the Super Bowl, the Giants (34-7) in no-nonsense fashion. New York's only points in Super Bowl XXXV came off of a kickoff return.

defensive back

n. back, ballhawk, DB, defensive halfback, jitterbug; SPECIFIC corner/cornerback, Eagle back (EB), dime/dimeback, nickel/nick-elback/5¢, safety/safetyman/safety man; see **cornerback**, **safety**

- A defensive back who seems to always be around the football is a *ballhawk* and is said to "have a nose for the ball." University of Michigan head coach Fielding Yost preferred the term "ball hound."

defensive backfield

n. secondary; SPECIFIC four-man backfield, five-man backfield (nickel), six-man backfield (dime), seven-man backfield (quarter/prevent), eight-man backfield (half-dollar/prevent); see **cornerback**, **defensive back**, **free safety**, and **strong safety**

- See "Dime, Nickel, and Prevent" under **defense**.

Notable Named Defensive Backfields

- *Legion of Boom*, Seattle Seahawks, 2013-2014, comprising cornerbacks Richard Sherman and Brandon Browner (2013) and Jeremy Lane/Byron Maxwell (2014), and safeties Kam Chancellor and Earl Thomas III. The Legion's reign might well be extended back a season to 2012, but everything came together for Seattle's bombastic secondary during their run to a dominating Super Bowl XLVIII victory. (Browner departed to New England following the season, where he won a second Super Bowl ring.)
- *No Fly Zone*, Michigan State Spartans, 2013, comprising cornerbacks Darqueze Dennard (who came up with the name) and Trae Waynes and safeties Kurtis Drummond and Isaiah Lewis. Dennard went on to win the Jim Thorpe Award as the nation's top defensive back and was selected in the first round of the 2014 draft, 24th overall, by the Cincinnati Bengals.

defensive end

n. DE, end (E), O man, outside man; SPECIFIC 3-4 defensive end, 4-3 defensive end, call-side call end (K), closed-side end (CE), defensive left end (DLE), defensive right end (DRE), edge rusher, elephant end, flex-E, open end, openside end (OSE), pass rusher, pass-rush specialist, Predator, read end, rush end, solid-E, speed rusher, strong end, strongside/strong-side defensive end, tightside end (TSE), weak end, weakside/weak-side defensive end, weak-side end (WE); see **defensive lineman**

"I can't figure it out—it's like a speed skater coming around a corner, he's so low to the ground, almost flat, with offensive lineman literally chasing him."—Buffalo Bills center Kent Hull, describing Bruce Smith's pass rush

Terms and Jargon

- The defensive end earned his name from his positioning

on the end of the defensive line, with the defensive guards (now defunct) and defensive tackle(s) between him and his counterpart.

- A defensive end who *stays home* remains disciplined in his area on a play that flows away from him, protecting against a counter, reverse, trap, or play-action bootleg that brings the play right back into his area.
- On the offensive line, the tight end's side is termed the *strong-side* or "closed side," while the opposite is the *weak-side* or "open side." The defensive end is thus called accordingly—a *weak-side end* or *open end* (*openside end*) always knows to line up on the other side of the line from the tight end.
- The other side of the line features the *strong-side end/ closed-side end*, working opposite the tight end. If this defensive end is able to give the tight end a good jam/ chug at the line, making it difficult for him to enter his pass pattern, and yet still put forth a solid pass rush, he earns the title of elephant end.
- The defensive end works to one side of the line and is responsible for setting *contain* (controlling the edge and denying outside room to a running back or a scrambling quarterback) and bringing pressure on the quarterback on passing plays. As such, the defensive end has more room to work with, allowing for speed and diversity in his pass-rushing techniques and tricks. If the quarterback gets outside of the defensive end, he *breaks contain*. As Minnesota sackmaster Jared Allen told former teammate Darren Sharper in a 2013 video interview for *Vikings.com*, "We have a little thing that's called reading on the run." Explained Allen, he didn't want to come to the line with his pass-rush move planned in advance. Instead, he preferred to watch the offensive lineman's stance and form and then react accordingly.
- On obvious passing plays, a defensive end understands that it is his job to get to the quarterback. A defender going entirely after a sack is said to *pin his ears back* and go.

- A *rush end*, *edge rusher*, or *pass-rush specialist* is employed because of his talents in getting to the quarterback. A defensive end who is at his best in pass rushing is often substituted on third down and long, or other logical passing situations. If his best pass rush trait is his speed around the outside, he earns an even more specific label: a *speed rusher*. In the Arizona Cardinals' current 4-3 under scheme (which was then brought to Philadelphia with the arrival of Chip Kelly as head coach), the pass-rush specialist is the "Predator."

Pass Rush Moves/Techniques

bull rush, chop and flip, conversion, crossing the face, inside rush, outside rush, rip, speed rush, speed (rush) to power (rush), spin move, swim move, swipe and punch

- A *bull rush* is built on power and leverage, with the rusher charging directly at the offensive lineman, extending his arms, and driving the blocker backward. (Add pace, and it becomes a *speed bull rush*.) Many pass rushes begin with the bull rush before switching into the rip or swim.
- With the offensive lineman punching forward, the rusher can choose to *chop* the hands and *flip them aside*, forcing his way through. This is related to the *swipe and punch*, which also literally describes how a rusher forces his way through his blocker.
- When *crossing the face*, the rusher decoys a speed rush, getting the lineman to start to lumber out to meet him. At that moment, the rusher cuts back to the inside, thereby crossing the lineman's face.
- The *rip* sees the rusher dip his inside shoulder, then punch upward, ripping underneath and through the extended arm of the hopeful blocker. Since the move goes to the inside, this is also often termed an *inside* rush.
- A *speed rush* sees the pass rusher use his feet to outpace the blocker, usually in an outside rush.
- In a *speed to power rush*, also called *conversion*, the rusher

starts toward the outside on a pure speed rush—and then, when the blocker shifts out to try to cut off the angle, shifts in a powerful bull rush straight at the blocker. The vice versa can also hold true, a power rush that turns into a speed rush.

- While the rip goes underneath, the *swim move* goes right over the top, powering over and past the blocker's shoulder with a motion akin to swimming's front crawl.

defensive line

n. defensive front, d-line, d-linemen, down linemen, forward wall, front, front four (on a four-man line), front-liners, the line, linemen, rush line, wall; POSITIONS defensive end/end (DE), defensive tackle/tackle (DT), nose/nose guard/nose tackle (N/NG/NT)

"A good defensive lineman has to be part buffalo and part ballet dancer."—defensive tackle Merlin Olsen

Terms and Jargon

- Across the line in a 4-3 defense (an *even* front): defensive end, defensive tackle, defensive tackle, defensive end; abbreviated as DE, DT, DT, DE.
- From left to right across the line in a 3-4 defense (an *odd* front): defensive end, nose tackle, defensive end; abbreviated as DE, NT, DE.
- A defender who lines up directly across from an offensive lineman is *head up* on that lineman. If he lines up toward the lineman's inside or outside shoulder, he's *shaded* to that shoulder.
- A defensive lineman *covers up* an offensive lineman, lining up head on or shading him; otherwise, that offensive lineman is left *uncovered* (or "vs. air"). The area surrounding an uncovered offensive lineman is a *bubble*.
- When a defensive lineman *crashes*, he angles his momentum hard toward the ball. A defensive end "crashing down," for instance, roars off the perimeter of the line as hard as he can toward the center of the play.
- A *one-gap* (1-gap) *technique* asks the lineman to occupy

one of the gaps in the line. A *two-gap* (2-gap) *technique* is even tougher, requiring the lineman to occupy two gaps. Those gaps: Left A (between left guard and center); Right A (between right guard and center); Left B (between left tackle and left guard); Right B (between right tackle and right guard); Left C (between tight end and left tackle); Right C (between tight end and right tackle); Left D (outside the tight end on the left side); Right D (outside the tight end on the right side).

- A defensive lineman who *loses gap integrity* allows the offensive line to open up a hole for the ball carrier directly where his assignment required him to have the gap sealed.
- A *forklift* sees the defensive lineman take the offensive lineman blocking him and lift him off of his feet.
- *Rush line* is an archaic term. From humorist George Ade, published in *Liberty* magazine, November 16, 1929: "The ball would be snapped into play and the enemy would come into contact with our rush line, whereupon our warriors would fall backward, still with their fists clenched, and lie upon the turf moaning feebly, while somewhere someone in possession of the ball would carry it to any point which might suit his whim or fancy, because there was none anywhere near him to disarrange his plans."
- If faced with the need for a short-yardage stop, the defensive linemen can *submarine* the offensive line, lining up in four-point stances (both hands on the ground), and aiming for the o-line's knees at the snap of the ball, trying to get low and disrupt a run.

Techniques and Gap Assignments

Credit Bum Phillips for developing the idea of numbered techniques, assigning positions and responsibilities along the defensive line, while coaching high-school football:

- The 0 technique (*0-tech* or *zero-technique*) lines the nose tackle head up on (nose to nose with) the center.
- The 1 technique (*1-tech* or *one-technique*) sees the nose

tackle line up in the A gap, between center and offensive guard; he is expected to occupy both linemen. If his stance brings him in close to the football pre-snap, he's said to "hug the ball." As described by Greg Garber in an *ESPN.com* article on December 1, 2009, "The nose tackle occupies the most lucrative real estate in football, patrolling the swath of ground—gaps "Left A" and "Right A" on either side of the center—that are the most direct path offenses must choose if they want to reach the end zone. If a nose tackle can stand his ground, take on two and sometimes three blockers (tight ends and fullbacks sometimes try to take him out), he can force the play outside."

- The 2 technique (*2-tech* or *two-technique*) puts the defensive tackle head up on the offensive guard. In the *2i technique*, the tackle is shaded to the guard's inside shoulder—the 'i' stands for inside.
- The 3 technique (*3-tech* or *three-technique*) lines the under tackle up in the B gap, between offensive guard and tackle. He is expected to shoot through the gap and disrupt the play. (For *under tackle*, see **defensive tackle**.)
- The 4 technique (*4-tech* or *four-technique*) has the defender head up on the offensive tackle. In the *4i technique*, he shades to the tackle's inside shoulder.
- The 5 technique (*5-tech* or *five-technique*) sees the defensive end responsible for both the B and C gaps (C signifying the gap outside the offensive tackle).
- The 7 technique (*7-tech* or *seven-technique*) places the defensive end in the strong-side C *gap*, outside of the offensive tackle, on the same side as the tight end, prepared to snuff out a run.
- The 9 technique (*9-tech* or *nine-technique*) locates the defensive end in the weak-side C *gap*, outside of the tackle, on the opposite side as the tight end, prepared to rush the passer.
- When describing a linebacker, a 0 is added to each technique's number. A 00 technique, for instance, places the linebacker head up on the center; a 70 technique has the linebacker set up in the strong-side C gap.

- If all of the techniques are shifted toward the strong side of the offensive formation, the defense is aligned in an *over* front. If the opposite is true, with the defensive linemen shifting toward the weak side of the formation, they're playing an under front. (This is termed "setting their front.") Tampa Bay Buccaneers defensive coordinator Monte Kiffin, the godfather of the Tampa 2, was the force behind showing how the under front could cause havoc.

Defensive Line Pass Rush Moves
n. cha-cha, cross-rush, deal, game, inside stunt, limbo, loop, outside stunt, pirate stunt, stunt, tackle-end twist, twist

- The defensive line need not rush the quarterback using a straightforward path. Instead, using a *stunt* (also called a *deal*, *game*, or a *twist*), they can trade assignments or gaps, befuddling the offensive line and helping one or more defenders find a way to the quarterback. This occurs through cross-rushing, with the linemen criss-crossing their way forward, or through patience, with one lineman firing off the ball and occupying blockers while the other waits back before working in behind his teammate and finding a free lane. In *Instant Replay*, Jerry Kramer described the game played by the 1960s New York Giants' defensive line: "On pure passing situations—on third down with ten yards to go, for instance—the Giants often use what we call a tackle-end twist. The end, instead of rushing his normal way, will cut inside the tackle's rush, and the tackle of course will come outside. They reverse positions, trying to confuse the offensive line."
- The *cha-cha* and *limbo* are described in Mickey Herskowitz and Steve Perkins's *Everything You Always Wanted to Know About Sports*. In the *cha-cha*, the two defensive tackles work a stunt in tandem. In the *limbo*, the defensive end presses inside while the tackle circles around the outside.
- A *loop*, like a stunt or twist, can describe the exchange for either defensive tackle and/or end, though it

specifically describes the looping path for the trail
defender, taking his time to circle around his teammate
before finding a free avenue toward the quarterback.

- The *pirate stunt* "involves three defensive linemen,"
wrote Pat Kirwan, "two crashing down inside and the
nose tackle looping outside."

- George Perles, defensive coordinator of the Pittsburgh
Steelers (and their dominant Steel Curtain front four)
before joining Michigan State University as head coach,
rode the 4-3 stunting defense, flummoxing offensive
lines at both the pro and college levels. Notable Perles
stunts, quoting from his piece for AFCA's *Defensive
Football Strategies*, include:

The Tom game ("we slant our weak side tackle into the
center-guard gap and loop our strong side tackle into
the face of the weak side offensive guard").

The three game ("It is run like the Tom game, except the
defensive end also runs an inside slant."). This was
changed to the "four game" in the pros.

Storm ("This is like the four game, except the outside
linebacker comes on the inside slant.").

Ram ("The end and linebacker stunt to the inside, with
the middle linebacker on a scrape off to the outside.")

Me ("We use the me call between the weak side end
and linebacker…. If we call the 'open me,' that involves
the strong side end and tackle. In the stunt, he steps to
the offense and then loops to the outside while the
linebacker comes on a down slant.")

Notable Defensive Lines

- *The Fearsome Foursome*, Los Angeles Rams, 1963-1968,
comprising defensive ends David "Deacon" Jones and
Lamar Lundy and defensive tackles Merlin Olsen and
Roosevelt "Rosey" Grier (later replaced by Roger
Brown). It was football's version of "Tinker to Evers to

Chance," quoted by Mickey Herskowitz and Steve
Perkins: "Olsen, Rosey, Lundy, and Jones / A Fearsome
Foursome to rattle your bones / When the quarterback
asks which were the ones / Tell him Olsen, Rosey,
Lundy, and Jones."

- *The Purple People Eaters*, also called the *Purple Gang*,
  Minnesota Vikings, 1967-1974, with defensive ends
  Carl Eller and Jim Marshall and defensive tackles Gary
  Larsen and the honorable Alan Page, who was later
  elected a Minnesota Supreme Court justice. (To extend
  the People Eaters' reign, Larsen was replaced by Doug
  Sutherland during the 1974 season.) The Vikings
  reached four Super Bowls while the Purple People
  Eaters were in their heyday, their moniker borrowed
  from Sheb Wooley's #1 hit in 1958.

- *The Steel Curtain*, Pittsburgh Steelers, 1971-1977,
  starring ends L.C. Greenwood and Dwight White and
  tackles "Mean Joe" Greene and Ernie "Fats" Holmes (the
  "charter members," said Steelers voice Myron Cope).
  Credit 14-year-old Greg Kronz with the invention of
  the Steel Curtain name; his submission won a 1971
  contest seeking the proper descriptor for Pittsburgh's
  dominating front. "To be fair, though, [Kronz] was just
  one of 17 people who submitted the 'Steel Curtain'
  moniker to the WTAE contest, necessitating a drawing
  for the grand prize," Ruth Ann Dailey wrote for the
  Pittsburgh Post-Gazette, January 30, 2006. "His age also
  meant that his parents got to enjoy the prize—a four-day
  trip to Miami just a few weeks later to see the Steelers
  play the Dolphins. 'I sent them on a second honeymoon,'
  says Greg."

- *New York Sack Exchange*, New York Jets, 1981-1983, with
  ends Mark Gastineau and Joe Klecko and tackles Abdul
  Salaam and Marty Lyons. Wrote Jerry Eskenazi for
  NFL.com, "A fan at Shea Stadium held up a bed sheet on
  which he had scrawled 'New York Sack Exchange.'
  Frank Ramos, the Jets' public relations director, used the
  nickname in a press release and a legend was born."

- *NASCAR*, New York Giants, 2012, devised by defensive

coordinator Perry Fewell and featuring a four-man defensive line of all pass-rushers: Mathias Kiwanuka, Jason Pierre-Paul, Justin Tuck, and Osi Umenyiora. NASCAR stands for the National Association for Stock Car Auto Racing, and no team planned on revving its engines and getting after the quarterback like the Giants' defensive front. But while 2012 had the catchy name and scheme, it was the 2007 and 2011 *Big Blue Wrecking Crew* defenses who took home Super Bowl titles.

defensive lineman

n. d-lineman, down lineman, lineman, redwood; see **defensive end, defensive line, defensive tackle**

"Now that I'm retired, I want to say that all defensive linemen are sissies."—Quarterback Dan Fouts

defensive tackle

n. DT, I man, interior man, tackle; SPECIFIC call tackle, defensive left tackle (DLT), defensive right tackle (DRT), five tech (five-technique tackle), middle guard, nose (N), nose guard (NG), nose tackle (NT), three tech (three-technique tackle), under tackle (UT); see **defensive line, nose tackle**

Basics

- The defensive tackle works in the middle of the line, and thus is often big, bulky, and physical.
- The under tackle is smaller and quicker than the average hulking defensive tackle and is utilized solely in 3-technique, and so is often nicknamed the *three tech*. In an April 30, 2014, article for the *Chicago Tribune*, "NFL Draft Preview: Defensive Tackle," reporter Dan Wiederer wrote, "In the Bears' system, [general manager Phil] Emery calls the under tackle position 'the engine that drives the defense.' "

down

n. attempt, play, snap, try; see **play**
v. see **defeat**; see **tackle**

Terms and Jargon

- Football plays all begin with the *down* and *distance* in mind: What down is it, and how far does the offensive team need to travel in order to pick up its next first down or score a touchdown? When the first-down system was first concocted in 1882, a team was given four plays (*downs*) to travel at least five yards. That was soon widened to ten yards once the forward pass was legalized and offenses began to open up.
- When a football team takes over possession of the ball, their down and distance always starts at "1st and 10," signifying first down—the first play—and ten yards needed to be traveled to gain a new first down. The lone exception: if the offense starts at the opposition's 10-yard line or closer. Since a first down is impossible without scoring a touchdown, the down and distance is termed "1st and Goal."
- Should the offense gain four yards on that first play, the down and distance becomes 2nd and 6—second down (the second play of the series) and six yards required.
- In order to aid television viewers, a yellow line was graphically added to the screen to indicate the yard line needed to be reached. Either the offense attains that first-down line in these four downs, or it hands the ball over to the opposition (in a *turnover on downs*).
- Each new first down gives the offense a new series or set of downs, moving the first down chains farther and farther downfield. See **first down** and **first down line** for more.
- When at last a team reaches the opposition's ten yard line or closer with a new series of downs, their down and distance becomes *1st and Goal*, or *1st down and Goal to Go*. They must score in the next four downs or else turn the ball over.

- On third down, if the offense remains a ways away from the first down line, the more general description of "long" is given for distance in the down and distance designation. A 3rd and 8, for instance, is a "3rd and long." (A 3rd and 17 would be considered a "3rd and very long.") If the offense is only a few yards away from the first down line, "short" may be substituted. A 3rd and 1, a 3rd and 2, or a 3rd and 3 could all be termed "3rd and short." In between "long" and "short" is considered "intermediate" or "manageable."
- With two yards or fewer needed—three yards required is the very border—the offense is in a *short-yardage situation*, determined by the offense's ability to run for the first down, instead of being forced into a near-certain pass play.
- First down is signaled by officials with a raised index finger, two fingers indicate second down, and three fingers signal third down. Fourth down, conversely, is indicated with a raised fist.

One Down Too Many...

- Four downs is all a team should get in American football. After the fourth, the ball is turned over on downs to the opposition. At least, that's what ideally should happen. On November 16, 1940, head linesman Joe McKenney lost count of the downs in a goal-line moment between #2 Cornell and upset-minded Dartmouth. On the fateful fifth down, the Big Red pushed into the end zone for a controversial 7-3 victory. When notified of the miscall, however, referee Red Friesell openly admitted his crew's error, after which Cornell telegrammed their rival: "In view of the conclusions reached by the officials that the Cornell touchdown was scored on a fifth down, Cornell relinquishes claim to the victory and extends congratulations to Dartmouth."
- Twenty-one years later, the Green Bay Packers were extended the benefit of a fifth down by referee George Rennix's crew in the third quarter of the NFL

Championship Game against the New York Giants. As chronicled by Dan Daly in *The National Forgotten League*, the crew became confused by a Bart Starr second-down fumble that was wiped out by a Packers illegal-motion infraction. When the penalty was assessed, the down marker was incorrectly reset to 1st down. This was followed by three consecutive Packer snaps that garnered only 11 yards, and culminated in a Boyd Dowler fifth-down punt. The Pack didn't need too many other breaks in the game, topping the Giants by a lopsided 37-0 margin.

- On October 6, 1990, the Colorado Buffaloes became the latest recipients of officiating inattention—and it aided the Buffaloes in winning a share in the 1990 national championship. In the final minute, down 31-27 to Missouri, Colorado arrived in the vicinity of the Tigers goal line and then 1) spiked the ball, 2) had an Eric Bieniemy run stopped short (with the down marker remaining at 2nd down), 3) watched Bieniemy again get stuffed, 4) again spiked the ball, and 5) scored the game-winning touchdown on a quarterback keeper as time expired. There was no postgame conceding telegram. (The Buffs went on to edge Notre Dame in the Orange Bowl, 10-9, and were voted national champs by the Associated Press.)

...and One Too Few

- On December 8, 1968, the Los Angeles Rams trailed the Chicago Bears by a point, 17-16. Attempting a last-second drive, the Rams made their way into Bears territory. A first-down holding penalty pushed them back, followed by three consecutive Roman Gabriel incompletions. At this point, when it should have been only fourth down, the officials handed the ball over to the Bears. "Commissioner Rozelle admitted the error the next day," wrote Bob Carroll, "and suspended the officials for the remainder of the season. Small consolation for the Rams. With two losses on their record, they could only finish second to the Colts."

E

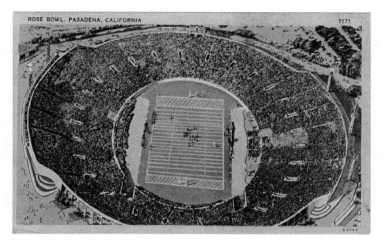

The Rose Bowl, Pasadena, California.

end zone

n. goal, the house, paint, pay dirt, paydirt, promised land, six-town (6-town)

History, Terms, and Jargon

- The rectangular end zone runs from *goal line*, signifying its start, to *end line*, signifying the back boundary line to the field. It stretches ten yards in length, with weighted pylons (usually bright orange) marking its four corners.
- At football's inception, wrote Robert W. Peterson in *Pigskin*, "There was no end zone. The area beyond the

goal line was called 'in goal,' but it had no rear boundary. There was no need for one because forward passing was prohibited. In order to score, the ball-carrier needed only to break the plane of the goal line."

- An offense driving into the *red zone*—inside the 20-yard line—and presenting a distinct threat of scoring is *knocking on the door*.
- A *goal-line stand* sees the defenders rise up at the doorstep of their own end zone and stop the offense on downs. (Red Matal, part of Columbia's goal-line stands against Stanford in the 1934 Rose Bowl: "We always knew where to line up; we just found our footprints in the mud from the last stand and dug in all over again.")
- An offense taking over possession inside its own 5-yard line is "in the shadow of the goal posts."

Furthermore

- The "Black Hole" describes the raucous and often costumed Raiders' fans who fill the south end zone in Oakland.
- Tennessee's orange-and-white checkerboard design draws notice, but there may be no more famous end zone pattern in college football than Notre Dame's angled white stripes. The significance, from NBC Sports' Keith Arnold: "Lest you think they are just diagonal lines, the year of Notre Dame's founding [1842] will be honored, with a total of 18 hash marks (nine in each) set at a 42 degree angle towards the Basilica and Golden Dome."

Brown v. Washington

- George Preston Marshall's Washington Redskins were the final team in the NFL to integrate, which raised the ire of *Washington Post* columnist Shirley Povich. Following a loss to the Cleveland Browns, Povich struck:

For 18 minutes, the Redskins were enjoying equal

rights with the Cleveland Browns yesterday, in the sense that there was no score in the contest. Then it suddenly became unequal in favor of the Browns, who brought along Jim Brown, their rugged colored fullback from Syracuse.

From 25 yards out, Brown was served the football by Milt Plum on a pitch-out and he integrated the Redskins' goal line with more than deliberate speed, perhaps exceeding the famous Supreme Court decree. Brown fled the 25 yards like a man in an uncommon hurry and the Redskins' goal line, at least, became interracial.

extra point

n. 1-point try, the point, point after, try, try point; see **PAT**

F

Ernie Davis of Syracuse University, the 1961 Heisman Trophy winner. (AP.)

fan

n. addict, admirer, aficionado, apologist, armchair quarterback, attendee, backer, bleacher critic, booster, buff, customer, devotee, diehard, enthusiast, fanatic, football junkie, freak, grandstand quarterback, grid fan, loyalist, nut, onlooker, partisan, rooter, spectator, turnstiler, twelfth man; SPECIFIC bandwagon fan, draftnik, fair-weather fan, fantasy football junkie, frontrunner, Monday morning quarterback, superfan, super fan, wolf; PLURAL assemblage, crowd, fanbase, mass, masses, mob, multitude, nation, rabble, throng, turnout

"A man must serve his time to every trade /
Save censure—critics all are ready made."
—*Lord Byron*

Terms and Jargon

- An *armchair quarterback* sits back in the comfort of his/her home and waxes eloquently (or not) and emotionally on what his/her favorite team *should* be doing. A *grandstand quarterback* does the same from the stadium, and rather loudly at that. The *Monday morning quarterback* waits until the day after an NFL game to share everything his/her favorite team did wrong and what they need to do now. It's a veritable fact of life that most every problem can be solved by either benching the starting quarterback or firing the head coach.
- Give full credit—or blame—to the Oakland Raiders, who are considered to be the first team to call their fan base a *nation.*
- In a "whiteout," all of the home fans wear white, thus "whiting out" the stadium in support of a team wearing white jerseys. (In a "blackout," all fans wear black, and so on.) Then there's the "Sea of Red" at the University of Nebraska, where the Cornhuskers faithful clad themselves fully in Nebraska red.
- *Wolves*, as defined in Zander Hollander's *Encyclopedia of Sports Talk*: "People who snarl because their team isn't winning. They may be alumni, fans, bettors—anyone who can put the heat on a losing coach."

"Football today is far too much a sport for the few who can play it well; the rest of us, and too many of our children, get our exercise from climb-

ing up the seats in stadiums, or from walking across the room to turn on our television sets. And this is true for one sport after another, all across the board."—President John F. Kennedy

Home of the 12th Man

- There are eleven players per side in football; the symbolic twelfth represents the fans.
- "The tradition of the Twelfth Man," reads the Texas A&M's website under Aggies Traditions, "was born on the second of January 1922, when an underdog Aggie team was playing Centre College, then the nation's top ranked team. As the hard fought game wore on, and the Aggies dug deeply into their limited reserves, Coach Dana X. Bible remembered a squad man who was not in uniform. He had been up in the press box helping reporters identify players. His name was E. King Gill, and [he] was a former football player who was only playing basketball. Gill was called from the stands, suited up, and stood ready throughout the rest of the game, which A&M finally won 22-14.... He came to be thought of as the Twelfth Man because he stood ready for duty in the event that the eleven men on the gridiron needed assistance....This tradition took on a new look in the 1980's when Coach Jackie Sherrill started the 12th Man Kick-Off Team composed of regular students through open tryouts....Later, Head Coach R.C. Slocum changed the team to allow only one representative of the 12th Man on the kick off team." And there the tradition has stood: Texas A&M, "home of the 12th man," where the students feel part of the action—and one of them literally is.

Drowned Out

- According to Chris Schenkel, an exuberant throng decided the victor in the 1963 Army-Navy game: "Ranked second in the nation, with its only loss coming via the upset route to Southern Methodist, the Middies led underdog Army 21-15, but their backs were to the goal line and there was still time for the Cadets to score. The 100,000 spectators boiled over, despite the December chill, and many blame the roar of the crowd for Army's failure to produce a game-tying touchdown....The clock read 1:38. The noise was deafening. Quarterback [Carl] Stichweh held his arms high in an appeal for quiet and even had to use a precious time-out to stop the clock. It was first down, the ball on the Navy seven. [Ray] Paske plowed in to the five. The clock continued. Then [Ken] Waldrop bulled in to the four. The seconds ticked. Again Waldrop plunged into the line, this to the two. Stichweh, in a frenzy with time running out, again raised his arms and asked for quiet—screamed for a time out—but the howling crowd absorbed his plea. The gun sounded, and Navy had won."

field

n. see **football field**

field goal

n. FG, goal, three-pointer; SPECIFIC chip-shot, made field goal, missed field goal, unhurried kick

"He kicks! And it's a beautiful kick! End over end! Terrific! And it's no good!"—radio broadcaster Harry Wismer

kick a successful field goal
v. cash in, convert, get, knock it through, make, put through, split the uprights, send through, slide in, slide through, sneak through

Term, History, and Changes

- A *chip-shot*, taken from golf jargon, is an easy field-goal attempt from short range.
- An *unhurried kick* sees the place-kicker attempt a field goal following a timeout or a spike, or at a time in the

game where there is no urgency. It is the preferred type of attempt, rather than the hurried kick, where the kicker and special teams unit has to race on the field and hustle to get off an attempt due to a dying clock. The term "unhurried kick" was credited by Chris B. Brown to Homer Smith, an offensive coordinator at UCLA and Alabama.

- On November 1, 1924, a freshman kicker for Montana State named Forrest Peters drop-kicked 17 field goals against Billings Polytechnic Institute to set the national record. It was his only season at Montana State; in 1926, 1928, and 1929, he suited up for powerful Illinois. Peters went on to play minor-league baseball in the 1930s before joining the American Association as an umpire.

- Did Don Chandler make his 22-yard field-goal attempt in the 1965 NFL Western Division play-off game? Only two minutes and change remained, with the Baltimore Colts leading Chandler's Green Bay Packers 10-7. "The kick wasn't Chandler's best," wrote Bob Carroll in *The Football Abstract*. "It climbed sky-high and twisted to the right. In fact, he seemed to think he'd missed it and turned away. But field judge Jim Tunney liked it and signaled it good. To this day, there's not a Baltimore fan who'd agree. Baltimore kicker Lou Michaels doubled as a defensive end and was on the field at the time. It was his expert estimate that the kick 'was at least three feet wide.' Chandler later admitted, 'It wasn't a real good kick, but I couldn't tell.' " But it had been ruled good, and that was the final verdict. Green Bay won in overtime on an uncontroversial Chandler field goal. The Pack went on to top Cleveland for the championship. An addendum from Carroll: "The NFL wouldn't admit it publicly, but two rule changes before the next season stemmed from Tunney's controversial call on Chandler's game-tying field goal. Two officials were required to stand near the goal line to make the call, and the uprights were extended another ten feet into the air to make high kicks easier to judge."

- There is no question that Matt Prater made his attempt on December 8, 2013, a 64-yard field goal that set a new NFL record. The previous record of 63 yards had been shared by Tom Dempsey (November 8, 1970), Jason Elam (October 25, 1998), and Sebastian Janikowski (September 12, 2011).
- A missed field goal may be returned by the defending team, and this uncommonly leads to a highlight-reel touchdown. In 2013, the SEC saw a missed field goal returned for a touchdown on two separate occasions: by LSU's Odell Beckham, Jr., on September 7 against UAB, and—in the play of the year—by Auburn's Chris Davis, Jr., with no time left to defeat Alabama in the Iron Bowl, launching Auburn into the SEC Title Game and (eventually) the BCS National Championship game. Both returns measured 109 yards, the farthest distance a touchdown could possibly be scored under the current field dimensions.

Field Goal Worth

- Originally, "goals from the field" were worth five points, while touchdowns were merely worth four points. In 1904, six years after scoring a touchdown was increased to five points, kicking a field goal was lowered to four points. In 1909, the number dropped again, with the current custom of three points awarded for a successful field goal.
- No one could ever accuse the World Football League of not being creative. During the WFL's 1975 preseason, the league experimented with awarding different measurements of points based upon the distance of successfully made field goals. If the ball was kicked from the 10-yard line or closer, only one point was given. Field goals booted from in between the 10- and 30-yard lines earned two points. Outside of the 30-yard line, a team received the full three points for a made field goal.

first down

n. first; SPECIFIC automatic first down

Terms

- A first down *moves the chains* and provides a *new sheet of downs* or a *fresh set of downs*, sometimes shortened to a *fresh set*.
- An *automatic first down* is given when the defense commits five-yard holding or illegal contact (also called illegal use of hands) penalties, even when moving the offense forward five yards is not enough for a first down.

first down line

n. the first, line to gain, marker, mark to gain, mark to make, necessary distance, necessary line, yellow line

- see "Working On the Chain Gang" under **official**

History, Terms, and Jargon

- In *The Paolantonio Report*, Sal Paolantonio argued that the creation of the first down in 1882 is the Most Underrated Moment in NFL History. "Without that rule change in 1882," wrote Paolantonio, "we would not have had offense and defense. We would not have had innovations to advance the ball, the 'quarter-back' running it and, of course, passing it. That rule change allowed for the institution of a vast statistical record of the game. Without it, there would be no specialization or, later, the need for substitutions." He finished with a flourish: "If that rule change had not been made in 1882, we'd still be watching rugby's slow-moving scrum. Or worse, soccer."
- Walter Camp's original words: "If on three consecutive fairs and downs a team shall not have advanced the ball five yards, nor lost ten, they must give up the ball to

opponents at the spot of the fourth down." Right from the start, there: The unit of measurement was laid down as the yard. (Also…what happened to that idea of losing ten yards causing a turnover?)

- Initially, teams were required to move the ball only five yards in order to pick up a first down, although they were only given three downs for their efforts. In 1906, the necessary first-down yardage was increased to 10 yards. Six years later, the fourth down was added to aid offenses.

- First downs are measured by two rods connected by a 10-yard chain, conspicuously held along the sideline to show the players the needed yardage for the next first down. These rods are also called the *chains, down and distance markers, markers,* or *sticks,* and they are operated by officials called the chain gang. If, after a measurement, the nose of the football comes up shy of the necessary yardage, the distance needed can range from yards to inches to—if the ball is remarkably close—links of the chain.

- The chain gang holds sticks indicating both the line of scrimmage and the necessary line to gain for a first down. A penalty or negative play that places the offense behind the original line of scrimmage (a false start penalty, costing five yards and leading to a 1st and 15, for instance) places the offense "behind the chains."

flank

n. flank zone, flat

- The *flank* describes the area of the field outside the numbers, toward the sidelines. The *flanker,* originally called the *flankerback,* received his name for regularly lining up in this area. (see **wide receiver**)

football (ball)

n. apple, ball, bladder, leather, oblate spheroid, oval, pig, pig rind,

pigskin, pig with a mohawk, prolate spheroid, pumpkin, rock;
SPECIFIC dead ball, deflated ball, dry ball, game ball, inflated ball,
K ball (or K-ball), laceless ball, live ball, loaf of bread, loose ball,
practice ball, wet ball

*"I decided finally to pack the football. It was a slightly used Spalding ball,
an expensive one, with the information printed on it that it was 'triple-
lined and lock-stitched.' Its sponsoring signature was that of Norman
Van Brocklin, the ex-Philadelphia Eagle quarterback. It seemed a little
deflated."—opening sentences of George Plimpton's* Paper Lion

Terms and Jargon

- The forward tip of the football is the *nose*.
- Any player currently in possession of the football is the
  ball carrier (sometimes seen as *ballcarrier* or *ball-carrier*).
- When a football is fumbled, it becomes a *greased pig,
  greased pigskin*, or *hot potato*. (see **fumble**)
- *Apple?* An excerpt from Chris Schenkel, describing a
  wild play for the Giants: "...[Frank] Gifford lateraled to
  Greg Larsen, the Giant center, who is not used to
  handling the ball in an upright position. Larsen quickly
  released the 'apple' to [quarterback Y.A.] Tittle, who
  broke into a smile as he flipped it back to Gifford."
  Disappointingly, the sequence ended in an incomplete
  pass.
- A player holding the football perilously out with one
  hand, rather than properly cradled against his body,
  holds it like a *loaf of bread*. It's an easy way to tempt fate
  and potentially lose possession.
- As for *oval*: Howard Roberts quoted Michigan's season
  in review in 1910 in "The Big Nine," " 'By making a
  grand running leap and turning half way around,
  [Stanley] Borleske caught the oval at a point 18 yards in
  advance of where it was put into play. Without a bit of a
  hesitation and before some of the Minnesota players
  knew what was coming off, the same play again was
  executed successfully. Borleske, after catching the oval,
  made a gallant effort to place it over the line, but he was

stopped on the four yard mark about 10 yards from the sideline.' "

- A football is the *rock* most commonly when a coach, player, or fan is exhorting his team to "Run the rock!" or "Give him the rock!"

"Styles and tastes change in football. Now, the forward passer has become the hero because of the large slices of enemy territory that can be vanquished by the accuracy of his heaves. But there is still no thrill comparable to the one furnished by a fast, shifty, elusive runner who tucks that windjammed pig rind under his arm and swivel-hips his way through a broken field to climax his effort by crossing the goal line standing up."—Paul Gallico

The Ball

- Interesting facts from the Wilson Football website: There is one lace on an official ball, with 16 lace holes and four panels; an average of 10 footballs can be made from a single cowhide; and 700,000 footballs are produced each year from Wilson's football-only factory in Ada, Ohio. Chicanery aside, a football is properly inflated to 13 psi, give or take 0.5.
- *The Big Nine*, written by Howard Roberts in 1948, begins in this fashion: "A football takes funny bounces. It's as perverse as a mule, as unpredictable as a woman. So is the game of football, which is decided by the antics of this leather lunatic and the men who kick it, throw it, and run with it."
- Robert W. Peterson accurately described the first football as "a rubber bladder encased in leather. It was a copy of the rugby ball; in fact, rugby balls imported from England often were used in the early days of American football. The ball was a cross between today's football and basketball–fatter than modern footballs and blunt at the ends. Sportswriters who fancied florid prose often called an American football a 'prolate spheroid.' "
- "Blimp," according to Zander Hollander and Paul Zimmerman, was "the name for the ball used in

football's early days. It was rounder in shape and looked like a cross between the modern football and a soccer ball."

- "Watermelon" and "cantaloupe" were other nicknames for the old ball. From George "Papa Bear" Halas's written words for *The Saturday Evening Post*, December 7, 1957: "[Benny Friedman] couldn't toss our 'cantaloupe' with the accuracy which Sid Luckman and Otto Graham later achieved with a streamlined ball, but he was accurate enough to jolt our defenses with unexpected passes on first and second down."

- We are accustomed to the current brown football, but the first night game in NFL history introduced a ball painted white for better visibility. The game was held between Providence and Chicago on November 6, 1929, with the local newspaper scribe reporting the ball "had the appearance of a large egg" and "there was a panicky feeling that the player who made the catch would be splattered with yellow yolk." The ball was still used into the mid-1950s.

"He merely lifted his arm, cracked his wrist like a whip and there through the sunlight went the shining, spinning spheroid."—Bill Cunningham, Boston Post, on Sammy Baugh, 1935

Spheroids, Oblate vs. Prolate

- It is closer to correct to say that a football is prolate rather than oblate. Indeed, according to George Halas, the *prolate spheroid* designation was how the "ball then was described in the [rules committee] manual." But the confusion is easy to understand. The *oblate spheroid* term comes from Hollander and Zimmerman's *Football Lingo* in 1967 (ball: also called a pigskin or oblate spheroid, a technical term meaning football-shaped). The difference between prolate and oblate—other than prolate being pointier at the sides—is similar to the difference between latitude and longitude, or horizontal and vertical. Consider a beach ball. To make that beach ball prolate, squeeze it together at its sides. To make it

oblate, squeeze it together from the top and bottom.
(The planet Earth is an oblate spheroid.)

The K Ball

- "Kickers and punters once resorted to strange measures
to kick the football further and gain more yards. They'd
put the ball in the microwave, hot tub or use a
blowdryer." Thus begins RaeAnn Dutto for *Chargers.com*,
explaining why the NFL introduced the K ball. Marked
with a K, the K ball is specifically set aside for kicking:
extra-point attempts, field goal kicking, kicking off, and
punting. "Once unwrapped, the footballs are hard and
slippery, making them difficult to handle compared to
the balls offenses uses. The official hands the K balls off
to a designated member of each organization, who is the
only person with the opportunity to rub down the
football....Kickoff begins with using ball number one
and continues to be in play until it is no longer an
option. Once unavailable, ball number two is brought
into play and the cycle continues throughout the game."

White Stripes and No Laces

- Footballs at lower levels can often be seen with a white
strip around each side, toward the tips, thus allowing
easier visibility in the evening.
- There are eight raised white laces on an official football.
Unless, that is, the football is laceless. From Megan
Watson's September 10, 2014, article for *The Ada Herald*:

  [Jon] Gruden had an idea that that he thought would
  reduce quarterback's dependency on football laces. He
  felt that by removing the laces from practice balls, it
  would train the players to just grab and throw vs. grab,
  line up laces, then throw. While the idea was strong,
  the big question was, could it be done?

  When Dan Riegle got the request from Wilson head-
  quarters for a prototype of a laceless football, he knew

that if it could be done it would be by recently retired employee Jane Helser….

Helser remembered that her sister, Lucille Cheney, used to hand-sew volleyballs for Wilson. The sisters spent a few days working on the project but finally developed something that would work.

The football had to be sewn almost completely together, air bladder inserted, and a small opening left at the tip. Helser then closed it by hand with two large needles. She had to be careful not to puncture the air bladder or get the thread tangled, because she was basically sewing it shut from the inside out….it took her two hours of nonstop work.

- The practice of learning how to throw a football without the laces might be recent, but unorthodox passing grips date back generations, a practice that includes quarterbacking icons. Wrote Dan Daly and Bob O'Donnell, "Sammy Baugh used only the seams, with the laces toward his palm. He felt he could only make the ball 'behave a little better that way.' The Packers' Arnie Herber did the same but had such short, stubby fingers that he couldn't actually hold the ball. He just rested it in his palm and heaved it the way a catapult would a stone….Y.A. Tittle used the laces but held the ball with his fingertips only. The rest of the hand just went along for the ride. Terry Bradshaw put only three fingers on the laces—middle, ring and pinky. His index finger was on the back point of the ball."

football (sport)

n. America's Greatest Game, America's passion, America's Spectator Sport, collision sport, game of attrition, game of autumn, game of inches, game of passion, grid game, The Game, King Football, Lord Football

"Baseball claims to be America's national pastime, but football is its true passion."—Pat Kirwan, Take Your Eye Off the Ball

Walter Camp

- "The Father of American Football." Such was the nickname given to Walter Chauncey Camp, a Yale end given significant credit for turning rugby into the current form of American football in the late 19th century. Historian Parke H. Davis wrote of how that occurred for the 1925 *Football Guide*:

  During these years, the closing years of the '70's, Walter Camp had been intensely studying the possibilities of the Rugby type of game in its natural laboratory, the playing field. Here he was confronted with the Rugby 'scrum' which gave to neither side the orderly possession, nor the right to put it in play and to execute the ensuing maneuver. With his penetrative mind, keen and powerful notwithstanding his youthful years, he perceived the vast improvement which would give to one side its undisturbed possession, thereby permitting a strategic and tactical preparation to advance it. Accordingly he planned a new device, the 'scrimmage,' and quietly awaited the coming of the next intercollegiate football convention. This eventually convened at Springfield October 12, 1880. It was composed of W.H. Manning and T.C. Thacher of Harvard, Edward Peace and Francis Loney of Princeton, Walter Camp, Robert H. Watson and W.B. Hill of Yale. Mr. Camp as a preliminary renewed his motion to reduce the number of players upon a side from fifteen to eleven, and this time the motion prevailed. Thereupon he suggested the following profound change in the rules, the phrasing of which he personally had penned:

  "A scrimmage takes place when the holder of the ball puts it on the ground before him and puts it in play while on-side either by kicking the ball or by snapping it back with his foot. The man who first receives the ball from the snap-back shall be called the quarter-back and shall not rush forward with the ball under penalty of foul." This proposition was accepted unanimously and thus Walter Camp at the outset of his football career became the inventor of the "eleven," the "scrimmage," and the "quarter-back."

- Walter Camp did much more than shaping the sport of football. He marketed it, too. Wrote David L. Porter, "Through his prolific writing Camp promoted football to a mass audience. He produced voluminous newspaper articles, wrote over 200 magazine articles, and edited Spalding's *Official Intercollegiate Football Guide....* From 1889 to 1925 Camp selected All-American football teams and consequently generated vast interest in the sport's stars."
- It should be mentioned that Camp campaigned against the forward pass in 1906, but the rule legalizing the play was passed over his protests and efforts.

50 Years Later

- Attendees to the Yale-Army contest in 1939 opening their game program found an excellent historical retrospective by William H. "Pa" Corbin, the captain of the Yale football team in 1888—a team that outscored its opposition by a combined 698-0 during a 13-game schedule. Corbin's piece began with a vivid comparison of 1888 football to the 1939 version:

It is a far cry from the football of word and sign signals, snapping the ball by the foot, continuous forty-five minutes halves, one to three games a week, thirteen to fifteen games a season, no substitutions without injury, no neutral zone, free use of the hands and arms, free ball, flying tackles, only one man necessary on scrimmage line, mass plays, "V's," flying wedges, hurling, "guards and tackles back" formations, absolute playing responsibility of captain or quarter-back, to this over-legislated, over-restricted, oversupervised, fifteen-minute-quarter pink tea, neutral zone, dead ball, curtailed tackling, hamstrung hands, helmets, armor menace, puppet, sideline managed, commercialized, basketball, Lady Luck spectacle—and few there be that care.

- To give a further illustration of early football, it's worth relating one further passage from Pa Corbin's piece, describing Amos Alonzo Stagg, shortly to become a 41-year-institution at the University of Chicago, in his initial work as a coach at Springfield: "At the time mass formations were permissible, only one man being required to be on the line of scrimmage to put the ball in play. In the YMCA game with Harvard, ten men formed in a mass, with their bodies bent over each, forming a 'turtle back,' several yards back of the center of the field. The ball was snapped back and disappeared into the middle of the mass. Soon all but one of the bunch started toward the side of the field in what appeared to be a 'flying wedge,' then much in vogue, with one man somewhat bent over and apparently carrying the ball, with nearly the entire Harvard team in pursuit. A minute later an unnoticed man on the ground, who all the time had the ball concealed under him, got up and ran down the other side of the field for a touchdown, much to the discomfiture of their opponents."

Wise Words

- A piece attributed to Detroit Lions quarterback Fred Enke for the *Tucson Daily Citizen*, December 30, 1948, began: "Since my return from Detroit last week many people have asked me if I really liked professional football. I say yes, for I believe a fellow has to like football to play football regardless of whether or not he is playing for pay. As the old pep-talk saying goes, 'Football is football wherever it is played and a football player plays football whenever he gets the chance.' "

Pittsburgh Steelers vs. Toronto Argonauts, Canadian Rules

- Canadian football and American football were both born from rugby but evolved separately. In August 1960, the two games were brought together in Toronto—the Pittsburgh Steelers were in town to challenge the Argos. From *The Pro Football Chronicle*:

  > There had been previous games between American and Canadian pro teams, but this was the first one played entirely under Canadian rules.

  > Well, almost entirely. The Steelers were granted concessions on blocking, timeouts and the time required to put the ball in play, but that was it. They still had to adjust to the 12 players, the three downs, the much bigger field and all the rest....

  > After spotting the Argonauts an early field goal, [the Pittsburgh Steelers] rolled to a 43-16 victory before 23,570 at Exhibition Stadium. It was 36-3 at the half. Bobby Layne threw three long touchdown passes to Preston Carpenter and Buddy Dial in a little more than two quarters' work.

  > This, by the way, was believed to be the first pro football game viewed on pay TV. Thousands of fans in the Toronto suburb of Etobicoke paid two dollars a set.

football field

n. arena, between the white lines, field, grass, green, grid, gridiron, grounds, playing field, playing surface, surface; ARTIFICIAL TURF carpet, concrete, plastic carpet, rug, synthetic grass, syn-thetic surface, turf, turface

"You can learn more character on the two-yard line than you can anywhere in life."—Paul Dietzel

- See **end zone**

Exterior of the field

n. edge, flank, flat, perimeter, sideline

Interior of the field

n. center, down the middle, heart, inside the hash marks, inside the numbers

History, Terms, and Jargon

- According to the NFL rulebook, "[t]he game shall be played upon a rectangular field, 360 feet in length and 160 feet in width." But, as Robert W. Peterson described, "When the first players were paid, football was very different than it is today. The field itself was different. It was 110 yards long from goal line to goal line—10 yards longer than that at present–and 53 yards wide, 1 foot narrower."
- Every five yards on the field is marked by a vertical white yard line that halts eight inches shy of the sideline, and every ten yards is indicated with a number on the field. Rare fields, such as LSU's Tiger Stadium, have the multiples of 5 painted on the grass as well, putting a number at every yard line.
- Each yard on the field is marked by two rows of *hash marks* (*hash, inbound lines,* or *markers*), "named after the service marks—one for every six years—a military man wears on his sleeve." (*Football Lingo*) When a play ends outside of the hash marks, the ball is spotted on the closest hash marks for the next play. Those hash marks were added to NFL fields in 1933, the same year that goal posts were relocated from the goal line to the end line. Before they were added, teams were forced to start each play from where the previous play ended, even if it brought them right up against the sidelines.
- Come deep winter, with freezing temperatures in effect in Wisconsin, the Green Bay Packers play on the "frozen tundra of Lambeau Field." (The Ice Bowl between Green Bay and Dallas for the 1967 NFL Championship featured a game-time temperature of 13 degrees below

zero. "I think I'll have another bite of my coffee," quipped announcer Frank Gifford.)
- Why is the football field nicknamed the *gridiron*? Edward J. Rielly shared an answer more complex and clever than you'd think:

> The quick and easy answer is that the football field with its lines designating yardage at 10-yard intervals looks somewhat like a gridiron. A gridiron is a flat framework consisting of parallel metal bars on which food, usually meat, is placed for cooking. The gridiron is then placed over a fire. According to *The Oxford English Dictionary*, the term *gridiron* has been used at least since the thirteenth century. Anyone cooking hamburgers or steaks in a backyard is likely experienced with a gridiron.

> There are other definitions for a gridiron, however; for example, the structure above the stage of a theater from which scenery and lights are hung by cables or ropes. Most of these definitions have no relevance to football, except for one. The gridiron was also a medieval instrument of torture. The person being tortured was placed on the gridiron and subjected to the horrible pain of being burned to death.

> The fusion of these two medieval uses of the word gridiron within the context of football occurred in a book by the prolific author of juvenile stories, H. (Harrie) Irving Hancock (1868-1922). Among Hancock's many books for youths is the High School Boys series, consisting of four books, among them *The High School Left End* (1910), also known as *Dick & Co. Grilling on the Football Gridiron*, as the books in the series had alternate titles....

> There is no actual torture, of course, despite the reference to the "grilling," but a metaphoric allusion to testing by the fire of competition. Dick is not burned to death but comes out a "real man": stronger, responsi-

ble, more morally mature, and ready for the next challenge.

Describing the Field

- The neighborhood of the 50-yard line is *midfield*; a player who takes the ball past the 50 brings it "across midfield."
- The field is described in *territory* (or "country").
- The *minus side of the field* describes one team's territory, from its goal line to the 50-yard line. The *plus side of the field* describes the opposition's territory, from the 50-yard line to its goal line. Imagine a game between the Seattle Seahawks and Indianapolis Colts, with the Seahawks proceeding at a vantage point from left to right across the field. The 1 to the 49-yard line from left to right is in Seattle territory; continuing forward, the 49 to the 1-yard line from left to right is in Indianapolis territory.
- A drive that begins deep in the offense's territory and climaxes in a touchdown sees the offense drive "the length of the field."

"Ground acquisition. That's what football is, football's a ground acquisition game. You knock the crap out of eleven guys and take their land away from them."—George Carlin, on Saturday Night Live, October 11, 1975

- The *far* and *near* sides of the field are all based on the fan's perspective. In the same sense, when judging from an upward angle (or watching on television/game film), the far side is the *top* side of the field and the near side is the *bottom* side of the field. An offensive unit proceeding from left to right with a receiver lined up to the left may be described as having that receiver on the "top side left" or "far side left."
- The *short side* or *boundary side* of the field is the side to which there is the least space at the snapping of the ball. If the ball is snapped from the left hash, for example, closer to the left sideline than the right sideline, the left

side is the short side. The opposite side (in this example, the right side) is the *field side*, *split side*, or *wide side* of the field.

- *Green zone, red zone*: An offense that reaches the other team's 20-yard line and in, closing in on a score, enters the *red zone*. The defense, meanwhile, is in the green zone—and in a lot of trouble, to boot.
- The Dallas Cowboys of Jimmy Johnson, Troy Aikman, Michael Irvin, and Emmitt Smith called the red zone the "green zone" for a different reason. Arriving into the green zone and then scoring touchdowns was how they made a different type of green money.

It Ain't Easy Being a Color Other Than Green

- In the Arena Football League, the LA KISS play on a silver field.
- In the Indoor Football League, the Nebraska Danger play on black turf.
- The Boise State Broncos play on the "Smurf Turf" at Albertsons Stadium in Boise, Idaho: artificial turf painted blue (and nicknamed "The Blue"). It was declared #1 on USA Today's Ten Best Fields in College Football by the College Football Fan Index, October 13, 2014, and you can give that ranking as much weight as you choose. Other colors represented by collegiate gridirons:

> Blue: Ralph F. DellaCamera Stadium, New Haven
> Gray: Rynearson Stadium ("The Factory"), Eastern Michigan
> Purple and gray: Estes Stadium, Central Arkansas
> Red: Roos Field ("The Inferno"), Eastern Washington
> Red and gray: Lindenwood Stadium, Lindenwood

football player

n. ballplayer, beefer, combatant, foot soldier, gladiator, gridder, leatherhead, modern-day gladiator, participant, (offensive/defensive) piece, player, two-way player (offense and defense), weekend warrior

"I've tried not to exaggerate the glory of athletes. I'd rather, if I could, preserve a sense of proportion, to write about them as excellent ball players, first-rate players. But I'm sure I have contributed to false values—as [sports editor] Stanley Woodward said, 'Godding up those ballplayers."—Red Smith, No Cheering in the Press Box

- *Leatherheads* came from the old leather helmets the players used to sport. (It later lent its name to a 2008 movie starring George Clooney, John Krasinski, and Renee Zellweger.)
- The final regular two-way player was Philadelphia's Chuck "60 Minute Man" Bednarik, who starred at center and linebacker for the Eagles from 1949-1962. In recent years, though, rare occasions have allowed other players to distinguish themselves on both sides of the line. Fearsome defenders ranging from William "Refrigerator" Perry to J.J. Watt have come in to aid the offense in goal-line situations, while game-breaking defensive backs like Deion Sanders, Champ Bailey, and Patrick Peterson have come in for occasional plays as receivers. The 2006 New England Patriots were forced to use wide receiver Troy Brown as a nickelback, where he acquitted himself well. Brown's teammate, linebacker Mike Vrabel, caught 10 regular season touchdowns and two postseason touchdowns as a goal-line tackle-eligible receiver. On December 14, 2003, the Baltimore Ravens started Orlando Brown at both offensive and defensive tackle. And on November 16, 2008, Denver Broncos rookie Spencer Larsen started at fullback, middle linebacker, and on kickoff coverage/return teams. "They needed me on defense," he said afterward. "We were real quiet about it. I was real excited about it, but I was able to keep my cool. It was fun and

challenging. At fullback, you really know what to do, but at linebacker, it's a different world." He finished the game with zero catches, zero rushes, and seven tackles.

football player, big

n. bear, behemoth, blimp, brick wall, bruiser, brute, caveman, elephant, giant, heavyweight, hippopotamus, house, jumbo, leviathan, mammoth, mass of blubber, mastodon, monster, moose, mountain, redwood, rhinoceros, skyscraper, space eater, whale

"When you're this size, you don't have sizes—all you have is Xs.... Right now I'm between 3X and 4X."—Nate Newton, Dallas Cowboys offensive lineman

- With great size comes great responsibility for a memorable moniker, including Gene "Big Daddy" Lipscomb (the "one-man gang tackler"), Ted "The Mad Stork" Hendricks, William "The Refrigerator" Perry (affectionately called "Fridge"), Tay "Mount" Cody, Terrance "Pot Roast" Knighton, and Damon "Big Snacks" Harrison.
- Wrote H.G. Bissinger in *Friday Night Lights*, "The [Midland High] Bulldogs were big, with a defensive line that average 220 pounds across, including one 263-pound tackle whom the Permian coaches described as a 'big 'ol humper.' "
- Any conversation on larger football players should include Les "Bingo" Bingaman, the largest man of his time. From Mickey Herskowitz and Steve Perkins: "Buddy Parker, the Detroit coach, took one look at Bingo in camp and decided he must weigh 400 pounds. Line coach Buster Ramsey defended him, saying his weight was closer to 300. They wagered a steak dinner on it. When they tried to weigh him on a locker room scale, the overburdened machine just went 'boinnnggg.' Ramsey located a grain scale at a feed store, and Bingaman checked in at 349 pounds, eight ounces.

Parker, a gracious loser, said his star lineman was in better shape than he thought.'"

football player, nonstarter

n. bench player, benchwarmer, body, fringe, JAG, LRP, no-name, reserve, second-stringer, sub, substitute, third-stringer

"This is not the time or the place to cry 'discrimination' ... I mean 'foul.' But why do the Heisman winners always have to be big guys? Why did 26 of the 28 winners have to be backs? Why do they have to be regulars all of the time? It's about time they recognized good, short substitutes!"—from Robert F. Kennedy's Heisman Trophy presentation, 1962

- A 1 is a starter (*first-teamer* or *first-stringer*); the others are reserves/backups: a 2 is a member of the second unit (*second-teamer* or *second-stringer*), a 3 is on the third unit (*third-teamer* or *third-stringer*), and onward. Florida A&M head coach Jake Gaither went a step further, naming his first unit "Blood," his second unit "Sweat," and his third unit "Tears," after Winston Churchill's 1940 speech to the House of Commons.
- In football's early days, the same 11 players stayed in for the entire game, playing both offense and defense, unless there was an injury. This ended with the introduction of the platoon system, credited to Fritz Crisler. The NFL legalized unlimited free substitution for good in 1950, allowing teams to bring players in off the bench whenever they pleased. For the NCAA, which had allowed free substitution since 1941, there was a reversal in 1953, rendering free substitution illegal. Things were finally turned around again in 1964, allowing the platoon system at the college level.
- A player who gets on the wrong side of the coach "lands in the doghouse" and is shunted to the bench.
- A *JAG* is "just another guy" or "just a guy"—i.e., unremarkable and replaceable.
- An *LRP* is a Jon Grudenism, standing for "limited role player."

- A player who does not play "gets some splinters" due to riding the bench.
- From locker room to locker room across the country, the Turk is dreaded. From John Feinstein's *Next Man Up:* "The Turk is one of football's oldest phrases. Whoever it is who gives a player the news that he's cut, or sends the message with the unmistakable request 'Coach needs to see you and bring your playbook,' is called the Turk. That is, unless you are Orlando Brown. He called the young scouts 'reaper,' and always turned his name tag away from them whenever they came near his locker, as if that might prevent them from knowing who he was."
- A tale of John Heisman, from Jack Wilkinson in the *Atlanta Journal-Constitution*: "In 1902, [John] Heisman and Clemson cost Tech fans a bundle of money. The day before the game, Clemson hopped off the train in Atlanta, checked into a hotel and proceeded to party until dawn. Tech fans who saw all this and couldn't wait to bet on the game didn't see another train of Clemson players—the varsity, not the decoy scrubs—arrive Saturday morning. The varsity, well-rested after a quiet night in Lula, Ga., trounced Tech 44-5."

football player, star

n. All-America, All-Everything, all-pro / All-Pro, All-World, artist on the field, best in the business, big gun, big play player, big shot, big-ticket item, box-office attraction, drawing card, elite, freak, frontline talent, future Hall-of-Famer, gamebreaker, game-breaking talent, game-changer, glamour/glamor boy, G.O.A.T., golden boy, grid hero, gridiron god, gridiron great, gridiron hero, gridiron star, hero, household name, idol, immortal, impact player, legend of the fall, main man, money player, mutant, name player, playmaker, premier player, prime-time player, rock star, sensation, star of the show, stud duck, superstar, toast of the town, weapon

Terms and Jargon

- The "All-America Team" (and term), honoring the top amateur players in the country, dates all the way back to 1889, selected by Casper Whitney, aided by Walter Camp.
- "All-Pro" Teams, honoring the top professional football players, have been selected by the National Football League since 1931.
- The great running back Jim Brown was a definite *big gun* for his Cleveland Browns, and as his coach, Paul Brown, said, "When you have a big gun, you shoot it."
- Above all other terms, *elite* now carries a controversial amount of modern weight, stirred up by the confident self-evaluations of quarterbacks Eli Manning (in 2011) and Joe Flacco (in 2012) that they were among the NFL's top QBs. ("Elite" came directly from Manning's mouth during a radio interview with WFAN radio host Michael Kay.)
- A football player who *flashes* shows the sparks of game-changing ability, but only every now and then. Young players often flash during preseason work.
- Defensive end Jevon Kearse was the original "Freak," designated as such for his combination of speed, size, and strength. In the same sense, Gerald McCoy said about defensive tackle Ndamukong Suh on January 22, 2015, on ESPN's Mike & Mike radio show, "He's what I like to call a mutant."
- G.O.A.T. is a modern acronym, standing for the Greatest Of All Time. From Oakland's Marcel Reese, quoted on *Raiders.com*, "C-Wood [Charles Woodson] is the G.O.A.T. He's kind of that DB that you talk about like the Jerry Rices and the Michael Irvins and the Deion Sanders. Charles Woodson is right there."
- The original golden boy was Notre Dame-turned-Green Bay running back Paul Hornung, who won the 1956 Heisman Trophy award. (One of the best Hornung stories, as told by Hornung himself: "...[T]here were rumors around that I was going to be traded to the New York Giants for Del Shofner. Just before the Giants' playoff game in '63 with the Chicago Bears, Giant coach

Allie Sherman called a team meeting. 'We've all been hearing these rumors about me trading Shofner for Hornung,' Sherman said. 'Well, let me tell you, I wouldn't trade Del Shofner for Paul Hornung and *all* his girl friends.' With that, Mo Modzelewski jumped up and cried, 'Wait a minute, Coach. Take a vote, take a vote!' ")

• Perhaps *stud duck* stood out to you? From *Friday Night Lights*: "Odell Beckham, the stud duck of the [Marshall] Mavericks, number 33, six feet, 194 pounds, 4.5 speed in the forty, punishing quick, able to take it up and out to the outside, a guaranteed lock for a major-college scholarship." Beckham went on to play running back at Louisiana State University; Odell Beckham, Jr., a wide receiver at LSU and a star in his own right, was drafted twelfth overall in 2014 by the New York Giants.

Strike the Pose

• Sculpted originally by Frank Eliscu, the Heisman Memorial Trophy Award—named for the great coach John Heisman and more commonly called the Heisman Trophy—goes, by vote, to the "most outstanding" college football player of the year each December. The first Heisman winner was the University of Chicago's Jay Berwanger in 1935, though it was known then as the DAC Trophy (since it was given out by the Downtown Athletic Club in New York, and also since Heisman was still alive; he died a year later, with the trophy renamed in his memory). Ohio State's Archie Griffin was the first (and to date, only) player to win two Heismans, thanks to his brilliant ground production in 1974 and 1975.

• The Heisman is, perhaps, the top individual athletic honor in the nation, and the "Heisman Pose"—the ball clutched in the left hand, the right knee flexed, the right arm extended for a classic stiff-arm—is iconic and oft-copied. (The website that prides itself in projecting Heisman Winners? *StiffArmTrophy.com*.)

• Dan Jenkins memorably wrote, in a column titled "The Old Fordham Halfback" (collected in *You Call it Sports, but I Say It's a Jungle Out Here*): "He doesn't have a nickname, such as Oscar or Emmy, which is probably just an oversight of the years, like some of the Sam Baughs and Jim Browns who never won him. He is only 18 inches tall. He weighs only 50 pounds. He costs only $452. He is, in fact, just an old Fordham halfback, a dark brown hunk of sculpture running and stiff-arming across a slab of ebony—and a bit ill-proportioned at that, considering that his head is too large, his shoulders are narrow, and his legs are short. For all of this, however, few relics in college football cause more melodrama than the Heisman Memorial Trophy, an award that is supposed to go to the outstanding player in the country each year, and sometimes does."

- Fordham aside, the Heisman Trophy's official website gives its model as "Ed Smith, a leading player on the 1934 New York University football team."

Other Notable Named Awards

- Reds Bagnell Award: Overall Contributions to the Game
- Chuck Bednarik Award: Top College Defensive Player
- Bert Bell Award: Top Professional Player
- Fred Biletnikoff Award: Top College Wide Receiver
- Dick Butkus Award: Top College Linebacker
- Walter Camp Award: Top College Player
- William V. Campbell Trophy: Top College Scholar-Athlete
- Lou Groza Award: Top College Place-Kicker
- Ray Guy Award: Top College Punter
- Jim Henry Award: Top High School Player
- Paul Hornung Award: Most Versatile College Player
- (Vince) Lombardi Trophy: Top College Lineman
- (Robert W. "Tiny") Maxwell Award: Top College Player
- George Munger Award: Top College Coach
- Bronko Nagurski Award: Top Defensive College Player
- Greasy Neale Award: Top Professional Coach
- Davey O'Brien Award: Top College Quarterback
- (John H.) Outland Trophy: Top College Interior Lineman
- Dave Rimington Trophy: Top College Center

- Jim Thorpe Award: Top College Defensive Back
- Doak Walker Award: Top College Running Back

football player, veteran

n. graybeard, long in the tooth, old man, old master, on the bad/ wrong side of thirty, senior citizen

- The Old Man of football was George Blanda, who broke into the NFL as a 12th-round pick in 1949 and provided capable quarterbacking (especially in relief) and place kicking until his retirement in 1975, age 48. This led to an amusing effect. As *The Pro Football Chronicle* relates: "Topps put out two George Blanda cards in 1975 because his record was too long to fit on one." (Before Blanda earned the moniker, quarterback Y.A. Tittle was considered the "grand old man of football.")
- In 1969, a made-for-TV movie titled "The Over-the-Hill Gang" was aired on ABC, starring Pat O'Brien, Walter Brennan, Chill Wills, Edgar Buchanan, and Andy Devine, among others. Two years later, the Washington Redskins' new head coach, George Allen, began adding seemingly past-their-prime players to their roster, including 35-year-old Jack Pardee, 34-year-old Boyd Dowler, 33-year-old Richie Petitbon, 32-year-old Myron Pottios, and 32-year-old Ron McDole. Including such stars as quarterback Billy Kilmer (32), Pat Fischer (31), Chris Hanburger (30), the experienced Skins soon became known as the "Over-the-Hill Gang." The strategy worked; before Allen, Washington had gone 6-8 in 1970. With him, they made the playoffs in four consecutive seasons, 1971-1974, including a trip to Super Bowl VII.

formation

n. alignment, arrangement, positioning, set, setup; SPECIFIC defensive formation, goal line formation, field goal formation, kickoff formation, kick return formation, offensive formation, onside kick formation, punting formation, victory formation; DEFENSIVE FORMATIONS one-gap, two-gap; (Psycho) 1-5-5, 3-3-5, 3–4 over, 3-4 under, 3-5-3, 4-2-5, 4-3 over, 4-3 under (Predator), (Notre Dame) 4-4-3, 4-5-2, 5-2 Monster, 5-3-3, (Okie or sliding) 5-4-2, (Umbrella) 6-1-4, 6-2-2-1, (goal line) 6-5, 7-1-2-1, (box) 7-2-2, 7-3-1, (goal line) 8-3, 9-1-1, 9-2, and many more variations; see **defense**; OFFENSIVE FORMATIONS A-11, A formation, B formation, double wing, Emory and Henry, flexbone, I formation, pistol, pro set, shotgun, single set back, single wing, stacked deck, T formation, V formation, wildcat, wing T, wishbone, Y formation

Terms and Jargon

- The *formation* describes how a team sets up before the start of a play.
- The *goal-line formation* describes both the offensive and defensive setup with the ball placed close to the goal line and big bodies inserted into the game.
- The *victory formation* is utilized for one play, and one play only: a kneeldown. It is used by a team with the lead and the game well in hand, needing only to kneel down to keep the clock moving and clinch the win. The quarterback takes the snap under center with a running back at each hip and a third back stationed behind him in case of a miscue.

Notable Defensive Formations

- When describing a defense—a 4-3-4, say—the first number (4) counts the defensive linemen, the second (3) counts the linebackers, and the third (4) counts the defensive backs. If a fourth number is used, it refers to a very deep safety or two. The most common current defenses are the 4-3 defense (the "Pro Four," the 4-3-4 used in the initial example, invented by Tom Landry in the 1950s with the Giants), or the 3-4 defense, a 3-4-4 look (evolved from the Oklahoma formation).
- The earliest defense was a 9-1-1 featuring a nine-man wall of standing defenders facing down the offense.

From there, the seven box defense (7-2-2) and seven diamond (7-1-2-1) were introduced, placing seven defenders on the line with either a box-shaped or diamond-shaped secondary supporting them.

- From Allison Danzig's write-up of Amos Alonzo Stagg, collected in Danzig's *Oh, How They Played the Game*: "In 1890 he departed from the nine-man line which had been commonly used in the days when the team with the ball had to gain five yards in three downs. He switched to a 7-2-2 alignment, known as a 'box.' In 1898 he used a 7-3-1 when he did not employ his center as a linebacker. In 1932 his team went into a 6-2-1-2 deployment and in 1943, when the T was becoming the vogue, he used a 5-2-1-2-1."

The Monster, the Umbrella, and the Okie

- With the Chicago Bears' reintroduction of the T formation in 1940, defenses were in trouble. "The response," Chris B. Brown wrote, "was the 5-2 Monster defense, which essentially dominated football for the next two decades. The 5-2 Monster involved five defensive linemen, each playing a two-gap technique over a specific offensive linemen. This allowed linebackers to roam free and match the offense's ball carriers. The 'Monster' referred to the safety who came down and created one of the first true eight-man-front defenses. The combination of five two-gapping defensive linemen with three second-level defenders, each attacking the ball and following potential runners, helped counteract the T formation offenses' misdirection."
- Attempting to combat the threat of Otto Graham and the Cleveland Browns' passing attack, head coach Steve Owen and the 1950 New York Giants unveiled their Umbrella Defense, a 6-1-4 look. "In this defense," wrote David S. Neft and Richard M. Cohen, "the two defensive ends dropped off the line to cover receivers, while backs Em Tunnell, [Tom] Landry, [Otto] Schnellbacher, and [Harmon] Rowe formed the 'umbrella' in the zone pass

defense." The Browns entered the NFL as the four-time defending All-America Football Conference (AAFC) champions; they lost to the Giants in both regular-season meetings, their only losses of the year. (In the playoffs, they finally beat the Umbrella, 8-3, and went on to win their first NFL title.)

- The *Oklahoma formation*, also called the *Okie defense*, was devised by Bud Wilkinson and was noted for its 5-4 front. It proved to be hugely influential. "The advantages of the Okie over the standard 4-3 pro defense," wrote Zander Hollander in 1976, "are that 1) there are two middle linebackers instead of one; 2) there are five short-pass zone defenses instead of four, making it difficult for receivers to find the gaps or seams, and there are still three men left to cover del routes; 3) any two linebackers can blitz, making it a five-man rush, and there are still two linebackers left to protect for the run and a free safety to play the ball; 4) if either of the inside linebackers blitz, it is much the same as a 4-3, but with the element of surprise; 5) the linebackers can stack [stand directly behind] the three down linemen, forcing offensive blockers to react quickly when these stacked linebackers move in either direction from their hidden positions. The New England Patriots were one of the first National Football League teams to use the Okie." The Patriots would not be alone; Wilkinson's seeming 5-4 morphed into the present-day 3-4 defense that can be found with multiple teams at every level.
- For Buddy Ryan's 46 defense, see **defense**

The 3-3-5

- The 3-3-5 defense was created in 1991 by Joe Lee Dunn, who ran the defense at Memphis State. Dunn had taken a look at Memphis State's next opponent, USC, and came up with a plan to defend against the Trojans' speed. "I didn't think we could just line up and play against USC," he told Tim Layden. "But I thought maybe we could run something that would confuse them. So here's what we did: We backed up the two defensive ends about seven yards off the line of scrimmage and about three yards outside the tight end, or where the tight end would normally be. We put those guys in space." The change of scheme paid off. Summed up Layden, "Moving the defensive ends back and outside turned Memphis State's 5-3-3 into a 3-3-5, with those defensive ends acting essentially as hybrid linebacker-strong safeties." Memphis State surprised USC, 24-10, and then went back to playing their usual 5-3-3 defense the next weekend.

- In 1996, now employed at Mississippi State, Dunn went right back to the 3-3-5 (explaining to Layden that he simply could not find enough big defensive linemen to recruit). "[A]t State," described Chris B. Brown, "Dunn went whole hog with the 3-3-5: almost every game, each defensive player blitzed at least once—and often much more often." The scheme was later instituted by Charlie Strong as the defensive coordinator at Florida, and was introduced by schools across the country as a potential antidote to spread attacks.

Notable Offensive Formations

The Original

- "The single wing," wrote Chris B. Brown for *Grantland.com*, "is, in many ways, football's original formation. Although hard to imagine now, there was a time in the NFL when using a quarterback under center was considered a gimmick, and nearly every team used some version of the single wing and other 'direct snap' formations." Drawn up by Glenn "Pop" Warner, the future coach of the Carlisle Indians (causing it to familiarly be known as the "Carlisle Formation"), the *single wing* featured an unbalanced line (two linemen on one side of the center and four on the other side), with four backs lined up and ready in the offensive backfield. In the main setup, a tailback and a fullback stood side by side several yards behind the center; the snap was tossed to either one of them. The quarterback's position as we currently know it did not exist yet; he was called a "blocking back," and he stood right behind the line. The last back was a wing back, placed outside the end of the line, one yard back.

- After many decades on top, teams began to turn away from the single wing, establishing the T and then the I formation in its stead. In the end, Keith Piper, coaching from 1977-1992 at Denison University, cut a lone figure in directing a single-wing offense. "The thing that people don't understand about the single wing," Piper told *Sports Illustrated* writer Rick Telander in 1982, "is that it was never caught up with or overrun. It works. But football is like men's fashions. Coaches don't run the single wing because they don't want to be out of fashion." The 21st century has seen a single-wing renaissance, with high schools rediscovering the effectiveness of Pop Warner's formation. There is now a National Single Wing Coaches' Association, formed in 1996, one year before Keith Piper's death.

The T

- The *T formation*, showcased in the Chicago Bears' overwhelming 73-0 NFL championship win over Washington in 1940, puts the quarterback under center, a balanced line flanking him, with three running backs behind him in the backfield standing side by side: a fullback bookended by a left and a right halfback. (The T formation setup, interestingly, was how Notre Dame would set up before shifting into its famed box in the 1920s.) Shirley Povich alluded to the formation's early origins in his write-up of the 1940 championship game for the *Washington Post*:

> Those Bears were wonderful, weren't they? That "T" formation is really dread stuff and Coach George Halas comes pretty close to being the No. 1 offensive genius in the land. The Bears' ball carriers were under way at full speed before they had their hands on the ball and at the rate they were galloping when they hit some-

thing, it didn't matter a difference whether there was a hole in the Redskins' line or not.

Halas' man-in-motion play was shaking his ball carriers loose through the middle, at the tackles and around the ends. The Redskins scarcely knew where the Bears would strike….The Bears' power plays were ghastly concentrations of blockers in front of ball carriers. The Redskins were first confused then so weakened physically by the pounding they were taking that they were helpless.

Halas turned back the clock to beat the Redskins. The Bears were getting their wondrous effects with the old "T" formation that was popular early in the century when the boys were playing the game in turtle-necks. Halas embellished it with some variations, but its form was basically the same with the quarterback taking the ball from center and handing it gently to a big back who was already in motion.

- The *Balanced T formation* uses a balanced line—three linemen on either side of the center.
- The *Full-House T formation* brought every possible back into the backfield, exploding upon the defense with power running. It was similar to the *Power T formation*, lining up with three backs, one quarterback, and two tight ends.
- The *Pro T formation* takes out a tight end and adds a wide receiver as an outside threat.
- The *Slot T*, used by the 1959 Philadelphia Eagles, placed the right halfback as a slot receiver between the tackle and the right end, maintaining two backs in the backfield—a halfback to the left and a fullback to the right. With the formation, the Eagles showed their desire to open up the field; they lost running effectiveness, but gained one-on-one matchups with their receivers. The *Double Slot T* caught on next, with a four-receiver, one-back formation featuring a slot receiver to each side. (The Double Slot T often

motioned one of the slot men into the backfield before
the snap.)

- The *Tight T* puts the offensive linemen close together,
while the *Split T* (credited to Don Faurot at the
University of Missouri) spaces the linemen out. For the
Split-Line T, invented by Jake Gaither at Florida A&M,
see **offensive line**.

Adding the Wing to the T

- Two of the main differences between the single-wing
formation and the T formation: The offensive line is
unbalanced in the single wing and balanced in the T;
and the positioning of the quarterback, spaced away
from center in the single wing (with the QB, halfback,
and fullback all able to take the snap), and set up under
center in the T. The idea of creating a mishmash of the
two formations dates to a duo with a dynamic idea,
Maine head coach Dave Nelson and line coach Mike
Lude in 1950. Wrote Tim Layden in *Blood, Sweat and
Chalk*:

  Come the summer of 1950, Nelson and Lude were
  convinced that they would put a quarterback under
  center. "Although," says Lude, "none of us even knew
  how to teach a center-quarterback exchange because
  all we had ever coached was the single wing." And they
  were loath to give up the diabolical blocking schemes
  so effective in the single wing and afraid to let go of the
  intricate backfield play fakes. They needed some sort
  of hybrid.

  They stayed up late every night, tinkering with plays,
  trying to marry single wing blocking and faking principles to an offense with the quarterback under center.
  "It was 3 a.m. on the night before the players reported
  for practice before Dave finally made his decision," says
  Lude. "He just all of sudden said, 'To heck with it; let's
  just go with it. He took all our blocking rules from the
  unbalanced single wing and converted them to a bal-

anced line." It was a mix of the single wing and T formations, but it was the first step in bridging the dominant offense of the first half of the 20th century.

It would eventually be called the wing T, because—simply enough—it looked like the T formation with a single wing wingback, and it appeared to have elements of both offenses. There was a quarterback under center and a balanced line (T formation), and here were two backs in the backfield and a wing flanked to the strong side of the formation (single wing). The name was intuitive and practical.

- While Nelson and Lude may have been the originators, it was Harold "Tubby" Raymond, first an assistant coach under Nelson at the University of Delaware, and then rising to UD head coach, who brought the formation into prominence with an effective passing game and option game.
- From the introduction of the wing T, coaches continued to experiment. The *double wing T formation* (or *double wing*) used two wing backs, one to each side, with a back in the backfield behind the quarterback.
- For the *Wildcat* formation, see "Types of Quarterbacks" under **quarterback**

The I

- The *I formation* places the tailback directly behind the fullback, and both of them behind an under-center quarterback. The innovation is given to Tom Nugent while coaching at the Virginia Military Institute (VMI) in 1950, and it soon spread through the 1950s and 1960s as one of the top formations for a rushing offense. Before Don Coryell became known for "Air Coryell," leading high-powered passing attacks, he used the I to run over the opposition at San Diego State.
- If the backs are not quite behind one another, they can create a *broken I*, *offset I*, or *staggered I*.
- In an *offset I*, the fullback is lined up behind one of the

two offensive tackles, with the tailback remaining deep and behind the quarterback.

- Jerry Kill's University of Minnesota Golden Gophers use the *Golden-I* formation, lining three backs in a row directly behind their quarterback under center. The formation was introduced by the aforementioned Tom Nugent, coaching the University of Maryland Terrapins from 1959-1965. It was called the *Capital I* or the *Maryland-I*, later gaining the name of the *full-house I*, *Stack*, or the *Stack-I*. It's a powerful formation, with the stacked backs often consisting of tight ends and/or fullbacks.

The Wishbone

- The *wishbone formation*, or *bone*, describes the alignment of three backs in the backfield, with a fullback behind (and closest to) the quarterback, with a halfback set back on either side of him. Their shape forms a wishbone. The wishbone formation was used to run the *triple option* offense—the three options being a (1) handoff/fake to the fullback, followed by the quarterback dashing around one side ("Option left" or "Option right") with a running back trailing him, able to (2) keep it himself, or (3) pitch the ball to the running back.
- The triple option began with the veer formation, invented by the University of Houston's Bill Yeoman in 1965. (The "veer" referred to the course taken by the first option, the veering path of the back approaching the line.)
- From Yeoman's introduction, Emory Bellard took the veer concepts, added a third back to the backfield, an additional read for the quarterback, and a lead blocker, and installed the offense at Texas in 1968. (The origin story, from Layden: "According to historian Bill Little, one of the reporters asked Royal what he should call this new offense, albeit such an unsuccessful one in the opener [a 20-20 tie]. Said the writer, 'It looks like a Y.' From near the door Mickey Herskowitz of the *Houston*

Post said, 'It looks like a pulley-bone.' That sounded about right to Royal, who said, 'O.K. The wishbone.' ")

- What killed the wishbone? "[T]he option became stigmatized as failing to prepare star players for the pro game," wrote Tim Layden, quoting Lenny DiNardo as saying, "When I was coaching at Colorado, I can't tell you how many programs beat us up in recruiting by telling kids, 'You won't be able to play in the NFL because you won't be learning the passing game.' "

- The *Inverted Wishbone* (or *Y formation*) turns the three-man backfield around, with a halfback in the center and two nearer fullbacks stationed on either side of him.

- The *Flexbone formation* is similar to the Double Wing, with a receiver to each side, a split end (or wing back) to each side, and one running back behind the under-center quarterback.

- The *I-Bone formation* lined up the backs in the I before running the option offense. This was the favorite formation for Nebraska in the 1970s under Tom Osborne, beginning in the I and then optioning to the left or right.

Box, Diamond, Empty, Full House, and Pro Set

- The *box* formation, utilized to great effectiveness by Notre Dame in the 1920s and '30s, saw four players stationed in the offensive backfield, switching into a trapezoid shape just before the snap.

- The *diamond* formation uses four players in the backfield along with the quarterback, either in a three-man straight line (quarterback in the middle) with a deep back, or in a true diamond shape, with the quarterback several steps behind center (in the *pistol*), flanked on either side with running backs set up a bit behind him, and a tailback directly behind the quarterback.

- A formation with zero runners in the backfield is an *empty backfield*, *empty set*, or *naked backfield*.

- A formation with three running backs behind the quarterback is a *full house*.

- The *split-back formation* places two running backs on the same horizontal plane with a space between them, with the backs located either directly behind the guards or behind the tackles. When used with two receivers, one tight end, and the quarterback under center, this is the *Pro Set* (or *Pro-Set*). The *Pro-Slot* moves both receivers to the same side of the formation (one receiver split wide, one in the slot), and places the tight end on the other side, keeping two running backs in the backfield.
- For **pistol** and **shotgun formations**, see "get the snap from center" under **quarterback**.

Less Orthodox Formations

- The *A formation* gives the center options. A wing back sits to one side, a spit end to the other, and there are three backs in the backfield—the blocking back closest, the quarterback slightly farther off (the only back behind the strong-side of the unbalanced line), and the fullback deepest. The center has the ability to snap the ball to any of the three. It was the New York Giants' offensive formation throughout the 1930s and 1940s.
- Introduced at Emory & Henry College during the 1950s, the *Emory and Henry* presents the unorthodox alignment of spreading the field out with three different groups of three, one to the far left (comprising a tackle and two receivers), one to the middle of the field (comprising the center and guards), and one to the far right (comprising the other tackle and two other receivers). The snap is taken in by one of two players waiting behind the center.
- The *Stacked Deck* was a Philadelphia Eagles innovation in 1961: one receiver to one side of the field and three receivers stationed in a vertical line on the other side of the formation, spaced toward the line of scrimmage a la the I formation. "Philadelphia used this play eight times against New York for a net gain of 92 yards," wrote Chris Schenkel, "one of them going for a 52-yard pass from Sonny Jurgensen to Tommy McDonald, the right [solitary] flanker."

The Fleeting A-11

- The brainchild—and it was a thunderous one at that—belonged to Piedmont High School head coach Kurt Bryan and Piedmont High School director of football operations Steve Humphries. The necessity that led to their innovation, wrote Michael Weinreb for *ESPN.com*'s Page 2, August 14, 2008, was "designing an offense that would allow Piedmont to compete against the other schools in its division, most of which have much larger enrollments, and are therefore much larger period." From an initial concept of an all-razzle dazzle offense, Bryan and Humphries soon hit upon the answer. It was called the A-11. Continued Weinreb:

> I am the farthest thing from an expert on football strategy, but here is what I can tell you about the A-11: It is one of the weirdest things I have ever seen. What's weird about it is that it violates all of our basic instincts about the game, those noble truths we gleaned from [NFL Films voice] John Facenda about the game being won in the trenches by men the size of water buffaloes. It shouldn't work, and yet it does. The A-11 is the spread offense, evolved to its most advanced stage. On film, the A-11 often resembles a hybrid of the spread and an elementary-school fire drill gone wrong.

> Here's how it works: On every play in the A-11, there are two quarterbacks in the backfield at one time, both set up seven yards behind the line of scrimmage. Every man on the field wears a number that potentially makes him an eligible receiver. Potential receivers set up in "pods" at each end of the field. The line, in the base set, consists of two tight ends and a center. Once the ball is snapped, up to six players (including both quarterbacks) become eligible receivers. All of this is legal because technically, according to the rules of high-school football, the Piedmont players are lined up in what is known as a 'scrimmage kick' formation (hence the quarterbacks placed behind the line, so as to

comply with the rules), and therefore, normal eligibility issues do not apply.

On every play, the possibilities are virtually limitless. Draws, wedge plays, screen passes, the run-and-shoot, the option—all of them can be employed, depending on how the defense reacts and on how your own players execute blocks in the open field.

It all sounds dazzling, doesn't it? Fast forward a bit. A notice on *Yahoo.com* written by Matt Hinton, dated February 13, 2009: "Sad news to end the week: Everyone's favorite crazy gimmick offense, the 'All-11,' was effectively declared illegal today by the far-reaching National Federation of State High School Associations (NFSHA), which closed the 'scrimmage kick' loophole the A-11 exploited for its existence. A moment, please, for innovation."

free safety

n. ballhawk, center fielder, deep safety, FS, S, safetyman, safety man, weak-side safety; see **safety**

Terms and Jargon

- The *free safety* was used originally on the weak-side of the formation, opposite the strong safety (on the "strong-side"). While the strong safety received his name for his location, the free safety received his common name, wrote Zander Hollander, "because he is free to play the ball or his choice of men."
- The *free safety* plays deepest of all the defenders, and is used as the center fielder, playing downfield and making plays on deep passes as if they were fly balls to flag down.

fullback

n. back, battering ram, bowling ball, bruiser, FB, goat, lead blocker, load, power back, road grader, workhorse; see **running back**

"When you hit him, it was like getting an electric shock. If you hit him above the ankles, you were likely to get yourself killed."—Red Grange, regarding teammate Bronko Nagurski, fullback/linebacker/tackle/pro wrestling champion of the world

The Fullback

- "When America's space scientists began envisioning orbital flights," wrote Chris Schenkel in *How to Watch Football on Television*, "they had to come up with a power plant capable of tremendous speed and thrust to get that payload into free flight. Maybe they were thinking of the fullback in football when the right idea hit. This is the human power plant who absorbs more punishment than any other offensive back. He's a ball carrier who can be called upon to run either inside or outside. He's a pass receiver, he's leading interference for the halfback. This is the guy who must get you that yard for the first down or the touchdown, when about 2,500 pounds of bull-meat is intent on not letting it happen. And he's the same guy who must become a sprinter when he breaks into the open. And he's the same who becomes his quarterback's bodyguard as the pass patterns unfold." Tough to put it any better than that.
- Jim Murray had the time of his life describing Green Bay fullback Jim Taylor, the future Hall of Famer, in the *Los Angeles Times*: "Jim gains his yards only four at a time. Some say this is because he gets lonely in the open field when he runs out of people to knock down and so, smacks the ground instead. 'He loosens telephone poles on the way to the store just for kicks,' Joe Schmidt once wagered. He's known as an 'Oh my G-d' ballplayer. Because the defensive captain can be heard to say when he has the ball 'Oh, my G-d, it's Taylor.' … 'The Goat,' they called him on the old New York Giants where Sam

Huff did more dental work on Jim Taylor than a lifetime of dentists. Once, in Yankee Stadium, when the fans swarmed onto the field, a player is supposed to have hissed at Taylor, 'Quick, over here, there's a door!' and a teammate, baffled, protested, 'There's no door over there!' and the first fellow, gazing in satisfaction after the churning head-down Taylor, replied, 'Well, there soon will be!' "

- He was not talented anywhere near the level of the great Jim Taylor, but the New Orleans Saints' Craig Heyward believed in the same bruising ethos. From high school onward, Heyward was known as "Ironhead."

fumble

n. ball on the ground, fair game, free ball, greased pig, greased pigskin, hot potato, loose ball
v. cough up, drop, give away, give up, leave behind, lose the ball, lose the handle, muff, put on the ground/carpet, turn over

"The man who complains about the way the ball bounces is likely the one who dropped it."—Lou Holtz

force a fumble
v. dislodge, dispossess, free, jab the ball out, jar loose, knock out, pop out, punch out, rip away, separate the offensive player from the ball, slap out, smack free, strip, swipe, take away, wrench loose

- A *strip-sack* sees the defensive player sack the quarterback while simultaneously forcing a fumble. If the defender is somehow able to recover the fumble, too, credit him with a *strip/sack/recovery*.

recover a fumble
v. collect, come up with it, corral, cover up, gain, gather, get control of, jump on, pick up, scoop up, secure, smother

- In a *scoop and score*, a defensive player recovers a loose ball and returns it for a touchdown.

Other Terms and Jargon

- A fumble as described in the NFL Rulebook: "any act, other than a pass or kick, which results in loss of player possession." Thus lost, the football is now officially considered a *loose ball.*
- From Bill Pennington, writing in *The New York Times,* "[John] Heisman, standing before his players when he first met them, would hold aloft a football and ask, 'What is this?' Answering his own question, Heisman said: 'It is a prolate spheroid in which the outer leather casing is drawn tightly over a somewhat smaller rubber tubing.' Heisman would pause and add: 'Better to have died as a small boy than to fumble this football.' " (In a different version of the quote, Heisman adds that the ball is "an elongated sphere." The point remained the same: Don't fumble.)
- A *muff* is specifically the description of a fumbled punt, kickoff, free kick, or onside kick.
- When a fumble occurs, it often creates a *pile* or a *pile-up* on the field, as players from both teams swarm in; it's then up to the officials to unpile the scene / "get down to the bottom of the pile" and "sort things out."
- A fumble is often caused by a ball carrier holding the ball "low and away" rather than the more secure "high and tight." When the New York Giants' Tiki Barber had troubles with losing possession, this was one of the two changes he made. "The operative phrase during the transformation," Bob Glauber wrote in *Newsday* on September 11, 2013, "was 'high and tight,' signifying the positioning of the ball as he ran. Barber would carry a football everywhere, holding it to his chest, with his hand up near his shoulder and his elbow down at around a 45-degree angle....Barber also added another technique to secure the ball. Once he sensed that he was about to be hit, he would take the hand that wasn't carrying the ball and hold onto his opposite wrist to further protect the ball and add a layer of strength to deal with opponents trying to rip the ball away."

- Since the football is nicknamed the *pigskin*—see **football (ball)** for more—it makes sense that a fumbled football is a *greased pig*. Well, the pigskin was a bit more greased up than usual for a wild Monday Night Football game on December 7, 1998. The Green Bay Packers fumbled the ball eight times in a 24-22 loss to the Tampa Bay Buccaneers, though they lost it only twice.

The Fumble

- The AFC Championship Game held January 17, 1988, between the Cleveland Browns and Denver Broncos was a classic. The previous season had seen "The Drive," in which Denver quarterback John Elway led a 98-yard march to a game-tying touchdown in the snow; a Rich Karlis field goal in overtime put Denver into the Super Bowl. On this occasion, it was Cleveland's Bernie Kosar who looked to play the part of the hero. Down 28-10 in the second half, the Browns rallied to tie the score. Elway came back with a go-ahead scoring strike to Sammy Winder, putting Denver up 38-31 and leaving Kosar only four minutes to answer. What transpired in those closing minutes became known as "The Fumble," two words that would torment Cleveland's faithful. From Gerald Eskanazi at *The New York Times*:

  Cleveland got down to the 8, and visions of what Elway did last year surely cropped up in the minds of football fans. But today, the Browns' mirror cracked.

  The versatile Earnest Byner took the ball on a play that was designed to send the runner inside. Instead, the middle was blocked and he ran to the outside, on his left, then cut back to the inside. He barreled to the 3, but was hit by Jeremiah Castille, a defensive back used in passing situations. Byner actually passed Castille, but the ball didn't. Castille stripped it, then pounced on Byner's fumble at the 3. Sixty-five seconds remained.

Snatching Defeat From the Jaws of Victory

- To New York Giants and Philadelphia Eagles fans, "The Fumble" might connote an entirely different play. It was the "Miracle at the Meadowlands": November 19, 1978: One more clean snap, and the Giants would secure a 17-12 victory over the Eagles—but instead of asking quarterback Joe Pisarcik to fall on the ball, offensive coordinator Bob Gibson called for a rush. There was a miscommunication between Pisarcik and back Larry Csonka, the ball popped free, and the Eagles' Herman Edwards swooped in, plucked it, and tore for the end zone and a shocking Philadelphia win.

Furthermore

- To set the scene with black and white details: New England Patriots 14, New York Jets 0; November 22, 2012; MetLife Stadium; East Rutherford, New Jersey. On a 1st and 10 from the Jets' 31-yard line, New York quarterback Mark Sanchez took the snap and turned to hand off to a back, whether running back Shonn Greene or fullback Lex Hilliard. But the play broke down and Sanchez found himself without a teammate to give the ball to. Trying desperately to salvage the play, the quarterback took off toward the line—and ran directly into the rear end of right guard Brandon Moore. Sanchez went down, the ball popped out, and New England's Steve Gregory arrived, scooped it up, and took off for an easy touchdown. The Patriots went on to score 35 points in the second quarter, on their way to a 49-19 win, and the play went down in infamy as the Butt Fumble.

G

Steve Van Buren with Philadelphia Eagles teammates Al Wistert (l) and Alex Wojciechowicz (r) in 1947.

gain

n. headway, pickup, plus, positive; SPECIFIC breathing room, chunk of yardage, healthy gain, hefty gain, huge gain, minimal gain, modest gain, nice gain, not much, short yardage significant gain, sizable gain
v. advance, attain, make headway, pick up yards

Terms and Jargon

- See **move about the field**
- Since distance is measured in football in yards, gains are measured in *yardage.*
- Gains are often given an eating metaphor: A ball carrier can *chew up, eat up,* or *gobble up* yards. (It's understandable, then, that a negative play would give a coach indigestion.)

game

n. affair, ball game, barnburner, battle, bout, brawl, business trip, chess match, clash, classic, cliffhanger, confrontation, contest, date, duel, encounter, engagement, excursion, get-together, main event, match, matchup, meeting, nail-biter, rumble, scrap, shootout, showdown, skirmish, slobberknocker, slugfest, social call, struggle, test, thriller, tilt, tussle, war; SPECIFIC bowl game, (national) championship game, conference game, exhibition game, grudge match, intersectional game, nonconference game, playoff game, Poll Bowl, postseason game, preseason game, rematch, return match, rivalry game, scrimmage; see **Super Bowl**

"When you're playing for the national championship, it's not a matter of life or death. It's more important than that."—Duffy Daugherty, Michigan State head coach

play against
v. see **play**

History and Terms

- The very first organized football game took place on November 6, 1869, pitting Rutgers against Princeton in East Rutherford, N.J. The game was a cousin of both rugby or soccer; it was prohibited, for instance, to either deliver the ball to a teammate by hand or run with it.
- The Rose Bowl is "The Granddaddy of Them All," though it began inauspiciously. First, the back story, from Herb Michelson and Dave Newhouse: "Before the turn of the century, the Valley Hunt Club represented the creme de la creme of Pasadena. There was a

discussion among some of its members in the winter of
1889 about the absurdly frigid weather in the East.
Rather than say, 'Let them eat snow,' Hunt Club figure
Dr. Charles Frederick Holder and his friend Dr. F.F.
Rowland suggested their colleagues count their
blessings and stage a celebration, a festival to salute their
land of sunshine, citrus and blossoms. Rowland named
the event the Tournament of Roses. Thus, on the first
day of 1890, many of Pasadena's 4,882 citizens gathered
at a local park for a day of fun and games, plus a small
parade which featured flower-bedecked horses and
carriages. Not to mention sporting events such as 'tilting
at the rings,' burro races and what the day's master of
ceremonies, C.C. Brown, called a 'football race.' " The
first Rose Bowl was held twelve years later, in 1902. It
was called the East-West New Year's Game, and it pitted
Michigan, Champs of the East, against Stanford,
Champs of the West. (To be fair, California was likely a
better club than Stanford, but it had refused the
invitation.) The game ended in a 49-0 Michigan
runaway, with Stanford waving the white flag and
forgoing the final eight minutes. ("If you are willing,"
said Stanford team captain Fisher to Michigan team
captain White, "we are ready to quit.") The
embarrassment was considerable, and there would not
be another Rose Bowl game until 1916; chariot-racing
was held in football's place.

- From the Rose Bowl's start, other big cities followed
  suit: a crew of civic officials and businessmen in Miami
  created the Orange Blossom Bowl, later to be shortened
  to the Orange Bowl, in 1933; publisher Colonel James
  M. Thompson and sports columnist Fred Digby brought
  the Sugar Bowl to New Orleans in 1935; and oil
  magnate J. Curtis Sanford welcomed teams to the
  Cotton Bowl in Dallas in 1937.
- Dan Jenkins fancied the term "Poll Bowl" to describe a
  game between the two top collegiate teams in the
  country according to the polls. "A Poll Bowl," wrote
  Jenkins, "is a Crucial Showdown, a Battle of Giants, a

Big Shootout. It is sometimes a Game of the Year, a Game of the Decade, and in rare instances a Game of the Century. This is all generally decided by sportswriters, who have never played in a Game of the Year, a Game of the Decade, or a Game of the Century."

A Compilation of Select Bowl Game Names From the Past and Present

Alamo Bowl, All-American Bowl, Aloha Bowl, Armed Forces Bowl, Aviation Bowl, Bacardi Bowl, Bahamas Bowl, Birmingham Bowl, Bluebonnet Bowl, Bluegrass Bowl, Boardwalk Bowl, Boot Hill Bowl, Cactus Bowl, California Bowl, Camellia Bowl, Charity Bowl, Cherry Bowl, Chigger Bowl, Cigar Bowl, (Florida) Citrus Bowl, Copper Bowl, Cosmopolitan Bowl, Cotton Bowl, Delta Bowl, Dixie Bowl, Fiesta Bowl, Fish Bowl, Fort Worth Bowl, Freedom Bowl, Garden State Bowl, Gator Bowl, Glass Bowl, Gotham Bowl, Great Lakes Bowl, Hall of Fame Bowl, Harbor Bowl, Hawai'i Bowl, Heritage Bowl, Holiday Bowl, Houston Bowl, Humanitarian Bowl, Independence Bowl, International Bowl, Iodine Bowl, Kickapoo Bowl, Las Vegas Bowl, Liberty Bowl, Mercy Bowl, Military Bowl, Music City Bowl, New Mexico Bowl, New Orleans Bowl, Oahu Bowl, Oil Bowl, Orange Bowl (originally known as the Orange Blossom Bowl), Outback Bowl, Pasadena Bowl, Peach Bowl, Pecan Bowl, Pelican Bowl, Pineapple bowl, Pinstripe Bowl, Poi Bowl, Poinsettia Bowl, Presidential Cup Bowl, Raisin Bowl, Refrigerator Bowl, Rose Bowl, Salad Bowl, San Francisco Bowl, Seattle Bowl, Shrine Bowl, Spaghetti Bowl, St. Petersburg Bowl, Sugar Bowl, Sun Bowl, Sunflower Bowl, Sunshine Classic, Tangerine Bowl, Texas Bowl, Tobacco Bowl, Turkey Bowl, Vulcan Bowl, Wheat Bowl

Furthermore

The 1944 Orange Bowl, pitting Texas A&M against Louisiana State, was nicknamed the "Teenage Bowl" by

one of the writers who covered the game, and for good
reason. It was, wrote Richard Whittingham, "one of the
more unusual bowl games in that the war had depleted
the college football ranks, so 17- and even 16-year-olds
were escalated to the college level." The star of the
game was LSU running back Steve Van Buren. "The
Aggies displayed a strong passing attack, but Van
Buren set the tone of the game in the first period, running the ball in from the 11 for one touchdown and
tossing a pass for another. Then in the third quarter, he
ripped off a dazzling 63-yard run, and that provided
the winning margin." LSU won the Teenage Bowl,
19-14.

This might sound strange now, but the NFL used to
hold an annual Playoff Bowl, also known as the
Runner-Up Bowl, at the Orange Bowl in Miami. Official name: the Bert Bell Benefit Bowl, honoring the late
commissioner/team owner, as well as fans of allitera-
tion. Vince Lombardi's label: "a rinky-dink game."
From 1960 to 1966, the competitors were the second-
place teams from the Eastern and Western Divisions.
(The Detroit Lions won each of the first three Runner-
Up Bowls.) When Eastern and Western Division
Championship Games began in 1967, the loser of each
of those championships was sent off to the Orange
Bowl for one last game. It all ended during the offsea-
son of 1970, when the NFL and AFL merged. There
were discussions about continuing the game with a
meeting of the losers of the new NFC and AFC Championship Games. To the gratitude of many a player and
coach, it did not come to fruition.

A football doubleheader? It was a Cleveland Browns
preseason tradition, the brainchild of owner Art Mod-
ell in 1962 and lasting through 1971. Contrary to what
you might think, and thankfully for the players'
healths, the event merely featured back-to-back contests involving different squads. In 1969, for instance,
the Buffalo Bills and Chicago Bears hooked up in the

opener before the Browns took on the Green Bay
Packers in the second act.

Notable Named Games

- *The Apple Cup*: Washington vs. Washington State
- *The Backyard Brawl*: Pittsburgh vs. West Virginia
- *Battle for Nevada*: Nevada vs. UNLV
- *Battle of the Brazos*: Baylor vs. Texas A&M
- *Battle of the Brothers*: Utah vs. Utah State
- *Battle of the Ravine*: Henderson State vs. Ouachita Baptist
- *Bedlam*: Oklahoma vs. Oklahoma State
- *The Biggest Little Game in America*: Amherst vs. Williams
- *The Big Game*: California vs. Stanford
- *The Border War*: Missouri vs. Kansas (rebranded as *The Border Showdown*)
- *The Civil War*: Oregon vs. Oregon State
- *Clean, Old-Fashioned Hate*: Georgia vs. Georgia Tech
- *Deep South's Oldest Rivalry*: Auburn vs. Georgia
- *Duel in the Desert*: Arizona vs. Arizona State
- *The Egg Bowl*: Mississippi vs. Mississippi State
- *Farmageddon*: Iowa State vs. Kansas State
- *The Game*: Harvard vs. Yale
- *The Governor's Cup*: Kansas vs. Kansas State
- *The Holy War*: Brigham Young vs. Utah; Boston College vs. Notre Dame
- *The Iron Bowl*: Alabama vs. Auburn
- *The Lone Star Showdown*: Texas vs. Texas A&M
- *The Magnolia Bowl*: Louisiana State vs. Mississippi
- *The Palmetto Bowl*: Clemson vs. South Carolina
- *The Red River Showdown*: Oklahoma vs. Texas (formerly known as *The Red River Shootout*)
- *The Rio Grande Rivalry*: New Mexico vs. New Mexico State (formerly called *The Battle of I-25*)
- *The Rivalry*: Lafayette vs. Lehigh
- *The Rocky Mountain Showdown*: Colorado vs. Colorado State
- *Rumble in the Rockies*: Colorado vs. Utah
- *The South's Oldest Rivalry*: North Carolina vs. Virginia
- *Textile Bowl*: Clemson vs. North Carolina State

- *The World's Largest Outdoor Cocktail Party*: Florida vs. Georgia

Games Fought Over Notable Trophies

- Houston vs. Rice, for the Bayou Bucket
- Colorado State vs. Wyoming, for the Bronze Boot
- SUNY Cortland vs. Ithaca, for the Cortaca Jug
- Iowa vs. Iowa State, for the Cy-Hawk Trophy
- Iowa vs. Minnesota, for Floyd of Rosedale (a bronze pig)
- Arkansas vs. Louisiana State, for the Golden Boot
- Mississippi vs. Mississippi State, for the Golden Egg
- Iowa vs. Wisconsin, for the Heartland Trophy
- Northwest Missouri State vs. Truman State, for the Hickory Stick
- Southern Methodist vs. Texas Christian, for the Iron Skillet
- Notre Dame vs. Southern Cal, for the Jeweled Shillelagh
- Cincinnati vs. Louisville, for the Keg of Nails
- Illinois vs. Northwestern, for the Land of Lincoln Trophy
- Michigan vs. Minnesota, for the Little Brown Jug
- Michigan State vs. Notre Dame, for the Megaphone Trophy
- Indiana vs. Michigan State, for the Old Brass Spittoon
- Indiana vs. Purdue, for the Old Oaken Bucket
- Fresno State vs. San Diego State, for the Old Oil Can
- Brigham Young vs. Utah State, for the Old Wagon Wheel
- Minnesota vs. Wisconsin, for the Paul Bunyan Axe
- Michigan vs. Michigan State, for the Paul Bunyan Trophy
- Missouri vs. Oklahoma, for the Peace Pipe
- Illinois vs. Purdue, for the Purdue Cannon
- Lamar Tech vs. Southwest Louisiana, for the Sabine Shoe
- The Citadel vs. Virginia Military Institute, for the Silver Shako
- Stanford vs. California, for the Stanford Axe
- Missouri vs. Iowa State, for the Telephone Trophy
- Arizona vs. Arizona State, for the Territorial Cup

- Cincinnati vs. Miami (OH), for the Victory Bell
- Missouri vs. Nebraska, for the Victory Bell

goal posts

n. uprights, posts

kick one off the uprights or the crossbar
v. bang, bounce, carom, crack, deflect, doink, glance, graze, knock, pinball, rebound, ricochet, shtoink, skim, skip, smack, strike, thud, thwack, whack into it

- If the ball hits the post, it makes *church music.*

History, Terms, and R.C. Owens

- From Jimmy Stamp's history of the American football field on *Smithsonian.com*, September 24, 2012:

  "Goal posts originally consisted of two separate vertical posts with a cross bar between them, and were installed on the goal line at the front of the end zone. As you might imagine, this did sometimes lead to players colliding with the goal posts (in Canada, goal posts are still located on the goal line, which still results in some nasty collisions). Today's model, known for obvious reasons as the 'slingshot' goal post, was first proposed in 1967 by Joel Rottman, a retired magazine and newspaper distributor and part-time inventor who came up with [the] idea while eating a steak lunch and noticing the prongs on his fork…. [T]he original design called for 10-ft uprights. The uprights were extended at the request of Pete Rozelle, who then agreed to allow their use in professional play. Within the year every NFL team was using the new slingshot uprights. In 1974 the goal posts were moved from the goal line, where they had been since the first rule changes in 1933, to the back of the end zone."

- Goal posts originally used to be wooden; they are now aluminum.

- As prescribed in the NFL's rules, the *crossbar* stands 10 feet above the field and horizontally stretches 18 feet, six inches along the boundary of the end line. The uprights, specifically mandated to be painted "bright gold" (also called "yellow glow paint"), are 30 feet tall with a 42-inch ribbon affixed to the top of each upright.
- *Offset posts* are goal posts that feature two supports rather than one.
- A successful field goal or extra point down the middle *splits* the uprights. (See **field goal** and **PAT** for more.)
- On December 8, 1962, Baltimore's R.C. Owens gained distinction with a basketball-esque rejection of a Bob Khayat field goal attempt. Owens stationed himself in front of the goal posts and leaped up as the ball neared, smacking it aside. "Man," said Owens afterward, "I've been just waiting for the chance to do that. What a thrill." He later mused, "Now that I've done it, you don't think they're going to outlaw it, do you?" In 1985, the NFL did.

Tear it Down

- College fanbases celebrate big wins, especially upsets, by storming the field and tearing down the goal posts. Usually such an act is performed solely by the home team—but Kansas State Wildcats fans ripped down the goal posts of their rival Kansas Jayhawks in 2007. Five years earlier, the Iowa Hawkeyes' fans (stymied by their own hinged posts in Iowa City) marauded onto the field in the Metrodome, bringing down the University of Minnesota's goal posts. It was also in 2002 that the University of Mississippi was forced out of necessity to reattach a torn-down goalpost following an upset of Florida; the Rebels didn't have a backup post on site.
- To some institutions, it doesn't even matter which goal posts are being torn down. Georgia Tech went to #1 Virginia in 1990 and upset the powerful Cavaliers, leading the Yellowjackets' students back in Atlanta to jubilantly march into their unused home stadium and claim the goal posts in triumph.

- Lastly, consider the parade of the Northwestern University Wildcats. Upon ending their embarrassing record-setting 34-game losing streak on Sept. 25, 1982, the Wildcats' students brought down the posts, carried them out of the stadium, and dumped them in Lake Michigan.

H

University of Wisconsin's David Schreiner wearing helmet and uniform of the era, 1942. He was killed in action in June 1945 during WWII. (UW Athletic Communications)

halftime

n. half, intermission, rest period

handoff

n. delivery, feed, give, service, transfer; SPECIFIC flip, pitch, toss

hand off

v. deliver to, distribute, feed, give, hand, put the ball in the belly (of), present to, ride, serve, slip, transfer; SPECIFIC flip, pitch, toss

Terms and Jargon

- The *handoff* is often a literal description, as the quarterback personally places the ball into his running back's arms for a generic rushing play. This is not the fastest way of delivery, though, leading to the introduction of the *toss*, an *underhand spiral*, and the *pitch*, a chest-high flip of the wrist.
- "One of the most important things for a quarterback to learn is the running game and how it affects his steps from center," wrote John Czarnecki and Howie Long. "Some running plays call for the quarterback to open his right hip (if he's right-handed) and step straight back. This technique is called the six o'clock step. The best way to imagine these steps is to picture a clock. The center is at twelve o'clock and directly behind the quarterback is six o'clock. Three o'clock is to the quarterback's right, and nine o'clock is to his left."

helmet

n. bonnet, dome, hat, headgear, headpiece, lid

History, Terms, and Parts of the Helmet

- The *crown* is the top of the helmet. It is illegal for a defender to lead with the crown of his helmet; this is *spearing* and a 15-yard penalty.
- The helmet was not a part of early football. The only facial protection utilized was a rubber piece worn over the nose (a "nose mask"). Creative measures were tried to add safety. "For one year during the 1890s," wrote Robert W. Peterson, "there was a vogue for long hair." Chicago Bears end Dick Plasman was the last NFL player to take part in a game without a helmet,

participating in the Bears' 1940 73-0 championship rout of the Washington Redskins. Dan Daly's research turned up more fascinating details about Plasman, "who ditched his helmet because whenever he looked up to catch a pass, 'the flap always fell down over my eyes so that I couldn't follow the flight of the ball.' " ("And anyway," continues Daly, "if Plasman hadn't been driving with the top down, as it were, he might not have been knocked cold when he ran into the Wrigley Field wall while chasing a pass in 1938. And if he hadn't been knocked cold, he wouldn't have met the woman of his dreams in the hospital—the nurse who kept him supplied with aspirin.") As a postscript, helmets were made absolutely mandatory in the NFL in 1943.

face mask

n. bars, birdcage, cage, face bars, face guard, grill, mask

- From Peterson's *Pigskin*: "[Paul] Brown is often credited with inventing the face mask, and he did in fact devise and patent a double protective bar for helmets after Browns quarterback Otto Graham was smashed in the face. But face masks were already being used during the 1930s, though the helmets in those days were so floppy that it was hard to attach a bar to them. Even earlier, in 1928, Bucknell halfback Eddie Halicki…wore a mask to protect his broken nose. It was basically a leather extension of his helmet that covered his nose and cheeks like the mask of Zorro."

Furthermore

- As depicted in the movie *Rudy*, the paint Notre Dame uses to freshly spray its "golden dome" helmets each week includes actual flecks of gold.
- Uniforms are usually, yes, uniform. That is, identical for all players on a team. Not so Alabama. Each Crimson Tide helmet features that player's jersey number on the sides, making that helmet unique. They were first introduced in 1957.

hit

n. clout, collision, crunch, crushing blow, greeting card, pop, stamp, stick, thump, wallop, whack; SPECIFIC blind-side hit, clothesline, decleater, groundhog hit, late hit
v. administer (a blow), annihilate, bang, bash, belt, blast, blindside, blow up, bring the hammer, bury, bust, clobber, clout, crack, crumple, crunch, crush, deck, de-cleat, deliver (a blow), demolish, destroy, detonate, drill, drop, drum, ear-hole, explode through, flatten, give a lick, greet, hammer, jack, jack up, jar, knock his block off, knock into next week, knock off his pins, lay the lumber, level, lower the shoulder, maul, nail, plant, plow, pop, pound, pulverize, pummel, punk, punish, put a lick, rack, rag-doll, rock, rough up, run over, run through, savage, say hello to, slam, smack, smash, smear, smother, stamp, steamroll, stick, tattoo, thump, truck, turn his lights out, unload on, waffle, wallop, welcome, whack, wipe out, wreck; ILLEGAL clothesline, spear; see **tackle**

"Football isn't a contact sport—it's a collision sport. Dancing is a contact sport."—Duffy Daugherty

Specific Terms and Jargon

- A *blindsided* player never sees the hit coming.
- The *clothesline*, an illegal blow that's more at home in a wrestling ring than a football field, was a favorite of Dick "Night Train" Lane: the defender holds out his arm at neck/head height, as straight as a clothesline, and either lets the ball carrier run into him or runs through the ball carrier. Contemporary Fred Williamson had his own vicious trademark. As he described, quoted in Dan Daly's *The National Forgotten League*, " 'The Hammer' is a stiff-armed tackle aimed in the area of the Adam's apple, much like Night Train Lane's old clothesline tackle. Only difference is I've refined the trick. You can throw 'The Hammer' two ways. You can throw it in a perpendicular plane to the earth's latitude or you can launch it from a horizontal plane. Night Train used to clothesline them when they got the ball. I wait until after they catch the ball before chopping them down. I

personally favor the perpendicular stroke because it lands on top of the head and tends to stun the opposition."

- A *de-cleating* hit takes a player off his feet. ("Cleats" are a football player's shoes, with raised studs on the sole for better traction.)
- A *groundhog*, as defined by safety Jack Tatum, who put it into practical use: "a perfectly timed hit to the ankles just as the receiver is leaping high to catch a pass. The Groundhog isn't as devastating as it looks on TV but it does have a tendency to keep the receiver closer to the ground on high passes." (Tatum also used the Hook, learned from George Atkinson: "flexing your biceps and trying to catch the receiver's head in the joint between the forearm and the upper arm….The purpose of the Hook was to strip the receiver of the ball, his helmet, his head, and his courage.")
- Uncomfortable in retrospect: ESPN's *Monday Night Countdown* spotlighted the top five hits of the week in 2003 with a "Jacked Up" segment. (With each hit, the talking heads jubilantly chorused, "He got *jacked up!*")
- A big-hitting player *packs a punch*.
- *Pins* refer to a player's legs, as do *pegs*. To be "knocked off his pins" refers to a player who is knocked off his feet.
- A player who gets *rag-dolled* is treated so violently, limbs splaying, that it is as if his tormentor is playing with a rag-doll, rather than a fellow human being.
- A slight note of nuance: A defender hits an offensive player; when the roles are reversed, the ball-carrier *trucks* the defender, running him over. The *Madden NFL 06* videogame was the first to feature a "truck stick" to empower hard-running ball-carriers to steamroll defenders.

huddle

n. conference, grouping, meeting; SPECIFIC circular huddle,

typewriter huddle
v. confer, get together, huddle up, meet, talk it over

"Football features two of the worst aspects of American life—violence and committee meetings."—George Will

History and Terms

- Credit for the invention of the *circular huddle* is sometimes given to hearing-impaired Gallaudet College quarterback Paul Hubbard in 1894, who, it was said, noticed that other teams were able to steal his teammates' signs at the line. The resourceful Hubbard gathered his mates together in a circle before each play, thus sharing the play call while preventing the other team from gaining any advance knowledge.
- Robert W. Peterson does not mention Hubbard in *Pigskin*, his history of football's early days. Wrote Peterson: "Amos Alonzo Stagg said that he had his team huddle in an indoor game in 1896, but Bob Zuppke of Illinois apparently was the first to use the huddle regularly in 1921."
- Counters Tim Layden in *Blood, Sweat and Chalk*: "Use of the huddle dates to the earliest days of football, but the implementation of organized, every-play huddling is widely credited to H.W. (Bill) Hargiss at Oregon State in 1918."
- The *typewriter huddle* was devised by Florida State coach Tom Nugent in the 1950s, placing the quarterback in front of his teammates, his back to the line of scrimmage, with the waiting offensive players divided into two rows in front of the quarterback like keys on a typewriter. In one setup, the skill players are placed in the first row of the typewriter, bent over, while the offensive linemen stand upright in the second row.
- The *no-huddle offense*, often synonymized with the *hurry-up offense*, sees the offensive unit forgo the huddle and hurry to the line, pushing the pace and keeping the defense on its heels. It started with Boomer Esiason, Sam Wyche, and the 1984 Cincinnati Bengals. "The

Bengals played a West Coast offense," wrote Pat Kirwan, "and when they came out in 12 personnel [one back, two tight ends], Boomer found that the defenses treated one of the tight ends as a receiver and countered with nickel personnel [adding a fifth defensive back]. On the next play, the Bengals went without a huddle to keep the defense from substituting and virtually assured themselves a favorable matchup if they ran the ball."

The K-Gun

- After the Bengals introduced the NFL to the no-huddle concept, it was Marv Levy, Jim Kelly, and the Buffalo Bills who turned the no-huddle offense into a regular order of business (over a decade before Chip Kelly made an impact with the blur offense in Oregon—see "Pushing the Pace" under **offense**). The Bills' attack was called the K-Gun, named for tight end Keith McKeller, who was added in place of the usual receiver in the run-and-shoot scheme. With Kelly passing, Thurman Thomas running and receiving, and such talents as Andre Reed and James Lofton catching aerials downfield, the Bills dominated the AFC on their way to four consecutive, albeit unsuccessful, Super Bowl trips.

I

Y.A. Tittle of the New York Giants injured in 1964. (AP.)

injured

n. ailing, banged up, hobbled, less than 100%, limited, playing with pain, shaken up

Times Have Changed

- In the very early days of football, injuries served an important purpose. "Once a game started," wrote John Heisman, "a player could not leave until he actually was hurt, or, at least, plead injury. Accordingly, whenever the captain wanted to put a fresh player into action, he whispered, 'Get your arm hurt, or something.' In one game my captain whispered to me, 'Get your neck broke, Heisman.' "

interception

n. boo-boo, gift, INT, intercept, mistake, pick, pick-off, takeaway; SPECIFIC gift-wrapped interception, pick-6 (pick six), pressure pick

intercept a pass

v. pick, pick off, take away

Terms and Jargon

- A quarterback who limits his dangerous throws and is subsequently hurt by few interceptions is said to "take (good) care of the ball." His opposite number, who makes tempts fate with passes into traffic, "takes risks with the ball."
- When a quarterback *gift-wraps* an interception, he throws it directly to the opponent.
- A *pick-6* is an interception returned for a touchdown.
- A *pressure pick* is the opposite of the coverage sack, an interception tossed due to pass-rush pressure applied, usually in the first three seconds after the snap.
- A quarterback adept at finding the opposition with his passes is considered "generous," sarcasm font on in full.

K

PRICE 10 CENTS

NEW YORK FOOTBALL GIANTS
vs.
PHILADELPHIA EAGLES

HARRY NEWMAN

POLO GROUNDS   OCTOBER 15, 1933

kick

n. boot, drive; SPECIFIC boomer, coffin-corner kick, drop kick, extra-point attempt, fair-catch kick, field goal attempt, free kick, kickoff, line drive, punt, quick kick, returnable kick; see **field goal, kickoff, punt**

v. boot, drive, elevate, get it away, get off, hoist, knock, launch, lift, loft, power, put in the air, put the leg to, put the toe to, strike, swing the leg through, tee up, tee it up, toe, toe it up, toe up; SPECIFIC boom, bounce, chip, drill, ground, hop, kick off, pop up, punt, skip, squib; KICK POORLY flub, hook, knuckle, mis-hit, miss, pull, shank, slice, spray

"Our kicker had only one bad day last year—Saturday."—Gary Darnell, Tennessee Tech head coach

Descriptions, Terms, and Jargon

- Based on its spin and rotation, a kicked ball may be described as *dancing, end-over-end, fluttering, spiraling, sidewinding, knuckling,* or *wobbling.* A *boomer* has a high arc; a *line drive* has a low trajectory.
- In the air, it can *drift, die, fade, flutter, hook, knuckle, slice, soar,* or *tail.* As such, descriptions of a kicked ball may call to mind the image of a golf shot or a fly ball in baseball.
- A successful extra point or field goal is *good* or *true.*
- A *fair-catch kick* may be opted for after the fair catch of a free kick, kickoff, or punt—see **catch**—and is an undefended kick in the style of a field goal from the spot of the fair catch, worth three points if successful.
- A *free kick* follows a safety, and is kicked to the team that has just recorded two points. It may be either punted or kicked off from a tee.
- The *kicking game* describes every kicking aspect for a team—kicking off, placekicking, and punting.
- A kickoff or punt that lands in the end zone or goes through the end zone is a *touchback,* with the ball brought out to the 20-yard line.
- "On my extra points," said kicker Bruce Gossett in 1970, quoted in *Inside Football,* "I try to hit the bottom half of the football on the ground because I want the ball to get up in the air. On the longer field goals, I try to hit the middle of the ball so that I get a slow spin."

kicker

n. specialist; POSITIONS field-goal kicker, kickoff specialist, placekicker (K or PK), punter (P); SPECIFIC all-purpose kicker, barefoot kicker, combination kicker, drop-kicker, side-foot kicker, sidewinder, soccer-style kicker, soccer-styler, straight-on kicker, switch-kicker

"There are twenty-two guys locked in a feud. Sometimes they can't settle it. So they call on the hit man. He fires that one shot nobody else will. He makes it, or misses and takes the blame from everyone else."—Benny Ricardo, New Orleans Saints, quoted by Gary Smith

- A placekicker has an *educated toe* (or *educated foot*).

Drop-Kicking, Straight-On, Soccer-Style, and Barefoot

- The original style of kicking, especially with the early rounded ball, was the drop-kick. Steps 5 and 6 of "Drop Kicking With Instep" from 1939's *The Lost Art of Kicking* (as reprinted in Dan Daly and Bob O'Donnell's *The Pro Football Chronicle*) specifies "Right foot contacts ball just as same hits the ground. The angle of the ball as it strikes the ground allows same to land lengthwise on the instep of the arched foot; the right leg swings through with a snap of the knee as the leg straightens out with the follow through. Eyes still remain on the ball." These are similar instructions to that of "Point of Toe Drop Kick," which teaches young footballers how to boot with their toe first. ("Head down, eyes on ball!") As Daly and O'Donnell write, "Drop-kicking's biggest advantage was that it involved only the snapper and kicker and eliminated the holder. That meant there was one person fewer to screw up and one more to block. The drawbacks were that a drop kick usually didn't get as much distance as a place kick and wasn't as effective under bad conditions. The drop could be disrupted by a gust of wind and the whole kick thrown off if the tip of the ball got stuck in the mud…. When the ball was made slimmer in the 1930s to open up the passing game, the drop kick's days were numbered. Kickers now had to be much more precise on their drops, otherwise the ball wouldn't be straight at the moment of impact." The last successful drop-kick was performed by New England's Doug Flutie on January 1, 2006.

- The next step in kicking's evolution was the straight-on toe-kicker, approaching the ball from straightaway and kicking with entirely the front of their foot, booting the ball from out of the hold of a teammate. This brought power, but not necessarily accuracy. (One of the better kickers of the time wore his livelihood in his name: Lou "The Toe" Groza.) To help matters, new shoes were introduced, offering square-toed tips for greater strength.
- Nowadays, it is the rare placekicker who is not a *soccer-style kicker*, approaching from the side and connecting firmly with top/side of his foot in the same way that a soccer player kicks a soccer ball. (Many of these kickers come from soccer backgrounds.) Dan Daly performed extensive research into the history of the side-kicking style, crediting the Texas Longhorns' Fred Bednarski with the first successful attempt. "Bednarski, a strong-legged fullback, had been serving as the Longhorns' kickoff man when he was sent in to try a 38-yard field goal that day in '57….The week before [head coach Darrell] Royal had had him try a 55-yarder against Oklahoma, not expecting much. 'If you miss,' he told Bednarski, 'it'll be better than a punt, anyway, so go in there.' That boot, at the limit of Fred's range, had landed short; but the kick in Fayetteville—with Arkansas governor Orval Faubus in the crowd, rooting on his tenth-ranked Hogs—was nothing out of the ordinary. He'd made field goals that long many times in practice. And, sure enough, Bednarski knocked it through—with plenty of room to spare—to give the Longhorns a 3-0 lead."
- We remain in the soccer-style era, though there was a brief craze some decades back. Wrote Stefan Fatsis, "Barefoot kicking was a fad in the late 1970s and '80s. As long as it didn't hurt, the theory went, kicking sockless and shoeless eliminated the energy-absorbing and -dissipating layers of fabric and leather. And the barefooters said it didn't hurt, because they made contact on the hard surface of the instep, about an inch

down from where you would tie your shoes. In a 1982 article in the *New Yorker*, Herbert Warren Wind wrote that the right foot of Philadelphia's barefoot kicker, Tony Franklin, 'felt lifeless, wooden' with a shoe on it. 'He lost the rhythm and power on his kicks—the kind of feeling you get when you hit a 'fat' 8-iron in golf.' "

All-Purpose

- An *all-purpose kicker*, also called the *combination kicker*, handles all kicking duties for his team: kicking off, place-kicking, and punting. At the lowest levels, the all-purpose kicker is often the rule rather than the exception. In the college rank and professional ranks, though, it's the rare player who is placed in charge of all of his team's kicks, except in emergency situations due to injury. From *The Pro Football! Chronicle*: "Expanded rosters spelled the end of all-purpose kicker….The last who was effective in both roles was the Rams' Frank Corral, who played in the NFL until 1981." Most recently, the Atlanta Falcons experimented with using Michael Koenen as the team's combination kicker in 2006, but the results proved so disastrous that it was soon scrapped.
- Increasingly, three different kickers are sometimes included on rosters (usually on the college level), comprising the punter, the placekicker (who handles field goals and PATs), and the kickoff specialist. (Specific teams choose to utilize two different placekickers, too: one for shorter kicks and one with a heavier foot for deeper attempts.) In *A Few Seconds of Panic*, Fatsis quotes Denver Broncos standout place-kicker Jason Elam saying in defense of the kickoff specialist, "If I were a coach, I'd go out and get the best punter and then I'd go and get the best field-goal kicker and then I'd go get the best kickoff guy and I'd carry three. So it's an extra roster spot. Who cares? If you had a linebacker who could impact a game and make a difference of five or ten yards on every kickoff, that guy would be making ten million a year." Elam now looks prescient.

Furthermore

- On many teams, there is the feeling that a kicker may not truly be a part of the team. Sometimes, he literally isn't. "At Southern Cal," defensive back Don Doll recalled, "we had a guy who came out of the band to kick field goals and extra points." But the great Green Bay Packers offensive lineman Jerry Kramer empathized with his teammate, Don Chandler. "Kicking is a lonely chore," philosophized Kramer, "you don't have an opportunity to take out your emotions on anyone else. When I get real upset, real nervous, real emotional, I just hit one of those 280-pound defensive tackles, and all my jitters disappear." (Big Kramer knew a thing or two about kicking: On November 3, 1963, he converted four field goals for the Pack in a win against Pittsburgh.)
- As *Ace Ventura: Pet Detective* taught the viewing public, place-kickers prefer their holder to put the ball down "laces out." Pat Kirwan specifies further: "the kicker wants 'perfect laces' (laces out) and the ball tilted 6 degrees to the outside."

"I'm so strong, I could kick a flat ball over a mountain in a blizzard."—Stephen Gostkowski, New England Patriots, quoted by Tom Curran

kick off

v. put in play; see kick

kickoff

n. kick; SPECIFIC deep kick, onside kick, short kickoff, squib, touchback

"I'll never forget our first game in 1958 with the Detroit Lions. We opened by kicking off and I tore down the field, wild-eyed and screaming, praying I would find the man with the ball and make a tackle on my first play. I had just gotten to about the 20-yard line when I made contact

with Charley Ane, the Lions' all-pro center. My feet went over my head and I flew through the air for about five yards. I struggled up as the whistle blew and Charley slapped me on the back. 'Welcome to the National Football League,' he said smiling. 'Thanks,' I said, returning the smile."—Johnny Sample, "Confessions of a Dirty Ballplayer"

History and Terms

- If a twenty-first-century football fan attempted to watch a nineteenth-century football game, he/she would behold a different sort of kickoff. "[I]t was a fake kick," described John Heisman, "the center merely touching the ball to his toe and then tossing it back to a teammate who ran with it while the rest of the team gave him what interference it could."

- The current kickoff, performed at the start of each half and after every touchdown and field goal, sees the ball booted off a tee from the 35-yard line at the professional and college ranks. (The tee was first allowed in the NFL in 1948.)

- For decades, the ball was kicked off from the 40-yard line, but as kickers improved, the NFL moved the ball back to the 35-yard line in 1974 and back to the 30-yard line in 1994. In 2011, the ball was brought back to the 35. (A 2014 proposal to bring the kickoff to the 40-yard line in the NFL, completing the circle, was voted down.)

- An *onside kick* is a kickoff designed to be recovered by the kicking team, which must either wait for the ball to strike a member of the receiving team or wait for it to travel ten yards before they can gain legal possession.

- A *squib kick* is purposefully bounced down the field rather than struck deep. It is used to avoid the possibility of a big return, either late in the game with time running short or when facing a dangerous kick-returner.

- In the NFL, a kickoff downed in the end zone (or bouncing through the end zone) is a *touchback*, with the ball awarded to the offense at its own 20-yard line to start the possession.

- The basics in kickoff return plays: *return left, return*

middle, and *return right*, depending on how the kickoff return unit prepared its blocks.

- In a kickoff *reverse*, the return man starts toward one side of the field before handing the ball off to a teammate streaking the other way. In a kickoff *throwback*, the ball is brought toward one side of the field before the ball carrier stops and laterals the ball back across the field. (See **trick play** for a depiction of football's most famous throwback, the Music City Miracle.)

The Play

The Big Game between Stanford and California on November 20, 1982, looked like a dramatic Stanford win. With four seconds remaining, Mark Harmon's 35-yard field goal gave the Cardinal a 20-19 lead. ("Only a miracle could save the Bears, as Stanford piles out on the field," summed up Cal broadcaster Joe Starkey.) The ensuing celebration brought with it a 15-yard penalty, backing Stanford's kickoff to the 25-yard line. Harmon bounced the kick forward, where it was picked up Kevin Moen just across midfield. In desperation, Cal began a sequence of laterals: Moen tossed the ball to Richard Rodgers, Rodgers flipped it to Dwight Garner, Garner found himself surrounded by Cardinal players and went down, but managed to just get the ball loose at the last second to Rodgers. Stanford believed that the game was over—and that included the Stanford band, which stampeded onto the field through the end zone. From Rodgers, the ball was delivered to Mariet Ford, who brought the ball farther into Stanford territory before flipping the ball over his shoulder inside the 30. (Starkey's voice rose. *"Oh, the band is out on the field!"*) And there was Kevin Moen again, ready for Ford's toss, weaving through the band members and barreling into trombonist Gary Tyrrell in the end zone for a remarkable game-winning touchdown and a 25-20 finish. (A raving Starkey: *"Oh my God, the most amazing, sensa-*

tional, traumatic, heart-rending... exciting thrilling finish in the history of college football!")

Jake Curtis of the *San Francisco Chronicle* caught up with the key participants on November 20, 1997. "I had turned around to look at our drum major," trombonist Tyrrell told Curtis, "and I turned around again to see this guy. Time sort of stretched right there. I had this guy coming at me, and I thought he just wanted to get off the field to avoid the mayhem. And then I said, 'Oh, he has the ball,' and boom! It was a sobering experience literally. You could say I was more alert than before it happened." ("The trombone player was just in the wrong place at the wrong time," said Moen.)

Even more interesting were the comments by Charles Moffett, the referee:

> "I called all the officials together and there were some pale faces. The penalty flags were against Stanford for coming onto the field. I say, did anybody blow a whistle? They say no. I say, were all the laterals legal. Yes. Then the line judge, Gordon Riese, says to me, "Charlie, the guy scored on that." And I said, "What?" I had no idea the guy had scored.

> "Actually when I heard that I was kind of relieved. I thought we really would have had a problem if they hadn't scored, because, by the rules, we could have awarded a touchdown (to Cal) for (Stanford) players coming onto the field. I didn't want to have to make that call.

> "The (other officials) were shook. So I say, "I can't believe it happened, but we got to make a decision here. We got a touchdown. Anybody disagree with a touchdown?" No one did.

> "So I say, "Here we go." I wasn't nervous at all when I stepped out to make the call; maybe I was

too dumb. Gee, it seems like it was yesterday. Anyway, when I stepped out of the crowd, there was dead silence in the place. Then when I raised my arms, I thought I had started World War III. It was like an atomic bomb had gone off."

Credit Stanford with the last laugh. Cardinal students created a mock version of the Cal newspaper, the *Daily Californian*, and spread thousands of copies around the Berkeley campus the next week in place of the real edition. The headline on the paper: "NCAA Awards Big Game to Stanford."

kickoff returner

n. KR, returner, return man; see **return**

L

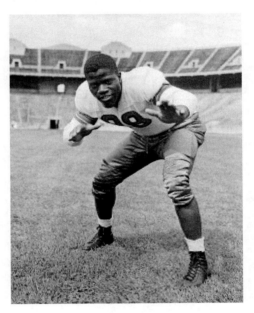

Hall-of-Famer Bill Willis of the Cleveland Browns.

linebacker

n. backer, LB, LBACK, thumper; SPECIFIC bandit, Buck, Cat, Dog, eagle linebacker, Elephant, drop linebacker, inside linebacker (ILB), Joker, left linebacker (LLB), Leo, middle linebacker, Mike, outside linebacker (OLB), plugger, right linebacker (RLB), rush linebacker, Sam, spy, stacked linebacker, Star, strong-side linebacker, Stud ($), tackling machine, true linebacker, two-down linebacker, Wanda, weak-side linebacker, Whip, Will; ARCHAIC roving center

"Linebackers are like caged tigers."—John Madden, One Knee Equals Two Feet

Terms and Jargon

- The linebackers form the *second level* of the defense, faster than defensive linemen and bigger than defensive backs. They are used all about the field: on the line, in pass coverage, and anywhere else that a defensive coordinator can put them in position to cause havoc.
- A *spy* is used to guard against the scrambling ability of a mobile quarterback. (If a linebacker is not up to the task, the spy may be a defensive back.)
- A *two-down linebacker* is used for first and second down before exiting the field before an obvious passing third-down situation.
- Since he's in the middle of most plays, an adept middle linebacker may be considered a *tackling machine* with a "nose for the ball"— as is, for that matter, anyone who racks up a heavy amount of tackles. Defensive linemen are used to canceling out offensive linemen and defensive backs have their hands full guarding passing, leaving linebackers to record the majority of the tackles. (As a general rule of thumb: If the defensive linemen collect the most tackles, the defense is strong. If the defensive backs have the most tackles, the defense is likely offensive in its mediocrity.)
- A linebacker assigned to pass coverage can *chug* or *jam* in preventing the receiver from gaining a free release, holding in the receiver while he is still around the line of scrimmage in order to foul up the rhythm of the designated pass pattern. (This technique is called *chucking, chugging, holding-in,* or *jamming.*)

Linebackers in the 4-3 Defense
Mike, Sam, Will

- Positions in a base 4-3 (four defensive linemen, three

linebackers): commonly divided into strong-side
linebacker, middle linebacker, weak-side linebacker;
uncommonly divided into left linebacker, middle
linebacker, right linebacker.

middle linebacker (in charge of the defensive play call)
n. M, MLB, the Mike, the Mike Backer, quarterback of the
defense, spokesman for the defense

- The *middle linebacker* plays in the middle of the second
  level and is in charge of the defensive play-call, earning
  him the title of "quarterback of the defense."
- In 1898, Amos Alonzo Stagg hit upon the idea of
  moving his defensive center back off the line to battle
  Penn's guards-back formation (later illegalized when the
  rules dictated first six, then seven offensive players had
  to be on the line of scrimmage). Half a century later, the
  middle linebacker was officially born: Pro Football Hall-
  of-Famer Bill Willis of the Cleveland Browns,
  who—along with Kenny Washington, Woody Strode,
  and the great Marion Motley—helped break the color
  barrier in 1946, a year before Jackie Robinson was
  called up to Brooklyn. "Until Willis came along," wrote
  Jeffri Chadiha for *ESPN.com* on November 30, 2007,
  "the position of middle linebacker didn't exist in the
  NFL. But since he was so quick and explosive as a
  middle guard in their five-man line, the Browns'
  coaches started moving him off the line of scrimmage
  and placing him a few yards in front of the center. The
  idea was to give Willis a chance to run down opposing
  ball carriers with his speed and relentless pursuit. He
  proved more than capable of handling the
  responsibility."

strong-side/strongside linebacker
n. S, SLB, the Sam, the Sam Backer

- The *strong-side linebacker* plays on the side of the
  formation with the most offensive players—this is
  usually the side with the tight end. Since most offenses

are "right-handed" and line up with their tight ends to the right, this puts the strong-side linebacker on the left side of the defense.

weak-side/weakside linebacker
n. W, Wanda, WLB, the Will, the Will Backer, Willie, or Bill

- The *weak-side linebacker* plays on the side of the formation with the fewest offensive players (the side without the tight end, usually on the right side of the defense).
- From Ben Zimmer's September 9, 2012, article in the *Boston Globe*, "How Sam, Mike, and Will became football positions":

  > Where did this welter of names come from? The earliest examples I've found are decidedly less manly than today's Sam, Mike, and Will. It was Tom Landry who pioneered the 4-3 defense as defensive coordinator for the New York Giants in the late 1950s, before going on to coach the Dallas Cowboys. For the strong-side, middle, and weak-side linebackers, Landry used women's names: Sarah, Meg, and Wanda.

  > Giants linebacker Harland Svare explained Landry's system to *The New York Times* in November 1957. "Sometimes we want the weak-side linebacker to crash so we call Blitz Wanda," Svare said. "If it's the strong-side linebacker's job we call Blitz Sarah. You understand. W is for weak side, and S is for strong side."

  > *Life Magazine* had some fun with this gender play in its Dec. 14, 1959, issue, running a photo spread of the three burly Giants linebackers signed with corresponding code names: "Faithfully, Wanda," "Constantly, Meg," and "Devotedly, Sarah." The article didn't actually explain the mnemonic role of the names, but then, as Michael Oriard wrote in his book *King Football*, "the incongruity of feminine names for hypermasculine football players was the real point."

Linebackers in the 3-4 Defense

Buck, Cat, Dog, Elephant, ILB (inside linebacker; left—LILB, LIB, right—RILB, RIB), Joker, Leo, Mike, OLB (outside linebacker; left—LOLB, LOB, right—ROLB, ROB), plugger, Sam, Star, Whip, Will

- Positions in a base 3-4 (three defensive linemen, four linebackers): strong-side outside linebacker, strong-side inside linebacker, weak-side inside linebacker, weak-side outside linebacker.

Inside Linebackers

- The inside linebackers in the 3-4 defense are the *Mike*, the middle linebacker and quarterback of the defense, who plays on the weak-side, and the *Buck*, the boundary linebacker, who plays on the strong-side. (On certain defenses, the Mike is moved to the strong side, with the *Will* linebacker placed on the weakside in the interior of the defense.)
- The *plugger* is a 3-4 inside linebacker whose specific responsibility is run-stopping.

Outside Linebackers

- The outside linebackers in the 3-4 defense are given multiple responsibilities, expected both to pass-rush off the edge and defend tight ends in coverage. In this scheme, the *Will* (also termed the *Leo*) is the weak-side outside linebacker; the *Sam* (sometimes called the *Dog*) is the strong-side outside linebacker. The Will is usually bigger and more physical, while the Sam is quicker and better in pass coverage. When the Will is moved inside, the *Jack* (or *Cat*) takes his place as a pass-rusher extraordinaire off the edge and at times a fourth defensive lineman. (As you might well imagine, teams use either "Jack" and "Will" linebackers or "Cat" and "Dog" linebackers, with little overlap.)
- "The original 'outside' linebacker in a 3-4 defense," wrote John Madden, "was Bob Matheson of the Dolphins' No-Name Defense.... Bob was inserted on

passing downs, replacing a defensive lineman. Bob's number was 53, which prompted Bill Arnsparger, then the Dolphins' defensive coordinator, to call it the '53' defense."

- Other interesting nicknames/roles: the *Elephant* is a bigger outside linebacker (perhaps even as big as a defensive end); the play-making *Joker* lines up on either side of the field and keeps the offense on its toes; and the athletic *Star* and fleet-footed *Whip* are used in hybrid outside linebacker / nickel corner / safety roles.

Notable Linebacking Units

- *The Crunch Bunch*, New York Giants, 1981-1983, comprising outside linebackers Lawrence "L.T." Taylor and Brad Van Pelt and inside linebackers Harry Carson and Brian Kelley. These were the first three years in the game-changing career of the great Taylor, the second overall pick in 1981 out of the University of North Carolina, who went on to strike fear in the hearts of quarterbacks throughout the NFL until his retirement following the 1993 season.
- *The Dome Patrol*, New Orleans Saints, 1986-1992, comprising outside linebackers Rickey Jackson and Pat Swilling and inside linebackers Sam Mills and Vaughan Johnson. Before the quartet came together, the Saints had never won more than eight games in a season and had never made the playoffs in the team's 19 seasons in existence. During the seven seasons of the Dome Patrol, the Saints won at least nine games in five of those years (including two 12-win seasons) and punched a ticket to the playoffs on four occasions.

line of scrimmage

n. line, LOS, no man's land, the pit, the pits, scrimmage line, the trenches, up front

the great battle at the line

n. between the tackles, fray, interior, meat grinder, mix, pile, scrum, traffic, wash

Terms and Jargon

- The neutral zone is the area, as wide as the length of the football, separating the offensive and defensive lines before the snap. According to John Heisman in Frank Menke's *Encyclopedia of Sports*, the neutral zone was initially introduced in 1903 by Bert Walter. Before this, it was a mess, as Heisman depicted:

  > There was only an imaginary scrimmage line drawn through the center of the ball. Naturally the rush line players of both teams were constantly striving to crowd this imaginary hair line in order to get the jump on their opponents.

  > This led to endless wrangling between teams and officials as to how many players were a hair's breadth over this hair line on each down. This resulted in so much charging and counter-charging, pushing and wrestling that it often took the quarterback a full minute to get the ball in play.

- A defensive lineman who gets himself as close as he can to the football before the snap *crowds the ball.*
- The convergence of the massive men on the offensive and defensive lines at the snap creates a *redwood forest* for a diminutive quarterback. (A big man on either line is a "redwood.")
- The central battle of a football game is *up front* or *in the trenches,* with each team seeking to control, dominate, or own the line of scrimmage, driving the opposite line backward. Everything is about the *push*—which line can push the other back? If a pile develops, who moves the pile and which way does it move? (Also: Who can get lowest? The lowest linemen gain the best leverage.) If the defense can *hold the line,* they win the battle in the trenches.

- A defensive player who crosses the line of scrimmage too early, trying to anticipate the snap, *jumps*.
- The *point of attack* (POA) is the central focus of the play; a run between right guard and right tackle, for instance, focuses that area as the key place for the offense to open a hole and for the defenders to *clog*, building a traffic jam of bodies—this defensive maneuver is called "stacking the point."
- A defender who gets lost in the middle, swept out of the play by a mass of bodies, gets *washed down*.

lose

v. choke, collapse, come up short, cough up, crater, drop, fall, fall apart, fall on their face, flame out, get boat raced, give away, give in, go down to, lie down, melt down, run out of time, sink, skid, slide, slip, stumble, surrender, trip up, wave the white flag

"The disappointment of losing a football game is in direct proportion to the amount of energy expended in trying to win it."—Green Bay end Dave Robinson, quoted in Instant Replay

loss (of a game)

n. see **defeat**

loss (of yardage)

n. going the wrong direction, minus, moving backward, negative, negative play

M

Chicago Bears running back Gale Sayers, 1969. (Pro Football Hall of Fame)

move about the field

v. accelerate, advance, angle, backpedal, bang, barge, barrel, bear
down on, boot, bounce (to the outside), break away, break past,
bull, bull rush, burrow, burst, bust, bustle, canter, change field,
chase, churn, corkscrew, crash, crawl, crumple, curl, curve, cut, cut
back, cut loose, dance, decelerate, deke, dive (in), drag (tacklers),
drive (forward), ease, elude, escape, evade, explode, fall, feint, fight
forward, fight his way, find daylight, find freedom, finesse, float,
flow, forage, gain ground, gash, get loose, get upfield, get vertical,
glide, grind, gut, hasten, head east and west, head horizontally,
head north and south, head vertically, hesitate, high-step, hurry,
hustle, make headway, make one's way, hurdle, hurry, in pursuit,
jog, juke, jump, jump-cut, jump-stop, knife, lope, lumber, lunge,
lurch, make a beeline, maneuver, matriculate, muscle, penetrate,
pick his way (forward/through traffic), pinball, plow, plunge,
power, press, probe, pump the brakes, pursue, ramble, reverse,
roar through, roll over, rumble, rush, scamper, scramble, scurry,
scuttle, separate, shoulder, skirt, slam, slant, slash, slice, slide, slip,
slither, smack, smash, snake, sneak, spill (to the outside), squirm,
squirt through, stampede, steamroll, surge, switch gears, swivel-
hip, swoop in, tear, test the line, thread, throttle down, tiptoe, trot,
turn the corner, turn upfield, twist, vault, wade through, weave,
wind, wind back, work forward, zag, zig, zigzag; SPEEDY blaze,
bolt, dart, dash, flash, fly, gallop, gun it, hightail, jet, pelt, race, run,
scoot, speed, sprint, spurt, take off, throttle up, zip, zoom; HALF-
SPEED dog, loaf, jake; DIVE lay out, lunge, sell out

*"[Paul Brown] had a favorite saying where he asked if you were running
as fast as you could. Now if you look at it, that's just a simple question
with a simple answer. But if you say yes, then that means you're too
slow. If you say no, that means you're loafing. So the best answer is not
to answer and we used to tell guys, 'Don't answer that question because
whatever your answer, it's the wrong one.'"—Sherman Howard,* Gridiron Gauntlet

Terms and Jargon

- When a ball carrier cuts back and reverses field, taking
the ball against the flow of the play and the other players

on the field, he's moving *against the grain*. When the ball carrier starts improvising on his own accord, the gridiron becomes chaotic and the ball carrier is termed a *broken-field runner*.

- A player's *burst* describes his ability to accelerate, whether as an offensive player speeding away from the defense, or as a defensive player "narrowing the gap" to a ball carrier. Such a player *explodes* forward.

- *COD*, a scout's term, judges a player's change of direction ability—can he stop on a dime, and cut back? How much speed does he lose in stopping and then re-accelerating?

- Ball carriers search for *daylight*, as Vince Lombardi termed it: an uncrowded area of the field without defenders. This is also considered *in the clear, freedom, the open, open field*, and *in space*.

- Everything beyond the line of scrimmage is *downfield*. This is not to be confused with *upfield*, which refers to the area of the field in front of a player. As long as a player is moving forward, he's heading upfield.

- When a ball carrier realizes that he's going to be brought down, he can choose to *finish* the run, driving forward (often through defenders) to pick up as many final yards as he can. This is especially notable near the sidelines: some ball carriers step out of bounds to avoid a hit, others plant their foot and barrel ahead, delivering a hit of their own.

- A player moving *horizontally* ("east and west") heads laterally toward the sideline, parallel to the line of scrimmage. If he is forced to run laterally by a disciplined crew of defenders, this is termed "stringing the play out." A player moving *vertically* ("north and south") heads straight ahead, down the field. Running south and running downhill are synonymous: racing down the field, building up momentum. A *straight-line player* is one who does well vertically, but loses speed and effectiveness when forced to cut to one side or the other.

- A *human pinball machine* is a ball carrier who bounces off tacklers like a pinball. This is also called "Plinko," referring to the popular *Price is Right* game. At 5'10" and 210 pounds, Don Nottingham took things a bit further; he was nicknamed "The Human Bowling Ball" for his ability to get low and roll through the opposition.

- The high-kicking style of 49ers running backs Roger Craig (in the 1980s) and Ricky Watters (in the 1990s), bringing the knees up and stepping away from lunging tacklers, had a precursor: Brooklyn's "Shipwreck" Kelly had his high-knee style described as a "sewing machine" technique on his 1935 National Chicle Company football card—the first pro football trading card set ever released.

- The *pursuit* refers to the defense chasing after the ball carrier, whether he realizes it or not.

- If the ball carrier appears to be stopped before giving one last push, lunge, or twist forward, his second *effort* is credited for any extra yardage gained. (For certain determined players, it's not just their second effort, it's their third, fourth, and fifth efforts that pick up first downs or touchdowns.)

- A far larger and slower player, in the parlance of ESPN's Chris Berman, goes "stumbling and bumbling."

- Speed in football is often placed in terms of 40-yard dash times, shortened to "the 40," and it, like so many things in modern football, can be traced back to Paul Brown. From a Mark Kram article for McClatchy-Tribune News Services, February 24, 2008: "Originally, [former Cowboys personnel chief Gil] Brandt says that Cleveland Browns head coach Paul Brown had players run the 40 once they got to training camp. 'He did it as a way of deciding which players to keep,' Brandt says. 'But we decided, "Why not get them to run a 40 before we have them in camp?' " From the Browns to the Cowboys to today, where every player runs a 40 in pre-draft workouts, most often at the NFL combine, so that teams can properly evaluate them.

- There are players who perform superbly in the 40-yard dash, but fail to see their speed translate on the gridiron, while the vice versa also may hold true—players who are slow on the track but play fast on the field. This is evaluated and described as *playing speed*: speed in pads. As quarterback John Elway said, "I'm probably about a 4.9 normally, but when a 280-pound guy is chasing me—I'm a 4.6."

avoid/break tackles

v. angle, bob and weave, bounce, brush aside, cross up, cut, cut back, dance, dead leg, deke, dodge, duck, elude, escape, evade, fight through, get away, high-step, hop, juke, put moves on, separate from, shake, shake and bake, shake off, shoulder, sidestep, slip, spin, shed, step away from, step out of a tackle, stiff-arm, straight-arm, stutter-step, trample, twirl, veer

- In the parlance of football, a *breakaway runner* "makes something happen with his legs." Inelegant, sure, but certainly accurate.
- A difficult ball carrier to tackle is described as *elusive*, *slippery*, or, in a popular football term that lasted through the decades, *swivel-hipped*. The opposite of this is a *straight runner*, defined by Red Grange as "one who doesn't try to get away from tacklers but instead opts to run right into them."
- The *dead leg* maneuver, used by players as diverse as Jim Thorpe and Chris Cooley, sees the ball carrier offer a leg to a tackler to grab onto—but sneakily placing zero weight on the leg, thus allowing them to break away easily from the defender's grasp.
- In today's video game society, a particularly deceptive deke/juke/feint is nicknamed "circle button" (spin move), "R1" (juke right), or "L1" (juke left) in reference to the button needing to shake a tackler in *Madden NFL*. To this end, Kansas City Chiefs breakaway returner Dante Hall, a player who demonstrated videogame-esque moves on a regular basis, was nicknamed "The Human Joystick."
- An outstanding move that leaves a prospective tackler empty-handed "breaks his ankles" or "leaves his jock(strap) on the field."

*"Really, I don't think anybody knows how fast [Gale] Sayers actually is.
Only time I've ever seen him is in the huddle. Once he tucks the football
under his arm, he's invisible."*—Henry Jordan, Green Bay Packers

Man in Motion

- The offense may send a *man in motion* parallel to the line
  before the snap. If he is moving forward at the snap, it is
  a penalty in college and pro football (though not in
  Arena League or Canadian football). If there are two
  different players moving in motion before the snap, it is
  also a penalty. The idea is credited to Amos Alonzo
  Stagg, who, wrote Allison Danzig in *Oh, How They Played
  The Game*, "used a man in motion as early as 1898. He
  called him a 'flyer.' He went laterally or backward to take
  a pass that could be thrown only to the side or to the
  rear."
- Sending a man in motion before the snap can indicate to
  the offense whether the defense is in man coverage (if a
  defender follows the man in motion across the
  formation) or zone coverage (if he is not followed).
- *Fly motion* or *jet motion* sees the man in motion speed
  behind the line of scrimmage directly in front of the
  quarterback, with the snap timed so that the quarterback
  can either fake or flip/shovel/hand off to his teammate
  in a *jet sweep/fly sweep*.
- *Orbit motion* or *rocket motion* brings the man in motion
  behind the quarterback, setting up the potential for an
  orbit sweep/rocket sweep.

Galloping Ghost

- When it came to dazzling the opponent and electrifying
  a crowd, the University of Illinois's Harold "Red"
  Grange was one of a kind. "If you have the football and
  11 guys are after you," said Red, "if you're smart, you'll
  run." Run he did, to the crowd's delight. His finest game
  saw him gain 402 all-purpose yards with five
  touchdowns in a 39-14 win over Michigan, October 18,
  1924, including four scores and 262 yards in the first 12

minutes of action. Originally called "The Wheaton Iceman," Grange received his famous nickname of "The Galloping Ghost" from Grantland Rice, who breathlessly penned: "A streak of fire, a breath of flame / Eluding all who reach and clutch; / A gray ghost thrown into the game / That rival hands may never touch / A rubber bounding, blasting soul / Whose destination is the goal."

Wrong Way

- In the 1929 Rose Bowl, playing defensive center for California, Roy Riegels picked up a Georgia Tech fumble, worked his way through traffic, got turned around, and unexpectedly found himself in the clear. "More than 66,000 fans sat dumbfounded as Riegels ran 80 yards the wrong way with his teammate Benny Lom in desperate pursuit," wrote Richard Whittingham. "Riegels made it into the end zone but Lom pulled him back to the 1-yard line where Georgia Tech tacklers brought him to the turf. On the ensuing play, California tried to punt out of danger (Riegels centered the ball) but it was blocked and the ball bounced out of the end zone. The 2-point safety proved to be the margin of victory at day's end, the final score Georgia Tech 8, California 7."

- On October 25, 1964, the Minnesota Vikings' Jim Marshall picked up a Billy Kilmer fumble, got turned around, and dashed 60 yards to daylight—to the wrong end zone. His teammates shouted at him to stop, but Marshall misunderstood them. "I thought they were cheering for me," he said later. "About the five-yard line, I looked around and things just didn't seem right." Then Marshall spotted quarterback Fran Tarkenton shouting and gesturing the other way. "I couldn't think anything else to do, so I threw him the ball," he explained. The safety brought the San Francisco 49ers within eight points of the Vikes, though Minnesota soon finished off a 27-22 victory. (A final quip, from back home in Minneapolis: "All the guys on the plane asked me to take over as pilot," Marshall said the Minnesota press corps. "They figured I'd land them in Hawaii.") During the fallout from Marshall's erstwhile dash, the Viking received numerous letters and messages, including one from Roy Riegels. It began, "Welcome to the club!"

- The name of Snooks Dowd might have also gone down in dubious history, except that, as the story goes, the lightbulb went on in time for ol' Snooks to become a hero. Penned Richard Whittingham, "Snooks Dowd of Lehigh, in college football's earlier days, ran 210 yards for a touchdown in a game against Lafayette. He ran the length of the field the wrong way, realized his mistake, circled the goal posts [which were then at the front of the goal line], and raced back the length of the field for a touchdown."

N

An original NFL team: The Canton Bulldogs—and team mascot Two Bits.

National Football League

n. Next Man Up, NFL, No Fan Loyalty, No Fun League, Not For Long, quarterback's league, The Shield

History and Thoughts

- Before there was such a thing as the NFL, Illinois coach Bob Zuppke addressed his graduating class of 1918. Said Zuppke, as related by Chris Schenkel, "Why is it that just when you players are beginning to know something about football after three years, you stop playing?

Football ends a man's career just when it should be beginning."

- "Vague talk about the need for a professional football league had been common in Ohio, and probably elsewhere, for fifteen years by the summer of 1920," wrote Robert W. Peterson. "The first step toward realization of the dream came on August 20 in the auto agency offices of Ralph Hay." Hay was twenty-nine years old. He dealt in Hupmobiles in Canton, Ohio, where his Canton Bulldogs (starring Jim Thorpe) were one of the top pro clubs going. Nine other pro teams sent representatives to meet with Hay, including 25-year-old George Halas of the Decatur Staleys. In Canton on September 17, 1920, the men worked together to create the American Professional Football Association, voting Jim Thorpe their president. The membership fee to join the APFA was $100. The champion that first year was the 8-0-3 Akron Pros, as determined by vote. They received the Brunswicke-Balke Collender loving cup for their efforts. (Three of the charter teams folded: the Muncie Flyers played only one game; the Detroit Heralds and Cleveland Tigers hung on for a season before closing up shop.) From Peterson once more, "In June 1922, the team managers, meeting in Cleveland, changed the name of their organization to the National Football League."
- In his December 30, 1948, print reminiscence of his first year in the National Football League, printed in the *Tucson Daily News*, Detroit Lions quarterback Fred Enke never referred to the NFL by name. Instead, he called it merely "professional football." The title of the piece: "Fred Enke Tells Of 1st Year in Professional Grid League."
- Those first few decades were difficult, but the NFL has staved off numerous challengers as the years rolled, absorbing the AAFC in 1950, merging with the AFL in 1969, and watching the WFL, USFL, and XFL burst into public consciousness and then shut down.
- "Pro football," said John Madden, "is a quarterback's

game." More recently, with rule changes specifying stricter discipline toward blows to the quarterback and impeding receivers' progress downfield, the sentiment has become even stronger: The NFL is a quarterback's league.

Initials

- "What does the N.F.L. stand for?" wrote Steve Wulf for *Time* magazine, December 11, 1995. "That's a question pro football fans are asking in Cleveland, Houston, Chicago, Tampa, Phoenix, Seattle and Cincinnati—all cities whose professional football teams are threatening to leave. It's the same question once asked by fans in Los Angeles, Baltimore, St. Louis, Oakland and New York—all cities whose teams did abandon them in the 1980s and '90s. No Fixed Location? No Fan Loyalty? National Flux League?"
- The NFL standing for "Not For Long" was coined by coach Jerry Glanville, and he used it often, whether with his players, the media, or (famously) to a sideline official during a game.
- The rejoinder came from referee Tony Corrente, interviewed by *Sports Illustrated*'s Peter King while battling cancer: "You hear it's the No Fun League, or it's Not For Long. I'll tell you what the league is—it's the National Family League. I've learned my glass isn't half-full. It's been full my whole life, and it's full now."
- "The Shield" moniker refers to the NFL's prominent shield logo.

nose tackle

n. middle guard, middle man in the line, N, NG, nose, noseman, nose guard, nose-T, NT, run-stuffer

History

- Before there was a nose tackle, there was a defensive *center* who lined up across from the offensive center (and usually played center when his team was on offense), soon to be called the *middle guard*. When Paul Brown moved middle guard Bill Willis off the line, creating the middle linebacker position—see **linebacker**—a void was created across from the center.

- It was not too long, though, that the void would be filled, with the *nose tackle* name chosen because he lines up on the nose of the football. The origin of the nose tackle position, courtesy of John Madden:

> You could always count on Hank Stram, the Chiefs' coach, to do something different. That's how Hank came up with the forerunner of today's nose tackle. Hank lined up one of his defensive tackles, Curley Culp, at what is known now as a nose tackle, playing opposite the center instead of a guard....
>
> Built like a sumo wrestler, Curley was 6 foot 1 and 270, as strong as any player I've ever known, and as physically suited to a position as any player I've ever known. For a defensive lineman, the worst possible stance is straight up. If he's straight up, he has no power, no leverage. If he's straight up, it's easy for an offensive lineman to push him back. The idea, especially for a nose tackle, is to be bent over. He has maximum power that way, maximum leverage, and that was Curley's natural stance.
>
> He even walked leaning forward, as if he was about to stare at the center, eyeball to eyeball.

O

An official trails the action in a 1942 Pittsburgh Steelers / Green Bay Packers game.

offense

n. attack, eleven, O, offensive unit, troops; SPECIFIC balanced offense, ball-control offense, the blur offense, conservative offense, fastball offense, hurry-up offense, K-gun offense, multiple, NASCAR offense, no-huddle offense, off-balanced offense, one-dimensional offense, two-dimensional offense, pro-style, quick-strike offense, red gun offense, run-and-shoot, spread, triple option, two-minute offense, up-tempo offense, veer, West Coast offense

- See "Notable Offensive Formations" under **formation** for descriptions of various offenses.

"Running a football franchise is not unlike any other business: You start first with a structural format and then find the people who can implement it."—Bill Walsh

Terms and Jargon

- The six *skill players*, *skill positions*, or *glamour positions* are the quarterback, running backs, tight end, and receivers – in other words, everyone except for the offensive line. Terrific skill players are *guns* or *weapons* for an astute offensive coordinator (and new skill-player acquisitions are *new toys*).
- An offense seeks *balance*, running the ball and passing the ball on a near equal ratio. An unbalanced offense *gets away from* passing or running the football, due to defensive design, ineffectiveness, or lack of quality control. An offense that, say, "abandons the run" or becomes "pass-happy," is an unbalanced unit. (Teams with a quality control coach charge him to keep track of how many running plays and how many passing plays they've executed, just in case they get off their balance.)
- A *ball-control offense* is based around running the football, "using clock," and keeping the opposition's offense off the field. The opposite of a ball-control offense is a *quick-strike offense*, which uses downfield passing strikes to jump on the defense in search of quick scores.
- A *conservative offense* takes few risks, using runs, underneath passes, and maximum protection to win the battle of field position and avoid making any mistakes.
- The *diamond* refers to the center, left guard, right guard, and quarterback, arranged in a diamond position at the time of the snap. These four spots are also called the "thinking positions." John Madden preferred to focus on a different grouping of players:

In the TV booth now, it's even easier to see all twenty-two than it was on the sideline. But when a play begins, I still watch what I call the "triangle" of those four players: the center, the two guards, and the fullback.

Nothing happens on a play until the center snaps the ball. But as soon as he does, everything starts.

By watching that triangle, it's easier to know what's happening. Unless it's an obvious passing situation, I always look for the run....

As a rule, if both guards pull and the other guard fires out straight ahead, it's an off-tackle run. If one guard pulls short, it's a trap—the runner won't be sweeping wide. If both guards fire out, it's a straight-ahead run.

- A *one-dimensional offense* can either run the ball or pass the ball, but not both. Something, whether fine defense, injuries, or a personnel deficiency, has taken away its ability to effectively both run and pass, allowing the defense to know exactly what to prepare for in the coming plays.

Personnel Groupings and Packages

- An offense's *personnel* is defined by the number of running backs and tight ends on the field, in that order. (Receivers, uncounted, are thus the number of players left over once the quarterback and five linemen are subtracted.) 23 personnel, therefore sees the offense utilize two backs, three tight ends, and zero receivers. 02 personnel ("double-tight") utilizes zero backs, two tight ends, and three receivers. And a wide-open formation with the quarterback, five linemen, and five receivers is 00 personnel, since there are no running backs or tight ends included.
- Each personnel grouping is given a nickname by its team. As Matt Bowen related on *NationalFootballPost.com*, his Washington Redskins called 01 "Kings," 02 "Joker," 10 "Jet," 11 "Posse" (honoring the team's great trio of wide receivers of the same moniker), 12 "Ace," 13 "Heavy," 20 "Houston," 21 "Regular," 22 "Tank," 23 "Jumbo," and 31 "Wildcat."
- A *jumbo* package, then, is one featuring two backs and three tight ends, perfect for picking up yards at the goal

line or in a similar short-yardage situation. Another names for the jumbo: *heavy set*.

Modern Passing Offenses

- The *West Coast offense*: "[B]y the 1990s, every NFL team had a rhythm passing game," wrote Michael Lewis in *The Blind Side*, following up with a quote from Bill Polian, the great front office man for the Buffalo Bills and the Indianapolis Colts: "In that sense, everyone in the NFL today runs Bill Walsh's offense. Because the rhythm passing game is all Walsh." The West Coast offense was developed by Walsh in the early 1970s, a system in which passes virtually turned into handoffs—quick, short, high-percentage passes that found receivers on the move. "Our argument," said Walsh, quoted in *The Blind Side*, "was that the chance of a completion drops dramatically over twelve yards. So, we would throw a ten-yard pass. Our formula was that we should get at least half our passing yardage from the run *after* the catch." Walsh masterminded the Cincinnati Bengals' offense under Paul Brown, moved on to run San Diego's offense, took the head coaching job with Stanford in 1977 and 1978, and then was hired as the head coach for the cellar-dwelling San Francisco 49ers in 1979. In 1980, Notre Dame third-round draftee Joe Montana joined the 49ers as the starting quarterback. In 1981, the team won their first of three Super Bowls under Walsh and the first of four Super Bowls in the next nine seasons.
- The *run-and-shoot offense*, sometimes termed the *red gun offense*, featured 10 personnel: one back, no tight ends, and four wide receivers. It was developed by Glenn "Tiger" Ellison" at Middleton High School in Ohio and was brought onward by Darrell "Mouse" Davis to the college ranks, the USFL, and the NFL, where it was a sensation in the early 1990s. "With no fullback or tight end to help in pass protection," Jeremy Stoltz wrote for *BearReport.com*, "the run-and-shoot forces the quarterback to get rid of the ball quickly....It is a read-

based offense, where the receivers decide which pattern to run based on their pre- and post-snap reads....It is a difficult assignment for the pass catchers as all four WRs must make the right decision on the fly. Additionally, the QB must make the exact same reads as his receivers, or else the execution of the play is compromised." Another difficulty presented by the run-and-shoot was its lack of pass protection for the quarterback. For Steve Spurrier's outstanding offensive teams at the University of Florida, the run-and-shoot became the fun-and-gun (or fun 'n' gun). To defensive guru Buddy Ryan, the run-and-shoot was nothing but the chuck-and-duck.

- The *Air Raid offense*, named by a marketing staffer at the University of Kentucky, was developed by Hal Mumme and Mike Leach with the Wildcats, evolving from LaVell Edwards's passing-based scheme for Brigham Young, which in turn had come from Sid Gillman's schemes at San Diego. The receivers ran short/underneath/flat patterns called "scat" routes (with the system termed "scat ball"), the running backs broke off huge gains on surprise draws and traps, and the previously punchless Wildcats started moving the ball all over the place on their tough SEC foes. The pirate-obsessed Leach was soon off to Oklahoma to work under Bob Stoops, and then Texas Tech to run his own team. Wrote Michael Lewis for *The New York Times*, December 4, 2005, "The [Texas Tech] offensive linemen positioned themselves between three and six feet apart—on extreme occasions, the five linemen stretched a good 15 yards across the field. At times it was difficult to tell the linemen from the receivers.... Leach spread out his receivers and backs too. The look was more flag than tackle football: a truly fantastic number of players racing around trying to catch passes on every play, and a quarterback surprisingly able to keep an eye on all of them."

- The *Air Raid* evolved, as football schemes so often do, along with a cousin now called the *spread offense* (or *spread-option offense*, if run by a mobile quarterback), begun by Urban Meyer and Rich Rodriguez.

ElevenWarriors.com's Ross Fulton explains how Meyer arrived at these schemes:

> Meyer's approach was to combine the one-back offense within the shotgun-to-run spread. Meyer and [fellow coach Dan] Mullen did not 'invent' anything new. Instead, their insight was in hybridization. They took the pro-style downhill run offense and fit it within the shotgun, using the quarterback as a run threat and adding reads and options off the base and inside run plays to create an arithmetic advantage [outnumbering the defense]....
>
> The spread's primary purpose for Meyer is not to open up the pass game. Instead, it is to provide greater opportunities for the power run game to succeed. It does so by A) making the quarterback a threat in the run game, requiring the defense to account for an additional threat, and B) by putting athletes in positions from where big plays are available on the outside through reads, options, screens, and motions off the inside run threat.
>
> A dangerous quarterback, placed back in the shotgun or pistol and executing ball-fakes—or did he?—forces defenders to watch the running backs, receivers, and the quarterback all at once. One slip-up, and an offensive player speeds toward the end zone.

Pushing the Pace

- *Tempo* defines a team's pace between the end of one play and the snap of the next play. When a team pushes the pace, hurrying to the line to begin the next play, it "goes tempo." A fast-paced team is a *tempo offense* or *warp speed offense*.
- The fastball offense. The NASCAR. The turbo. The Blur. They are the team-specific names given to an up-tempo, hurry-up, no-huddle offense, completing a play, racing upfield, and going right to the line of scrimmage for the next play, thus denying the defense a chance to

substitute. (The concept of hurry-up, no-huddle is abbreviated HUNH.) The fastball offense is found at the University of Alabama; the NASCAR comes from the University of Michigan and Penn State; the turbo offense belongs to the Washington Redskins; and the blur offense is run by Chip Kelly, first at the University of Oregon, and then brought to the Philadelphia Eagles.

- As Gregg Easterbrook described for *ESPN.com*, "The blur offense combines four existing ideas—the 'pistol' set developed at the University of Nevada; the single-wing run fakes used since football became a sport, then forgotten as old-fashioned, and now revived; the triple-option that is a standby of high school and college football, though very rare in the NFL; and the spread set that was considered radical a decade ago but now is practically conventional. The blur offense combines these four existing ideas then executes really quickly. Not only are Oregon's offensive players swift, but the team signals in plays so rapidly that an average of just 15 seconds passes from the spot of the ball to the next step."

- Hurrying to the line is no new concept. Starting in 1901, the powerful "Point-a-Minute" Michigan Wolverines were headed by Fielding "Hurry Up" Yost. "Speed was always Yost's order of the day," wrote Herb Michelson and Dave Newhouse in their Rose Bowl history. "When a play ended, Michigan quarterback Boss Weeks would be calling the next play even before enemy tacklers had crawled to their feet, brushed themselves off, and ambled to the line of scrimmage. The Wolverines used quick counts and snaps, and then alternated the counts to draw the offense offside." (Yost is also notable for his direction to his players: "Use your searchlights and jump the dead ones," though this was actually an example of him quoting Willie Heston's direction to the team in 1902.)

Cagers and the Flying Trapeze

- When it came to offensive innovation, the University of Illinois's Bob Zuppke was ahead of his time. According to University of Miami head coach Tommy McCann, from the *Miami News*, November 18, 1934, "[Zuppke] soon will be giving basketball players of the right build and temperament lots of consideration in scouting for gridiron talent. Mark my word on that." Top-notch former basketball players in modern day football include record-breaking tight ends Tony Gonzalez and Antonio Gates and impactful defensive end Julius Peppers. But Zuppke's originality went further than that. As Tommy McCann opined, back in 1934:

"Coach Bob Zuppke started something this year with his Illinois team that's bound to go a long way in revolutionizing football. In one season of his spectacular 'flying trapeze' offense he's done more to revise the basic principles of the game than rule-changers could accomplish in 20 annual sessions.

"Single, double and triple spinners; plays that start out looking simple and winding up with enough complications to set the defensive team on its ears from mental agony; all sorts of forward-lateral and lateral-forward passes, many of 'em followed by other laterals after the ball has been advanced far down the field. There you have just a few examples of why the football now being used by Zuppke and copied by other coaches will revolutionize the game."

offensive guard

n. G, OG; SPECIFIC backside guard (BSG), left guard (LG), offensive left guard (OLG), offensive right guard (ORG), off-side guard, on-side guard (OG), quick guard (QT), playside guard (PSG), right guard (RG), strong guard (SG); see **offensive line**

Terms

- The two guards on the offensive line are aligned in the interior, with the center separating them. There used to be defensive line guards as well, though these positions have evolved into today's defensive tackles.

- Who do offensive guards guard, earning their name? The center.
- Most offenses only refer to their guards as the *left guard* and the *right guard*, but there are exceptions.
- Since the majority of offenses line up with a tight end on the right side, making it the *strong side*, the *strong guard* is set up on the right side of the line while the quick guard is stationed on the left. The quick guard had better be quick—in this position, he'll be expected to pull in order to hustle out in front of running plays on the right side.
- The *on-side* or the *playside* is the side to which a play is being run. The other side is the *off-side* or the *backside*. If a play is run to the right side, for instance, the right guard is the *on-side* (sometimes onside) or *playside guard*, while the left guard is the *off-side* guard or *backside guard*.

offensive line

n. beef, big fellas up front, big uglies, blockers, bulwark, dancing bears, elephants on parade, forward wall, group, line, linemen, o-line, o-linemen, picket fence, protecters, protection, redwood trees, unit, wall; SPECIFIC balanced line, farm gate, overload, sieve, tissue paper, unbalanced line, undersized line; POSITIONS center (C), left guard (LG), left tackle (LT), right guard (RG), right tackle (RT), tight end (TE)

"We're in the security, protection, and insurance business."—Cincinnati o-line coach Paul Alexander, Take Your Eyes Off the Ball

Terms and Jargon

- From left to right across the line, by abbreviation: LT, LG, C, RG, RT. The tight end (TE) is usually placed to the right side of the line.
- The left guard, center, and right guard comprise the *interior* of the line; pressure through them (or running plays through their area) occur *right up the gut*.
- The tight end's side is on is the *strong-side*; the opposite

side is the *weak-side* or *offside*. If the tight end lines up on the right side, the offense is right-handed; if the opposite is true, the offense is left-handed.

- The holes between linemen are also numbered: 1 between center and left guard, 2 between center and right guard, 3 between left guard and left tackle, 4 between right guard and right tackle, 5 between the left tackle and tight end, 6 between the right tackle and tight end, 7 outside a tight end on the left side, and 8 outside a tight end on the right side.

- If the quarterback is right-handed, the left tackle protects his *blind side*—that is, keeps a pass-rusher from hitting the quarterback from behind, where the QB can't see the rush coming. If the quarterback is a lefty, his right tackle protects his blind side. The importance of making certain that the quarterback does not get blindsided gave rise to the tackle-as-superstar dogma in football, captured in Michael Lewis's *The Blind Side*, an alternating biography of young offensive tackle Michael Oher and an examination of the evolution in valuing the tackle position.

- *Splits* refer to the distance between linemen. (Offensive linemen who are *tight* set up close together.) From Samuel G. Freedman's *Breaking the Line*: "[Florida A&M head coach Jake] Gaither was an innovator who had devised an offense called the split-line T. With it, the Rattlers of the late 1950s and early 1960s scored nearly forty-two points a game. Gaither had even written a book about it for a big New York publisher. In the split-line T, Gaither set all his linemen a half step behind the center, and he widened the gaps between them so that the line's width stretched forty-eight feet, fifteen more than in a normal T formation. This design forced an opposing defense into impossible choices. If you played head on head along the line, within seconds a Florida A&M back was past you and through the hole. If you played the gaps, the blockers had the angle to knock you aside and clear the way for a sweep."

- It is a famous quote, and one that is written many

different ways and credited to many different coaches. The origin? Here's Richard Whittingham in *Rites of Autumn*: "Coach Gaither was explaining his formation at a clinic when Paul 'Bear' Bryant, who coached just up the road at Alabama, questioned Jake at length, then said he doubted the formation would work in big-time football. Irritated, Gaither challenged Bryant. 'I'll tell you what. I'll take my players and beat yours with it, and take your players and beat mine with it.' "

- Offensive linemen—and running backs and defensive backs, too, for that matter—set up each play in a specific stance. In the *up* or *two-point* stance, the player bends slightly over with his hands extended over his knees. In the down or three-point stance, the player crouches forward and puts the index, middle, and ring fingers of right hand on the ground. The *four-point stance*, used in preparation of short-yardage rushing plays, sees both hands placed on the ground.
- An offensive lineman who is pushed backward by a defender is *walked back* toward his quarterback, more colorfully described as being put "on roller skates." When the middle of the offensive line is pushed backward, it *sags*.
- A defensive player who *penetrates* has broken through the offensive line.

Types of Offensive Lines

- A *balanced line* sees the center flanked by three players on either side of him; an *unbalanced line*, also called an *overload*, puts more players on one side of the center than the other.
- A *farm gate*, *sieve*, or a *tissue paper offensive line* is exceedingly poor, allowing the defensive rushers easy passage. An offensive lineman who is a terrible blocker is a turnstile.
- The *picket fence* isn't just a play in *Hoosiers*: In describing new Cleveland Browns offensive coordinator Kyle Shanahan's zone blocking scheme for his o-line entering 2014, *The Morning Journal & The New-Herald*'s

Jeff Schudel wrote, "Picture a picket fence moving laterally instead of straight ahead....Kyle Shanahan wants his linemen to be smart, athletic and have quick feet."

- A *reshuffled* offensive line sees its linemen shifted about, changing positions, often due to injury.

Notable Offensive Lines

- *The Seven Blocks of Granite*, Fordham University Rams, 1929-1930, 1936-1937. The line's coach was Frank Leahy, future head man for Notre Dame; the moniker's creator was school publicist Timothy Cohane. The 1936 line featured future Packer head coaching icon Vince Lombardi alongside Al Barbartsky, Johnny Druze, Ed Franco, Leo Paquin, Natty Pierce, and Alex Wojciechowicz. The 1937 line might well have seen the Blocks of Granite at their best, though, with Franco and Wojciechowicz named to the All-America Team.
- *The Electric Company*, Buffalo Bills, 1973-1976. Beginning in 1973 with tackles Dave Foley and Donnie Green, guards Joe DeLamielleure and Reggie McKenzie, and center Mike Montler, the Electric Company turned on the juice—Hall of Fame running back Orenthal James "O.J." Simpson, "The Juice," who set single-game (250 yards) and single-season (2,003 yards) NFL rushing record.
- *Fort Knox*, Buffalo Bills, 1981. Working under head coach Chuck Knox, the 10-6 Bills featured tackles Ken Jones and Joe Devlin, guards Jon Borchardt and Conrad Dobler, and center Will Grant ably protecting 31-year-old quarterback Joe Ferguson.
- *The Hogs*, Washington Redskins, 1981-1991. Washington won three Super Bowls with three different quarterbacks thanks to its rough, powerful, and proudly uncouth offensive line. The origin of the name, from *One Knee Equals Two Feet*: "One day at training camp, Joe Bugel, Washington's offensive line coach, kept staring at Russ Grimm, the left guard at 6 foot 3 and 292. 'Russ,' he said, 'you are a prototype hog.' When the other linemen

heard that, they wanted to be hogs, too." Bugel took the name of "Boss Hog" and took initiative with the distribution of t-shirts emblazoned with a pig's face. The Hogs starred fixtures Joe Jacoby (left tackle), Russ Grimm (Hall of Fame left guard), Jeff Bostic (center), and Mark May (guard/tackle); early Head Hog George Starke; later additions Raleigh McKenzie, Mark "Stinky" Schlereth, and Jim Lachey; and tight ends Don Warren and Rick "Doc" Walker. As the nickname grew in glory, running back John Riggins campaigned for admittance, and the line eventually gave in, naming him an honorary "Ground Hog." From the Hogs soon came Washington's most memorable troupe of superfans, The Hogettes, founded by Michael Torbert, big men adorning themselves in dresses, floppy hats, and pig snouts, and cheering on their beloved "significant others" from 1983 onward, officially retiring in January 2013.

offensive lineman

n. bastion, big ugly, blocker, protector; see **center, offensive guard, offensive tackle**

offensive tackle

n. OT, T; SPECIFIC backside tackle (BST), blind-side tackle, left tackle (LT), offensive left tackle (OLT), offensive right tackle (ORT), off-side tackle, on-side tackle, playside tackle (PST), quick tackle (QT), right tackle (RT), strong tackle (ST); see **offensive line**

Terms

- The two tackles on the offensive line are set up to the outside hip of the guards. They are, by and large, the biggest of all offensive linemen.
- It is up to the tackle to protect the back (the *blind side*) of an unsuspecting quarterback as he sets up to throw. For a left-handed quarterback, it is the right tackle who

protects his blind side, thus making him the *blind-side tackle*.

- Most offenses only refer to their tackles as the *left tackle* and the *right tackle*, but there are exceptions.
- With a tight end on the right side, making it the *strong side*, the *strong tackle* is set up on the right side of the line and the *quick tackle* is on the left. The quick tackle uses his quickness to pull in front of a running play to the right.
- The *on-side* or the *playside* is the side to which a play is being run. The other side is the *off-side* or the *backside*. If a play is run to the right side, for instance, the right tackle is the *on-side* (sometimes *onside*) or *playside tackle*, while the left tackle is the *off-side tackle* or *backside tackle*.
- A story related by Zander Hollander: "Paul ('Bear') Bryant used to call his weak-side linemen weak guard, weak tackle, and so on, but he dropped the designation when a player's mother wrote, 'Why do you call my son a weak tackle? He weighs 220 pounds and I don't call that weak.' "
- The *tackle box* describes the area from tackle to tackle, starting from the time of the snap. A quarterback must exit the tackle box if he wishes to throw the ball away without incurring a penalty for intentional grounding.

Furthermore

- From 1928 to 1930, Bert Metzger played tackle at Notre Dame, setting up on both the offensive and defensive. In such a physical spot on the field, the slender Metzger stood 5-9 and weighed only 145 pounds. Because of this, he was called the "Watch-Charm Guard." That didn't bother Metzger, who earned All-America honors in 1930 and eventual induction into the College Football Hall of Fame.
- Michael Lewis's book, *The Blind Side*, did two things at once: It introduced football fans to the growing importance of the blind-side tackle, protecting a franchise quarterback's well-being, and it brought Michael Oher's remarkable story to the forefront. (It

was then turned into a much-loved movie, starring Sandra Bullock, which, a miffed Oher wrote afterward, "portrayed me as dumb instead of as a kid who never had consistent academic instruction and ended up thriving once he got it." But let's set that aside.) Lewis wrote, with regard to the blind-side blocker:

> The ideal left tackle was big, but a lot of people were big.…size alone couldn't cope with the threat to the quarterback's blind side, because that threat was also fast. The ideal left tackle also had great feet. Incredibly nimble and quick feet. Quick enough feet, ideally, that the idea of racing him in a five-yard dash made the team's running backs uneasy. He had the body control of a ballerina and the agility of a basketball player. The combination was just incredibly rare. And so, ultimately, very expensive.

official

n. judge, officiant, striped shirt, whistle blower, zebra; SPECIFIC back judge (B or BJ), chain crew, chain gang, field judge (F or FJ), head linesman (HL), instant replay official, line judge (LJ), linesman (L), sideline official, replay official, referee (ref, R), side judge (S or SJ), umpire (U), wing official

"Jim [Durfee] was penalizing the Bears 15 yards, and [George] Halas cupped his hands and yelled, "You stink!" Jim just marched off another fifteen yards, then turned and shouted, "How do I smell from here?"—Red Grange, foreword, The Chicago Bears—An Illustrated History

The Crew

- In both an NFL and a college football game, the officiating crew consists of the back judge, field judge, head linesman, line judge, referee, side judge, and umpire. The officiating crew in a high school game may feature as few as three officials, including the referee and excluding the chain gang.

- The *sideline official* or *wing official* refers to any official along the sideline.
- You'll notice that the pronouns used throughout this book are overwhelmingly masculine, as is much of the landscape of football play. On September 15, 2007, Sarah Thomas became the first woman to officiate at the Division I-A level during a game between Jacksonville State and Memphis.

Black and White

- "We can imagine the furor that would be created today should a referee appear on the field clad as Joe Turner was for the Wisconsin-Purdue engagement of 1893," wrote Howard Roberts in *The Big Nine*. "Turner, a law student at Wisconsin, officiated in the game while dressed in a derby, a light tan topcoat, light-colored spats, and patent leather shoes with pearl buttons. As a crowning touch, he carried a cane!"
- Forty years later, outfits remained formal. Officials often wore a beret of sorts, according to Uni-Watch editor Paul Lukas. As Dan Daly and Bob O'Donnell further detailed in *The Pro Football Chronicle*: "The well-dressed NFL official in the early '30s wore 'white trousers, white shirt, black [bow] tie and preferably black stockings.' Those, at least, were the league's instructions in 1933. Officials that year also were told to buy 'reduced rate weekend' train tickets. They were hired and paid by the home team, receiving $25 apiece."
- Unfortunately, those white officiating shirts were easy to mix up with teams wearing white jerseys. Most memorably, referee Lloyd Olds had a pass sent his way by a confused quarterback in 1920. (Hey, he was open.) So it was that Olds asked a friend in sporting goods, George Moe, to supply a shirt that would dispel any confusion. In 1921, he sported today's familiar black-and-white stripes, a look that would be adopted by the NFL in 1935, inevitably leading to the "zebra" nickname.
- In the early 1940s, the officials were forced to change

their wardrobes again. From Daly and O'Donnell's research: "Another of [new commissioner Elmer] Layden's ideas was to have each official wear a different-colored shirt—black and white for the referee, red and white for the umpire, orange and white for the head linesman and green and white for the field judge.... Everybody went back to black and white when Bert Bell became commissioner in '46."

- "In the early 1960s," wrote Pagan Kennedy for *The New York Times* on November 1, 2013, "the American Football League embraced a flamboyant shirt for its refs that featured tomato-red stripes. This was the era in which TV screens went color, and A.F.L. officials seem to have been caught up in the enthusiasm for the new technology. But when the A.F.L. ceased to exist, so, too, did the shirts."

Specific Roles
(quoting the NFL rule book for responsibilities, via NFL.com)

The **Referee**: One of the original NFL officiating crew, often shortened to *ref*, wears a white cap to distinguish himself from his black-capped colleagues. Other duties are as follows:

- At the start of the play, takes a position in the backfield 10 to 12 yards behind line of scrimmage.
- Responsible for general oversight and control of game, giving signals for all fouls and serving as the final authority for rule interpretations.
- Determines legality of snap, observes deep back(s) for legal motion.
- On running play, observes quarterback during and after handoff, remains with him until action has cleared away, then proceeds downfield, checking on runner and contact behind him.
- When runner is downed, determines forward progress from wing official and, if necessary, adjusts final position of ball.
- On pass plays, drops back as quarterback begins to fade

back, picks up legality of blocks by near linemen; changes to complete concentration on quarterback as defenders approach.

- Primarily responsible to rule on possible roughing action on passer and if ball becomes loose, rules whether ball is free on a fumble or dead on an incomplete pass.
- During kicking situations, has primary responsibility to rule on kicker's actions and whether or not any subsequent contact by a defender is legal.
- Announces on the microphone when each period has ended.

The **Back Judge**, added to the NFL in 1947:

- At the start of the play, takes a position 25 yards downfield from the line of scrimmage.
- In general, favors the tight end's side of field; keys on tight end, concentrates on his path and observes legality of tight end's potential block(s) or of actions taken against him.
- Rules from deep position on holding or illegal use of hands by end or back or on defensive infractions committed by player guarding him.
- Times interval between plays on 40/25-second clock plus intermission between two periods of each half.
- Makes decisions involving catching, recovery, or illegal touching of a loose ball beyond line of scrimmage.
- Responsible to rule on plays involving end line.
- Calls pass interference, fair catch infractions, and clipping on kick returns.
- Together with the Field Judge, rules whether or not field goals and conversions are successful
- Stays with ball on punts.

The **Field Judge**, added to the NFL in 1929:

- At the start of the play, takes a position 20 yards downfield from the line of scrimmage, on the same side of the field as the Line Judge.

- Keys on wide receiver on his side.
- Concentrates on path of end or back, observing legality of his potential block(s) or of actions taken against him.
- Rules from deep position on holding or illegal use of hands by end or back or on defensive infractions committed by player guarding him.
- Has primary responsibility to make decisions involving sideline on his side of field, e.g., pass receiver or runner in or out of bounds.
- Makes decisions involving catching, recovery, or illegal touching of a loose ball beyond line of scrimmage.
- Rules on plays involving pass receiver, including legality of catch or pass interference; assists in covering actions of runner, including blocks by teammates and that of defenders; calls clipping on punt returns.
- Together with the Back Judge, rules whether or not field goal attempts and conversions are successful.

The **Head Linesman**, one of the original NFL officiating crew:

- At the start of the play, straddles the line of scrimmage on side of field opposite the Line Judge.
- Primary responsibility is to rule on offside, encroachment, and actions pertaining to scrimmage line prior to or at snap.
- Generally, keys on closest setback on his side of the field. On pass plays, responsible to clear his receiver approximately seven yards downfield as he moves to a point five yards beyond the line.
- Secondary responsibility is ruling on any illegal action taken by defenders on any delay receiver moving downfield.
- Rules on sideline plays on his side, e.g., pass receiver or runner in or out of bounds.
- Together with the Referee, keeps track of number of downs and is in charge of mechanics of the *chain crew* (see "Working on the Chain Gang" below) in connection with its duties.
- Must be prepared to assist in determining forward

progress by a runner on play directed toward middle or into his side zone, then signals the Referee or the Umpire what forward point ball has reached.

- Rules on legality of action involving any receiver who approaches his side zone, calling pass interference.
- Rules on legality of blockers and defenders on plays involving ball carriers, whether it is entirely a running play, a combination pass and run, or a play involving a kick.
- Assists the Referee with intentional grounding.

The **Line Judge**, added in 1965:

- At the start of the play, straddles the line of scrimmage on side of field opposite the Head Linesman.
- Keeps the time of game as a backup for the clock operator.
- Along with the Linesman is responsible for offside, encroachment, and actions pertaining to scrimmage line prior to or at snap.
- Keys on the closest setback on his side of field and observes his receiver until he moves at least seven yards downfield; he then moves toward backfield side, being especially alert to rule on any back in motion and on flight of ball when pass is made.
- Has primary responsibility to rule whether or not passer is behind or beyond line of scrimmage when pass is made, as well as whether the pass flies forward or backward.
- Assists the Referee in determining intentional grounding.
- Assists in observing actions by blockers and defenders who are on his side of field.
- After pass is thrown, directs attention toward activities that occur in back of the Umpire.
- During punting situations, remains at the line of scrimmage to be sure that only the end men move downfield until kick has been made, confirms whether or not the kick crossed line, observes action by

members of the kicking team who are moving downfield to cover the kick.

- Advises the Referee when time has expired at the end of each period.

The **Side Judge**, added in 1978:

- At the start of the play, takes a position 20 yards downfield from the line of scrimmage on the same side of the field as the Head Linesman.
- Keys on the wide receiver on his side.
- Concentrates on the path of the end or back, observing legality of his potential block(s) and actions taken against him.
- Rules from deep position on holding or illegal use of hands by end or back and defensive infractions committed by player guarding him.
- Primary responsibility is to make decisions involving sideline on his side of field, e.g., pass receiver or runner in or out of bounds.
- Makes decisions involving catching, recovery, or illegal touching of a loose ball beyond line of scrimmage
- Rules on plays involving pass receiver, including legality of catch or pass interference; assists in covering actions of runner, including blocks by teammates and that of defenders
- Calls clipping on punt returns.

The **Umpire**, one of the original NFL officiating crew:

- Primary responsibility is to rule on players' equipment, as well as their conduct and actions on scrimmage line.
- Lines up approximately four to five yards downfield, varying position from in front of weak-side tackle to strong-side guard, looking for possible false starts by offensive linemen and observing legality of contact by both offensive linemen while blocking and defensive players while they attempt to ward off blockers.
- Moves forward to line of scrimmage when pass play

develops in order to ensure that interior linemen do not move illegally downfield.

- If offensive linemen indicate screen pass is to be attempted, shifts his attention toward screen side and picks up potential receiver in order to ensure that he will legally be permitted to run his pattern.
- Assists in ruling on incomplete or trapped passes when ball is thrown overhead or short.
- On punt plays, positions himself opposite the Referee in offensive backfield—5 yards from kicker, one yard behind.

Working On the Chain Gang

- The *chain gang* (or *chain crew*), under the jurisdiction of the head linesman, is in charge of the markers (also called the *chains*, *rods*, or *sticks*) indicating line of scrimmage and the necessary distance to reach a first down. Since they are not a regular part of the officiating crew, it is up to the home team to supply the members of the chain gang.
- The chain gang's gang: The two *rodmen*, who hold the markers, one standing at the first down's line of scrimmage, the other waiting ten yards down the field to indicate the necessary place needed to be reached in order to pick up a first down and move the chains. And the *boxman*, who holds an upright marker indicating the current down and line of scrimmage; his presence and accuracy is crucial.
- see **first down line**
- The chain gang is an unbiased part of any football game, important and unassailable. Except one preseason day in 1979, when Bubba Smith's pro-football career came to a screeching halt because, he claimed, he tripped over a chain or the aluminum down marker. After the ensuing knee injury basically ended his career, Smith sued the NFL for $2.5 million. As detailed in *The Pro Football Chronicle*, there were two trials. The first ended with a hung jury, the second ended with a unanimous decision for the NFL.

Rewind the Tape

- Instant replay was tried experimentally in the NFL in 1985 before an official introduction in 1986. A *replay official*, nicknamed the "electronic official," was added to each crew, aided by a communicator and a technician in the first "replay booth," which featured two different VCRs recording the game on video cassette. The system was controversial—"In one [1989] game it was used 14 times," according to a report published in the *Kokomo (IN) Tribune*—though it was renewed on a one-year basis through 1991.

  One early replay official was football coach-turned-officiant Nick Skorich, who had this experience, as told in Stuart Leuthner's *Iron Men*:

  The Bears were playing Cleveland in Chicago. As luck would have it, on the third play of the game we got a replay problem. The center snapped the ball and [Bears quarterback Jim] McMahon was in the shotgun. The ball went by his shoulder, they were on their own sixteen-yard line and started rolling toward the goal line. Everybody was diving for it and a couple of Cleveland players went for the ball, *zipppppp*, they're out of the end of the end zone. The officials on the play thought they had a touchdown, but it might be a safety. Did the player have possession before he went out of the end zone? They came to me and I sat looking at two tapes, and so far it was a safety because I couldn't see the ball. "Stand by," I told them, "I'm still looking." Then they come back with the reverse-angle shot from the end zone, and I could see the Cleveland player clearly got the ball about a yard from the end line, his knee hit, and then he went out. I told the referee, "You've got a touchdown."

  Don't you know the following week a few of the wire services had to carry the story that a former Cleveland Browns coach was doing the replay in Chicago and was that really fair? They doubted my integrity and I didn't take that too nicely.

- After a hiatus from 1992 through 1998, the replay system returned to the NFL in 1999 with a challenge system now in effect, and here it has stayed. If a head coach wishes to challenge a call (excluding turnovers, touchdowns, and plays in the last two minutes, all of which are automatically reviewed), he tosses—in some cases, drops—a red challenge flag onto the field.
- The onsite replay official has also been removed. In his place, the referee checked out the replays himself (going "under the hood" to see the different angles of the play in question) until, entering the 2014 season, a centralized replay station was instituted at the NFL's offices in Manhattan.

opponent

n. adversary, antagonist, archrival, the bad guys, bump in the road, challenger, competition, counterpart, enemy, foe, nemesis, obstacle, opposer, opposite number, opposition, the other guys, other side, rival, sparring partner, thorn in the side

- The oldest uninterrupted football rivalry belongs to Pennsylvania foes Lehigh University and Lafayette College, who first played one another in 1884. Their meeting at Yankee Stadium on November 22, 2014, was the 150th game between the two schools. In all sports, their rivalry is known as, bluntly, "The Rivalry."
- The NFL Network's Deion Sanders quipped about the punchless 2014 Oakland Raiders, "They're one of the best sparring partners in the league."

overtime

n. bonus football, extra period, extra session, fifth quarter, OT; SPECIFIC sudden-death

History

- The NFL introduced sudden-death overtime rules—with the first score determining a victor—for playoff games in 1941, though it took the 1958 NFL Championship for fans and players alike to understand how dramatic sudden death could be.
- The NFL's first unofficial sudden-death overtime game was a 1955 preseason contest between the Los Angeles Rams and the New York Giants. Coincidentally, the Giants ended up on the short end in both '55 and '58, losing 23-17 to the Rams just three minutes into sudden death.
- The longest game in NFL history came on December 25, 1971, with the Miami Dolphins defeating the Kansas City Chiefs 27-24 at 7:40 into the second overtime, thanks to a Garo Yepremian 37-yard field goal.
- In 1974, the NFL added sudden-death overtime to regular-season games.
- In 1996, the NCAA went to the "Kansas Playoff" rules to decide its own overtime games. The teams each have one possession starting at the opponent's 25-yard line. If they match one another in their scores (both kicking a field goal, for instance, or both scoring a touchdown), the game continues to a second overtime. Following the third overtime, teams are forbidden from kicking an extra-point after touchdowns, thus speeding up a conclusion. That didn't slow down the Arkansas Razorbacks, who played two separate seven-OT games, topping Eli Manning and Ole Miss 58-56 in 2001 and outlasting Kentucky 71-68 in 2003.
- In 2010, two Texas high schools topped everyone, as the Jacksonville Indians bested the Nacogdoches Dragons 84-81 in 12 overtimes. (Apparently, the players for the corresponding schools have felt pressure to live up to the legacy of that marathon: The 2014 meeting lasted five overtimes. Jacksonville triumphed again, 85-79.)
- Sudden death no longer exists in the NFL. In 2010, the league voted to adjust overtime rules in the playoffs so

that if the first team to receive the ball in OT kicked a field goal, the opponent would have an opportunity to match or top that score. In 2012, that regulation was extended to all games, regular-season and postseason.

The Greatest Game Ever Played

The silver screen's version of "The Greatest Game Ever Played" was about young golfer Francis Ouimet stunning Harry Vardon. Football's version was the sudden-death—"sudden victory" for the cleaned-up TV viewers—1958 NFL Championship, played in Yankee Stadium, nationally televised on NBC, and featuring the New York Giants against the iconic Johnny Unitas and the Baltimore Colts. The game has quite the title, but, wrote Bob Carroll, "From an artistic standpoint, it wasn't quite that. It was a first-rate affair, all right, but in any given season, you could find games with more spectacular plays or games in which the lead seesawed back and forth more often. Even drawing only from championship games, there have been more thrilling affairs. But the '58 championship between the Baltimore Colts and the New York Giants was different because its national telecast put the NFL in more living rooms than ever before—an estimated 10,820,000 homes across the country." That sizable TV audience saw the NFL's first postseason game to go to overtime.

"When the game ended in a tie," remembered Unitas in an *NFL.com* article, "we were standing on the sidelines waiting to see what came next. All of a sudden, the officials came over and said, 'Send the captain out. We're going to flip a coin to see who will receive.' That was the first we heard of the overtime period." The sudden-death nature of the game, with the first score determining a winner, was only recently enacted by Commissioner Bert Bell; first score won. The Giants received first, but punted. Given the opportunity, Unitas drove his Colts 80 yards for the championship, finished off by an Alan Ameche 1-yard touchdown run on 3rd and goal.

Three interesting notes that came out afterward:

First, the New York and Baltimore broadcasters, Chris Schenkel and Chuck Thompson, flipped a coin to divide up their tandem NBC play-by-play. Schenkel won, selected the second half—and Thompson became the voice of the memorable sudden-death climax.

Second, from Bob Carroll: "Ironically NBC nearly missed the winning play. Fans had inadvertently kicked a cable connection apart, plunging TV screens into darkness. Fortunately, a drunk staggered out onto the field and reeled around just long enough to allow the network to get the cable reconnected. Only later was it discovered that the fortuitous drunk was a cold sober NBC vice-president."

Third, from Jack Mann: "*Sports Illustrated*, which caused it to be called 'The Greatest Football Game Ever Played,' didn't actually use the word 'greatest.' Tex Maule, the pro football curator, wanted to use the word. But his magazine had a rule against it. So they settled on the word 'best,' and people got the idea anyway. Maule also remembers *S.I.* merely giving the 'Best Game' a two-page, one-picture spread. 'Pro football just wasn't Madison Avenue in those days,' he recalls."

P

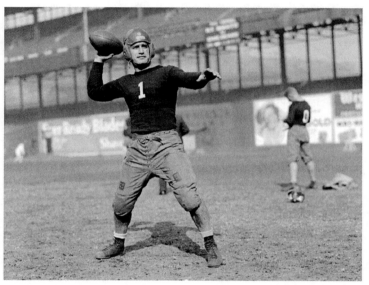

Michigan's Benny Friedman, considered the first great passer in the college game. (University of Michigan.)

pass

n. aerial, air shot, chuck, delivery, fling, flip, heave, overhead, pass play, pitch, spiral, throw, toss, throw, toss, wing; HARD BB, bullet, clothesliner, fastball, frozen rope, hummer, laser, missile, peg, seed, sizzler, strike; SPECIFIC arcing pass, back-shoulder pass, backward pass, balloon, bomb, checkdown, completed pass, dart, deep ball, deep pass, dying quail, end zone shot, feather pass, field position pass, flare, floater, flutterball, forward pass, Hail Mary, halfback pass, hanger, high arcing pass, hot read, hot-potato pass, incomplete pass, intercepted pass, intermediate pass, lateral, line drive pass, lob, lollipop, long one, long pass, looper, mallard, medium-range pass, moonball, play-action pass, play pattern pass, pocket pass, pop pass, quick-hitter, rainbow, shovel pass, shuffle pass, sideline pass, spike, swing pass, tackle-eligible pass, tailback pass, tipped pass, uncatchable pass, wide receiver pass, wobbler, wounded duck; see **pass route**

v. air out, bring, bomb, buggywhip, burn, cast, check down, chuck, crank, dart, deal, deliver, deposit, dish, distribute, drill, drive, drop a dime, drop off, dump, dump off, feather, feed, find, fire, fit in, flare, fling, flip, float, get rid of the ball, get the ball out, gift, go, go deep, go long, go to the air, gun, hang, heave, hurl, hum, jump throw, laser, launch, let fly, let rip, lateral, lob, loft, loose, offer, overhand, peg, pepper, pick up, pitch, pop, present, propel, pull the trigger, put right on the money, rainbow, release, rifle, rip, rocket, sidearm, send, serve, shoot, shotput, shovel, sizzle, sling, smoke, snap off a throw, spiral, steam, swing, take, take a shot, thread, throw, throw hot, twirl, toss, uncork, unload, whip, whistle, wing, wobble, zing, zip

"In football, technically, there are three kinds of forward pass: First, the spot pass, thrown to a spot where the receiver is supposed to be; second, the pass which is thrown to one definite individual; third, the choice pass, in which the passer, dropping back for protection, selects whichever of his eligible receivers is uncovered. This is the best pass in football, but the most difficult to execute."—Knute Rockne, Collier's Weekly, *October 25, 1930*

complete a pass
v. connect, connect with, find, get his man, hit, hook up with, lay the ball in the receiver's hands, locate, thread the needle

completed pass
n. catch, caught ball, completion, connection, hook-up; see **catch**

pass poorly
v. airmail, bounce, bury, flutter, have one slip, lose, miss,

overshoot, overthrow, sail, short-arm, skip, toss up a wounded duck, underthrow

- When a quarterback throws a pass too low, he didn't "put enough" (or get enough) on it. Perhaps a little more *gas* or *mustard* or *oomph* would've helped out, or perhaps the quarterback in question "doesn't have the arm (strength)" to make a certain throw. A pass too high is *too tall*, forcing the receiver to try *climbing the ladder* in order to snag it.

spike (deliberately throw the ball down at the field)
v. clock, dirt, ground, kill the clock, kill the play, turf

Passing Terms and Jargon

- The *back-shoulder pass* is thrown purposefully behind a receiver, toward his back-shoulder, foiling a cornerback's blanket coverage. This is usually a *back-shoulder fade*.
- A deep pass is called a *bomb*, *deep ball*, *long pass*, *long one*, or, since the quarterback "wants it all," a *home run shot*. The Raiders' Daryle Lamonica, who loved to throw the ball deep, was nicknamed "The Mad Bomber."
- A quarterback letting fly a deep pass is said to "take a shot downfield," "take a shot up the field," or simply "take a shot."
- A *catchable ball* is a pass that is easy for a receiver to collect. This is a skill, not merely a light lob of a toss. A quarterback who throws a soft, catchable ball even when humming a pass deep downfield is a popular man with his receivers.
- A checkdown is thrown (*dropped off* or *dumped off*) to an underneath receiver, often a running back, when all of the deeper receivers are covered. (This receiver is considered a *safety valve* for the quarterback.)
- An accurate pass is a *dart* and hits a receiver *in stride*. A quarterback who completes an impressively accurate pass through excellent coverage *drops (in) a dime*, *puts it right on the money*, or *threads the needle*, *fitting* the pass in

through a *narrow window*. The window is the area of a space where a quarterback can safely deliver a pass to a receiver—though windows have a way of closing in a hurry. Earl Morrall told George Plimpton that trying to throw against tight coverage was "like trying to drop a plug into a pond packed in solid with lily pads."

- A *field position pass* is a conservative pass thrown when the offense is backed up, looking to avoid a deep punt and losing the battle of field position.

- A *flutterball*, *mallard*, or *wounded duck* describes exactly how it looks, a football fluttering through the air or a football looking much like a wounded duck as it leaves the quarterback's hand—perhaps tipped at the line of scrimmage, or let fly just as the quarterback was being hit. A hanging pass is much the same, hanging lazily in the air to allow an easy interception.

- In a *Hail Mary*, taking place in the dying seconds of a half, particularly with the offensive team trailing and desperate for a miracle, the quarterback sends every receiver into the end zone and "heaves up a prayer." If the Hail Mary is caught, the "prayer is answered." The term traces back to the first half of the century, though it was put on the map by Roger Staubach's 50-yard touchdown pass to Drew Pearson in 1975, advancing the Dallas Cowboys past the Minnesota Vikings in the NFC postseason. ("After the game," remembered Staubach, "the press asked me about the play. I said I closed my eyes and said a Hail Mary.")

- For *hot read* (and *throwing hot*), see **audible**.

- A *hot-potato pass* leaves the quarterback's hand in a hurry, directly following the snap.

- In order for a pass to be considered a *lateral*, it must travel backward. If it isn't caught, the offensive team better be quick to recover it; that's a loose ball.

- A *balloon*, *lob*, *lollipop*, *moonball*, and *rainbow* all describe a pass with plenty of air beneath it. That said, a lob or rainbow pass is likely thrown purposefully with a high arc (as in a purposeful jump-ball, fade, or alley-lop pattern), while a balloon, lollipop, and moonball are

related to a wounded duck, hanging high for a potential
interception.

- The *launch angle* is the angle at which the quarterback
  throws the ball.
- A *quick-hitter* is any pass that is thrown in a hurry.
- A *shovel pass* (often corrupted into "shuffle pass") does
  travel forward, but not very far. Used often with low
  risk, the quarterback draws in the defense before
  flipping a short toss to a receiver/running back just in
  front of him. It is named because the pass evokes the
  image of the quarterback using a shovel to deliver the
  ball to his target. A shovel pass is used for the effective
  "fly screen."
- A *tipped pass*, like an *uncatchable pass* (or *uncatchable ball*),
  cancels a pass interference penalty. Once a pass is either
  tipped or thrown in an area where a receiver can't make
  a play on it, a referee cannot rule against the covering
  defender.
- See **pass route** for descriptions of more types of passes
  and routes

History... on a Checkerboard

- The aerial arrived in football just after the turn of the
  twentieth century. In 1903, the first year that Major
  League Baseball held a World Series between the
  American and National Leagues, coach John Heisman
  began lobbying for the pass to enter the game. Three
  years later, it did. "The first use of the forward pass,"
  wrote Robert W. Peterson, "probably was by St. Louis
  University in a game against Carroll College played the
  first or second week of September [1906]." The
  enthusiasm of the St. Louis players at the new offensive
  play was immediate. From a letter written by coach
  Edward B. Cochems to the *St. Louis Post-Dispatch*,
  printed November 8, 1940: "Just before our first
  practice [of the season], I told the players to put their
  fingers between the two lacings nearest the end of the
  ball where the diameter was shortest and throw it with a
  twist of the wrist, on its long axis. ... In about half an

hour Bradbury Robinson, all excited, came back and said, 'Coach, I can throw the danged thing 40 yards!' " SLU won every game it played in 1906.

- With the original forward-pass rule, there were several strict mandates: Uncaught passes became turnovers, with the opposite team taking over for the next play at the spot of the incomplete toss. Additionally, passes had to be thrown to flanks of the field; if a pass came within five yards of the center, the play was illegal. But how could it be determined if the pass was within five yards? Yes, five-yard stripes were added to the field, crisscrossing the existing yard lines and turning the field into a checked pattern. The field was returned to its previously striped look entering 1910, according to Peterson, "when rules makers decreed that the passer could throw anywhere over the scrimmage line but had to be at least five yards back when he threw." The game was on its way.

passing attack

n. aerial aptitude, aerial assault, aerial attack, aerial barrage, aerial circus, air raid, bombs away, dink and dunk, nickel and dime, pitch and catch; see **offense**

"I always preferred a running offense, but I was smart enough to put in one long incomplete pass per quarter just for the alumni."—Duffy Daugherty

- *Dinking and dunking* refers to a short passing style of 3- to 5-yard passes, "nickel and diming" one's way down the field with short bits of yardage, rather than large chunks.
- The passing game may be described and separated by the lengths of the passes. The *quick game* or *short game*, for instance, describes how a team's short pass routes.
- *Pitch and catch* is an aerial offense that looks easy due to excellent execution (and perhaps poor defense, too).

Airing it Out

- From Zander Hollander and Paul Zimmerman's *Football Lingo*, "Oklahoma's team of 1914 was the country's first great passing outfit. Coach Bennie Owen's Sooners averaged 40 points a game, throwing 30 to 35 passes—and this was in the era of oversized ball. The term 'aerial circus,' though, was first applied to Ray Morrison's SMU teams of the early 1920s, which passed more often than they ran and put Texas football on the map for the first time."

- At the professional level, the 1927 entrance of the University of Michigan's Benny Friedman, who, wrote Robert W. Peterson, "thought nothing of passing on first down (gasp!), which was heresy to traditionalists," followed by the 1937 introduction of TCU's sensational Slingin' Sammy Baugh into the NFL ranks hugely impacted the league's offensive philosophy. David L. Porter's *Biographical Dictionary of American Sports: Football* quotes the Pro Football Hall of Fame's Don Smith as opining, "More than any other person, the transformation of pro football from an infantry-type game to a pass-punctuated game offensive extravaganza can be traced to Baugh." Said TCU coach Dutch Meyer of Baugh's skills, "He could drop the ball on a dime from 30 yards with no more than wrist action."

- "The Greatest Show on Turf," coined by ESPN's Chris Berman in 2000, described the high-flying 1999-2001 St. Louis Rams. Starting quarterback Trent Green was lost due to major injury in the '99 preseason, causing former supermarket stocker/Arena League slinger Kurt Warner to gain the starting job. With Mike Martz calling the offense, Warner firing touchdown passes, running back Marshall Faulk causing havoc both on the ground and in the air, and a crew of dangerous wide receivers led by Isaac Bruce and Torry Holt, the Rams scored 1,569 points on their way to 37 victories over the three-season span. They won Super Bowl XXXIV (with Warner throwing for 414 yards), staving off upset-minded Tennessee, and then fell in an upset to New England in Super Bowl XXXVI.

- For a look at the West Coast, run-and-shoot, Air Raid, and spread offenses, see **offense.**

pass defense

n. coverage, pass coverage; SPECIFIC bump and run, cloud coverage, cover 0, cover 1, cover 2, cover 3, cover 4, four across, high-low, jam, man, man-to-man, man underneath, off, off and inside, off and soft, press, press bail, single coverage, soft, Tampa 2, tight, two deep coverage, vise coverage, zone

"Put a bull and a cat in an arena and have them run at each other. What do you think the bull is thinking? When I cover somebody, that's what I'm thinking."—Charles Woodson

- The three R's for a pass defender: read, recognize, and react. Make a *read* based on what was observed before the snap; *recognize* the play after the snap; *react* to the play.
- Well-disguised coverages are *muddied,* the better to confound the quarterback.
- A *busted coverage* describes a defensive miscommunication that leaves a receiver wide open. (In this case, a defender likely "missed an assignment," abbreviated *MA.*) If the coverage is performed correctly, though, here is how those coverages look:

Scheme: Man and Zone

- A *man defense,* also called *man-to-man* and *single coverage,* assigns a defender (or two, or three) to directly cover a specific receiver.
- In the *zone defense,* defenders dropping off into coverage are assigned to cover zones of the field. If a receiver enters their zone, he becomes their responsibility. If he leaves their zone, they pass him off to the next teammate. The edges of each defender's zone is called the *seam,* and it is up to the offense to find those seams in order to pass effectively against a zone. "The Cardinal

Rule of a zone defense is to never let a receiver get behind the defense," wrote George Allen.

- There are hybrid versions of *man* and *zone* defense, combining the two: *man underneath*, for instance, assigns specific coverage to receivers running shallow routes, even though there might be a zone in use downfield.
- Chris Landry points out that "there is a direct correlation to the amount of sacks and interceptions you have to how much man or zone coverage you play. When you are in man coverage, you get more sack opportunities but less interception opportunities. When in zone coverage, you get less sack opportunities but more interception opportunities."

Cushion: Press and Off

- In *bump and run*, *press*, and *tight* coverage, the defensive back gets right on top of the receiver. (The opposite of this is *off* or *soft* coverage.) A *bump and run* sees a literal bump at the line of scrimmage before the DB runs with the receiver.
- A *jam* sees the defensive back gets his hands on the receiver right off the snap, seeking to throw the play off of its timing and get the receiver off of his route (also termed *off of his line*).
- If the corner comes up, showing tight coverage, and then suddenly backs off the receiver just before the snap, he *bails*.
- The *cushion* is the distance that a corner gives to a receiver before and just after the snap.
- *Bracket coverage, cloud coverage, sky coverage, vise coverage,* and *high-low* sees tandem coverage by two different defensive backs on one receiver, allowing one to *front* the receiver, playing in front of him (*underneath*), while the other plays behind him (*over the top*).
- In *cloud*, indicated by its starting with a 'c,' the cornerback handles underneath/outside coverage. In *sky*, indicated by its starting with an 's,' the safety heads to the outside to handle any receivers in the flat.
- If the defense is concerned about a particular receiver, it

may *roll* the safety over to that receiver's side of the field, aiding the assigned defensive back.

- A *trail dog* is a defensive back playing underneath the receiver in bracket coverage, purposefully trailing the route.
- A *jam* sees the defensive back gets his hands on the receiver right off the snap, seeking to throw the play off of its timing and get the receiver off of timing and off of his route (also called *off of his line*).
- There are two types of *off* coverage, with the defensive back giving the receiver a cushion.
- In *off and inside* coverage, a man-to-man coverage scheme, the defensive back locks to take away inside routes (such as the slant).
- In *off and soft*, the defensive back drops back farther, working out of a zone, making sure to keep passes in front of him.

Cover 0, Cover 1, Cover 2, etc. ... and the Tampa 2

- Cover 1 and Cover 1 Robber are two of the most popular defenses run in the NFL and college football. As described by Chris B. Brown, "Cover 1 Robber works the same [as Cover 1], except that there are only four rushers and, along with the deep middle safety, another defender sits at an intermediate level reading the quarterback's eyes to 'rob' any pass routes over the middle, such as curls, in routes, and crossing routes. *Robber* is the most popular term for this technique, but [Nick] Saban's is *Rat*. (I was always partial to the word Homer Smith, the former Alabama and UCLA offensive coordinator, used: *floaters*, a far more descriptive term.)....The key is for the floater to be able to read run, screen, or pass, and to use his eyes to get to the receiver and the ball. It's particularly effective nowadays with the increased use of spread formations, which most offenses use to open up passing lanes over the middle. Rat players can stop these inside passes and make game-changing interceptions. Cover 1 Robber is useful—though not perfect—against spread offense teams with mobile quarterbacks because the floater may not only read the quarterback's eyes on passing downs but also to watch him for scrambles and to mirror him on run plays."

- In a Cover 1, also seen as a *cover-one* or a *one-deep safety* or *one-high safety*, there's a sole safety playing "center field" à la baseball, protecting the man-to-man defense deep against long passes.

- In a Cover 0, for instance, also seen as a *cover-zero*, there's no one back deep. Every player being used in pass-coverage is on a man-to-man basis and left to his own devices, allowing greater numbers to be used to bring pressure on the quarterback.

- The "Cover" schemes all relate to the number of safeties patrolling the deep field in what's described as an *umbrella* pass-defending alignment.

- The Cover 2, *cover-two* or *two deep coverage*, features a zone defense with two deep safeties, each responsible for half of the field. Wrote Sal Paolantonio of defensive guru Bud Carson: "[I]n Pittsburgh in 1972 it was Carson who implored Chuck Noll to stress quickness and athleticism on the defensive line. The foursome of Joe Greene, Ernie Holmes, L.C. Greenwood, and Dwight White was such a mobile, powerful, relentless force that it became known as the Steel Curtain. Carson also invented the cover-two defense, where the safeties from those four down linemen, the cover-two's umbrella frustrated offenses—particularly Bill Walsh's burgeoning system in Cincinnati with shifts and disguises."

- The Cover 2's heir was the Tampa 2, written often as the Tampa-two, devised by Monte Kiffin while serving as the Tampa Bay Buccaneers' defensive coordinator in the 1990s and 2000s. Same four-man pressure expected; same two-deep safety umbrella. From Paolantonio once more: "Kiffin's wrinkle was to have the inside linebacker run down the middle of the field with the inside receiver—first Hardy Nickerson, then, of course, the perennial Pro Bowler Derrick Brooks. In Chicago, it's

Brian Urlacher running deep down what they call the chute, between the hash marks. You got to be a hybrid player: hit like a linebacker, run like a safety. In Tampa, Kiffin was able to develop two players who could've played both positions at once: safety John Lynch hit like a linebacker, and linebacker Brooks ran like a safety." (Contrary to the notion that Tampa Bay solely used the Tampa 2, Chris Landry points out that "Kiffin actually played lot of man coverage on first down and some on second down as well. He plays mostly Tampa 2 looks on third downs, especially on third and long".)

- The Cover 3, or *cover-three*, is a zone that places three different defensive backs in charge of the deep area of the field: one to the left, one to the right, and one responsible for the deep middle.

- The Cover 4, another zone, also called *Four Across, four deep, cover-four*, or *quarters*, splits things even further: four deep defenders, cutting the field into quarters of responsibility. This usually begins even before the snap, with the two corners falling back as deep as the two safeties.

- Chris B. Brown considers the Cover 4 to be "the most important defensive scheme of the past decade." He explains, "At first glance, Cover 4 looks like an anti-pass prevent tactic, with four secondary defenders playing deep. But therein lies its magic. The four defenders are actually playing a matchup zone concept, in which the safety reads the tight end or inside receiver. If an offensive player lined up inside releases on a short pass route or doesn't release into the route, the safety can help double-team the outside receiver. If the inside receiver breaks straight downfield, it becomes more like man coverage. This variance keeps quarterbacks guessing and prevents defense from being exploited by common pass plays like four verticals, which killed eight-man fronts. The real key to Cover 4, however, is that against the run both safeties become rush defenders (remember, the outside cornerbacks play deep). This allows defenses to play nine men in the box against the run—a hat-tip to the 46's overwhelming force." The dynamic safeties who ushered in the Cover 4 were Baltimore's Ed Reed and Pittsburgh's Troy Polamalu.

pass route

n. pattern, route; SPECIFIC alley-oop, arrow, banana, bench route, bomb, buttonhook, circle, circle in, circle out, clearing route, combination, combo, comeback, comebacker, corner, criss-cross, cross, crosser, crossing route, curl, dagger, deep cross, deep post, delay, dig, double move, down-and-in, down-and-out, drag, drive, fade, flag, flare, flat, flood, fly, go, Hail Mary, hitch, hitch and go, home run ball, hook, in, jump-ball, look-in, option, out, out-and-up, pick, post, pump and go, Q-in, Q-out, read, rub, screen, seam, shake, shallow cross, shoot, shovel pass, skinny post, slant, sluggo (slant and go), smoke, square-in, square-out, squirrel, stick route, stop and go, streak, strike, swing, turn-in, turn-out, twirl, under, up, vertical, wheel, whip, Z, Z-in, Z-out; SCREEN PASSES bubble screen, fly screen, fullback screen, halfback screen, jailbreak screen, jet screen, middle screen, quick screen, slip screen, slot screen, slow screen, throwback screen, tight end screen, tunnel screen, wide receiver screen

"There's no thrill in football like popping the ball to a receiver who has a step on his man in the open."—Bob Waterfield

Terms and Jargon

- One receiver runs a *pass route*. Two or more receivers, working in concert, run a *pass combination*. (The term *pass pattern*, depending on whom you talk with, may be used to describe both solo routes and combinations or solely combinations.)
- A short pass route is *shallow* or *underneath*, since it is thrown underneath (in front of) the coverage. A quick crossing route, then, is a *shallow cross*. A short pass, completed at a high percentage of the time—sometimes called a *high-percentage pass*—is often considered the equivalent of a handoff by a passing team. (A *low-percentage pass* is a far more difficult route to complete.)

- A medium pass route is *intermediate*.
- A long pass route is *deep* and is thrown *over the top* of the defense.
- A deep pass route designed as a decoy to draw the attention of the deep safety is said to *take the top* off the defense.
- One of Darrell Royal's classic lines (also credited to Woody Hayes): "Three things can happen when you throw, and two of them are bad." Those three possibilities: completion, incompletion, and interception. Today's pass-happy football coaches would respectfully disagree with Woody's pessimism toward putting the football in the air.
- Pass routes *work* parts of the field. If a pass combination calls for out routes, the quarterback and receivers *work the sidelines*; in routes, and they're *working the middle of the field*.

At the Forefront

- Defensive guru Tom Landry, a former cornerback, gave full credit to one particularly talented Baltimore Colts receiver: "Raymond Berry was the guy who started moves in the NFL. He worked on and perfected those moves which started the demise of man-to-man coverage." Wrote Sal Paolantonio, "Berry claimed to have perfected 88 different moves. [Quarterback Johnny] Unitas knew each one. But they had one simple favorite, what they called the Q pattern. It was based on a 10-yard square pattern. 'I'd go down about 10 yards and make my break, like I was squaring inside,' Berry told *The Sporting News* much later. 'Then, when the defensive back made his move and tried to go inside with me, I'd plant my inside foot and head to the corner.' Simple but deadly. Berry led the league in receptions three straight years, from 1958 to 1960, and he caught a then-record 631 pass for 9,275 yards and 68 touchdowns in a 13-year career."
- Among coaches, the innovative Sid Gillman deserves a lion's share of credit, opening up the game as the head

man for the AFL's San Diego Chargers. "We developed passing lanes," Gillman told Bob Carroll. "We worked out what we called a 'field balance' system. The field was divided into several areas. First, from the sideline out to the numbers on the field is what we called the 'number area.' Inside the numbers to the hash marks is the 'hook area.' And the hash marks are six yards apart, and that's the 'hash area.' Then, starting from the other sideline, you've got the same thing, number, hook, and hash areas. That gives you six areas to throw to. We wanted to make sure in our field balance that there was always someone to throw to….Our receivers followed very definite patterns. The system demanded that." The head coach at San Diego State at the time was Don Coryell, who studied Gillman's offense and developed it into the high-powered 'Air Coryell' passing game.

Notable Pass Patterns

- The *alley-oop* (or *jump-ball*) is more associated with basketball than football, with a perfectly lofted pass allowing a soaring player to finish with a slam dunk, but San Francisco 49ers quarterback Y.A. Tittle and athletic receiver R.C. Owens brought the play to the gridiron. With the 49ers looking for a score, Tittle sent Owens into the end zone and rainbowed a pass toward him. The receiver did the rest, outleaping defenders to pull in touchdown after touchdown.
- The *arrow*, defined by John T. Reed: an "outward pass route along a path about 30 degrees from the line of scrimmage."
- The *banana*, defined by Steve Belichick: "A back that runs a pass pattern inside or outside the defensive end to a depth of about six to eight yards, and then breaks for the sideline approximately parallel to the line of scrimmage." If the back broke inward instead, toward the middle of the field, Belichick termed it the *flare* pattern.
- The *bench route*, similar to the *flat*, *out*, and *square-out*,

sees the receiver break toward the sideline, thereby
running a pattern toward his bench.

- The *corner*, or *flag*, is a deep route that sees the receiver
  break from the stem to angle for the deep corner of the
  field (racing toward the flag/pylon at the corner of the
  end zone).
- The *criss-cross* brings two receivers across each other's
  paths, shaking their defenders.
- The *cross*, *dig*, *in*, and *square-in* all ask the receiver to
  break from the stem and run directly toward the middle
  of the field.
- The *curl*, synonymous with a *button-hook*, *strike*, or *turn-in*,
  sees the receiver go out hard, putting the corner back
  on his heels, before spinning back toward the line of
  scrimmage. (A *curl in* takes the receiver break from his
  stem and circle toward the middle of the field; a *curl out*
  takes him toward the sideline.)
- The *fade* is lofted off the snap, with plenty of air,
  allowing the receiver to run a vertical route beneath it.
- The *flat* (or *quick out*) is a shallow route toward the
  flat—that is, the outside part of the field, beyond the
  numbers. It can be combined with other patterns (the
  curl-flat, slant-flat, etc.) to give the receiver a more
  specific route.
- The *fade*, *fly*, *go*, *streak*, and *up* routes all ask the receiver
  to do the same thing: race straight ahead on a vertical
  route, challenging the defense deep.
- The *fly sweep*, despite technically being a pass play, is
  described in the "Notable Rushing Plays" under **rush**. In
  it, a receiver comes in timed motion and is shoveled a
  pass by the quarterback right off the snap. (West
  Virginia calls its version a "quick sweep.")
- The *hook* and *stop* are related, using a flanker for the
  hook and a tight end for the stop: run straight ahead,
  then halt and turn around at the designated destination,
  be it the first-down marker or the goal line.
- The *post* is the opposite of a *corner*, a deep route that asks
  the receiver to take a 45-degree turn toward the middle
  of the field, thus angling his path in the direction of the

goal posts. A skinny post uses an angle less ("skinnier") than 45 degrees. Don Coryell's version of the skinny post was the Bang 8—the 8 route, post pattern, thrown in a hurry. (*Bang!*) The *Q-in* and *Q-out* (or *twirl*) are each routes, as defined by John T. Reed, that see the receiver take a 225-degree turn mid-route. In the Q-in, the receiver starts to angle out and then spins back in. In the Q-out, the receiver begins to angle in before spinning back to the outside.

- The *rub*, or *pick*, sees one receiver subtly (or not so subtly) run his route so that it takes the corner covering his teammate out of the play, allowing an easy open-field catch. Aye, but here's the rub: When done well, there is no contact between the receiver and the corner he's shielding. When done poorly, the receiver runs directly into the corner, blocking him aside before the pass is ever thrown, and that's worthy of an offensive pass-interference penalty from a watchful official.

- The *screen* is short and deadly, relying on drawing in the defense before dropping the ball off to a waiting receiver who advances behind a screen of blockers. Screens are described by the player they are thrown to (*halfback screen, tight end screen, wide receiver screen*) or their description (*middle screen, throwback screen*—which is thrown back across the field after initial misdirection).

- On slower developing screens passes, football parlance declares that the offense *sets up* the screen, with the offensive line giving the impression of a missed block, luring the rushers in, before getting out in front of the ball carrier.

- Other notable screen passes include *bubble screen*, which is fired at the snap to a wide receiver coming back and in toward the ball, with fellow receivers and pulling linemen tromping over to clear the way; the *jailbreak screen*, in which the entire pass rush is invited in on the quarterback, who tempts danger before delivering a pass to a running back with a cadre of blockers; and the *slip screen*, which is delivered to a split end in the same fashion as the bubble screen, occurring right off the snap to an receiver facing soft coverage. (Other names for similar quick screens to receivers include *slot screen* and *tunnel screen*.)

- The *slant* is usually quick, with the receiver taking an angled route toward the middle of the field to pick up easy yards on the run. The *sluggo* stands for a "slant-and-go," with the slanting receiver suddenly turning it into a go-route and racing vertically up the field,

- The deceptive *squirrel* route, defined by George Allen: "faking the quick 'out' and breaking back up, and breaking out again at 15 yards."

- A *swing* is a short, quick throw that finds a running back running parallel to the line and then curling around the corner into a vertical (straight ahead) route, looking to catch an aggressive defense off guard.

- A *timing route* is thrown toward a receiver before he's even turned toward it, developed on pre-rehearsed timing between the quarterback and his target to prevent defenders from interfering.

- The *wheel route* is similar to a swing: a running back leaves the backfield, running parallel to the line of scrimmage, and then arcs up the sideline in a deep pattern.

- The *whip* sees the receiver start inside, drawing attention, before whipping back outside. The Z (*Z-in/Z-out*) is similar, with the receiver either starting outside and zigging back inside or starting inside and zigging back outside.

The Route Tree

- In the *route tree*, or *passing tree*, each receiver has a combination of routes that he is ready to run, with each route given a number. The tree is a diagram of all of these routes, going further and further up the field with each larger number/deeper route (and each shorter route breaking off from the vertical *stem*). On *NationalFootballPost.com*, Matt Bowen numbered them as follows: Flat (1), Slant (2), Comeback (3), Curl (4), Out

(5), Dig (6), Corner (7), Post (8), Fade (9). In *Take Your Eye Off the Ball*, Pat Kirwan chose: 0 (Slant), 1 (Quick Out), 2 (Stop), 3 (Out), 4 (Dig/In), 5 (Curl Out), 6 (Curl In), 7 (Corner) 8 (Post), 9 (Fade). As Kirwan explains, "if you wanted the split end to run a corner pattern, the tight end to run a curl in the middle of the field, the Z [flanker] to run a post, and the tailback to run a swing route, what would the play be called? You got it: it's "768 Tailback Swing.""

- Though the intermediate and deep pass routes differ in their end destination, there is one important similarity—and it can help tip off a defensive back. From Bowen: "Outside of the 3-step game (Slant, Flat), every route breaks at a depth of 12-15 yards. Why is that important? Double moves. If you are playing defensive back and see the WR stutter his feet at a depth of 8 yards, expect him to get vertical up the field—because there isn't a route that breaks at 8 yards. However, remember one very important detail: If the WR doesn't break his route between a depth of 12-15 yards, you better open your hips and run. Because he is running straight down the field."

- Routes used in tandem—called *route combinations*, *route concepts* or *route schemes* (also seen with "passing" used in place of "route")—clear troublesome defensive backs from zones of the field and open up space for big plays. A *flood* sees the offense send more than one receiver into the same area of the field, thereby "flooding the zone," while a *clear* or *clearing pattern* seeks to clear defenders away from an area in order to bring in an open receiver. More specifically: In the *Flat-7*, a slot receiver runs a flat route (shallow, to the outside) to draw the corner's attention, while the flanker takes off in the 7-route (corner, deep, to the outside), testing the safety. In the *Dagger*, the slot receiver takes off vertically down the field, following the inside seam. Outside of him, the wide receiver suddenly carves in toward the middle with a square-in (or "dig") route. With the slot receiver drawing the safety's attention, the wide receiver finds the middle of the field nice and open, sticking the dagger into the defense.

Spider 2 Y Banana

- One pass pattern took on a life of its own thanks to Jon Gruden's Quarterback Camp on ESPN. The play-call was *Spider 2 Y Banana*, ably diagrammed by Andrew Luck to Gruden's delight: 21 personnel—two backs, one tight end. "Spider 2" refers to the blocking scheme for the line, bringing *slide protection* toward the strong side (the first two letters of slide protection indicated by the first two letters in 'spider'). The "Y" is the tight end, who leaves the line and bends down the field in the the *banana route*, a vertical, curving pattern down the sideline. The fullback charges out of the backfield at his assigned defender, as if readying a lead block, before slipping around the side. The defender, keying on a possible run, pays the passing fullback no mind—only to be met by a sturdy block from the halfback. This leaves the fullback wide open for a pass in the flank, giving the offense easy yardage.

President Nixon's Play-Call

- The *down-and-in*, in which the receiver breaks his route toward the middle of the field, took on special notice at Super Bowl VI in New Orleans in 1972. From Red Smith: " 'I think you can hit [Paul] Warfield on a down-and-in pattern,' the fan named Richard M. Nixon had told Don Shula, the Miami coach, after the Dolphins qualified to represent the American Conference in the playoff for the professional football championship of this mercenary world. Now it turned out that the fan could be mistaken like anybody else…During the regular season, the White House strategist urged George Allen, head coach for Washington, to use Roy Jefferson on a flanker reverse, sometimes described as the end-around play. Allen did, and Jefferson lost thirteen yards." The result of Nixon's advice stayed consistent:

Concluded Smith, "The Dolphins never did make it work with Warfield." Not too much worked for the Dolphins in general that day. The Dallas Cowboys won the Super Bowl going away.

A Surprise for Bucko

- A story from defensive tackle Mike Jarmoluk, as related to Stuart Leuthner in *Iron Men*:

> The game I remember best was when I played for the Bears and we beat the Eagles in 1947…
>
> We had a pretty good defensive unit and figured if we shut off [Steve] Van Buren, we could beat them. All week long [Bears head coach] George Halas was saying, "Jarmoluk, you're going to have to play end because Wilson and Kavanaugh are hurt. Ed Sprinkle is the only one left, so we're going to have to use you." I said, "Are you sure you want me to play end?" He said, "Yeah, but I'm only going to use you for blocking on end runs and off-tackle plays and to keep everybody off Sid Luckman when he's passing." The night before the game, "Bucko" Kilroy, who was playing with the Eagles, got in touch with me as soon as he got into town. I told him, "Bucko, I've got a big surprise. You won't have to worry about me doing too good against you guys tomorrow because I won't be playing my regular position."
>
> During the course of the game, the information came down from Luke Johnsos in the booth, "Throw Mike a short pass over the middle—nobody's paying any attention to him." In the huddle Sid Luckman looked at me, "Go down five yards, cut across five yards, and I'll hit you right in the hands." I said, "You've got the wrong guy. Sprinkle is on the other side."…He told me to shut up, hit me right in the hands, and I ran thirty-eight yards for a touchdown. I'll tell you, there I was,

standing in the end zone with those ivy-covered walls of Wrigley Field and the whole crowd roaring....

We beat them 49-7, and Bucko wouldn't talk to me after the game.

PAT (point after touchdown)

n. 1-point try, extra point, goal, kick, the point, point after, try, try point

kick the PAT
v. add, convert, knock through, make, put through, split the uprights, send through, slide in, sneak through, tack on

Extra Point and Two-Point Conversion History

- The extra point dates back to rugby, where a kick at goal follows a try. From wire reports, November 18, 1934: "On the seventh play of the second period, Allen Mahnke, 185-pound Wisconsin sophomore center, grabbed an attempted pass just as it left Les Lindberg's fingers and ran 25 yards for the winning touchdown....Mario Pacetti kicked the goal."
- "People have been trying to get rid of the extra point since 1933," wrote Dan Daly and Bob O'Donnell. "Giants owner Tim Mara was the first to propose it, and Bert Bell took up the fight during his commissionership from 1946 to '59. Like Mara, Bell considered the play a waste of time and supported a sudden-death period to break ties."
- In 1958, the NCAA introduced the option of a two-point conversion. Instead of kicking the ball for one point, a team could run a play with the reward of two points if it scored. The American Football League followed suit as it started up play in 1960, but the National Football League resisted the change.
- The short-lived World Football League loved the idea of an alternative to the extra point. Entering its inaugural 1974 season, the WFL instituted the "action point." The

new rule stated, "Touchdowns will be worth seven points and the extra point kick has been eliminated. Instead there will be an 'action point' attempt from the 2½-yard line for one additional point by running or passing."

- Finally the NFL followed suit: In 1994, the league allowed teams the option of a two-point try after a touchdown. Entering the 2015 season, the NFL moved the extra point attempt from the two-yard line to the 15-yard line (keeping all two-point conversion attempts at the two-yard line). In addition, the defense could receive two points for a successful return of a blocked or fumbled extra-point attempt or an intercepted or fumbled two-point attempt.

62 Yards for One Point

- The top continuing complaint about the PAT—as Tim Mara and Bert Bell argued—is that it does not add any additional unpredictability to the game. Well, there was a bit more excitement about a PAT on October 4, 2003, in Washington, D.C. The unique circumstance, as described in the *Washington Post*:

  First David Rosenbaum of Washington, D.C., Wilson High ran back a kickoff 69 yards for a touchdown. When all the celebrating was over, and three penalties were assessed, Rosenbaum faced a 62-yard extra point.

  Rosenbaum made the kick, believed to be the longest conversion in high-school play.

  "I did it before in practice," said Rosenbaum, a 5-foot-11 senior who has committed to Virginia. "I saw it as a chip shot. I have hit longer ones in practice."

pattern

n. combination, pass routes; see **pass route**

penalty

n. call, flag, foul, indiscretion, infraction, no-no, violation; SPE-
CIFIC dead-ball foul, double foul, five-yard penalty, ten-yard
penalty, fifteen-yard penalty, offsetting penalties, spot foul

*"You've been called for holding [Lawrence Taylor] six times in one
half!"—Buffalo Bills head coach Marv Levy, to center Will Grant*

*"Hey, Coach, that's really good. Because I've been holding him on every
down."—Buffalo Bills center Will Grant, to head coach Marv Levy*

accept a penalty
v. affirm, agree to, comply with, sign off on, take

decline a penalty
v. decide against, demur, forgo, refuse, reject, turn down

Types of Penalties
chop block, clipping, crackback block, defensive holding,
defensive pass interference (DPI or PI), defensive delay of
game, defensive offside, delay of game at the start of the half,
deliberately batting or punching a loose ball, deliberately/
illegally kicking a loose ball, encroachment, excessive crowd
noise, excessive time out(s), face mask, false start, failure to
wear required equipment, fair catch interference, forward
pass caught or touched by an ineligible receiver, hands to the
face, helping the runner, horse collar tackle, illegal bat, ille-
gal block above the waist, illegal block below the waist, ille-
gal block in the back, illegal contact, illegal cut, illegal
equipment, illegal formation, illegal forward pass (passer
entirely crossed the line of scrimmage), illegal forward pass
(passer entirely crossed the line of scrimmage, then returned
to throw the pass), illegal helmet contact, illegal kick, illegal
motion, illegal onside kick, illegal participation, illegal procedure, illegal shift, illegal substitution, illegal use of hands,
illegal touching (pass touched first by a receiver who went
out of bounds and returned), ineligible receiver downfield,
intentional grounding, interlocked blocking, illegal fair
catch signal / invalid fair catch signal, kick catching interfer-

ence, kickoff out of bounds, leaping, leveraging, neutral zone infraction, offensive delay of game, offensive holding, offensive offside, offensive pass interference, peelback block, personal foul, piling on, player running voluntarily out of bounds during punt coverage, removal of helmet, roughing the center, roughing the kicker, roughing the passer, running into the kicker, second forward pass behind the line of scrimmage, sideline interference, spearing (leading with the crown of the helmet), targeting, taunting, too many men on the field (twelve men on the field), tripping, twelve men in the huddle, unnecessary roughness, unsportsmanlike conduct

Notable Penalties and Terms

- For *chop block*, *clipping*, and *crackback block*, see **block**
- For *horse collar tackle*, see **tackle**
- A *dead-ball foul* occurs after a play is over.
- *Defensive holding* and *illegal contact* grant an automatic first down to the offense. They are balanced by *illegal forward pass* (thrown beyond the line of scrimmage) and *intentional grounding*, which each come with the penalty of a loss of down.
- By a wide margin according to *NFLPenalties.com*, the two most common penalties in the NFL are *offensive holding* and *false start*.
- If both teams commit penalties on the same play, a "double foul," the penalties *offset*, forcing the down replayed.
- Penalties that force a ball to be moved greater than half the distance to the goal line—say, a 10-yard penalty charged from the 14-yard line—are instead marked off at half the distance to the goal line. (The penalty in this example would move the ball to the 7.)
- Yes, an infraction is synonymous with a penalty, but it is particularly used to describe a *neutral-zone violation*. A fan rarely hears of a "holding infraction" or a "pass-interference infraction," for instance, but if a defender crosses the line of scrimmage before the snap, the

referee is highly likely to proclaim a "neutral zone infraction," as is specified by the rule book.

- A *spot foul*, such as defensive pass interference in the NFL, comes with a specific cost: the ball is placed at the spot that the penalty was committed.
- The spot foul offers the greatest potential for yardage for a penalty, since the ball will be placed as far downfield as the foul was committed. Otherwise, the greatest yardage charged because of a penalty is 15 yards.
- This was not always the case. Clipping, a potentially dangerous action, particularly back in football's early days, came with the cost of a 25-yard penalty. It could be even worse. Wrote Dan Daly and Bob O'Donnell, "Before '41, fighting, punching a referee, anything that called for automatic ejection could result in a half-the-distance-to-the-goal-line penalty *from anywhere on the field*. (There was one instance of a 40-yard markoff.)"
- If an offensive penalty, such as holding, is committed in the offensive team's own end zone, a safety is recorded, with two points given to the defending team. The Dallas Cowboys found this out first-hand on September 23, 1962: Andy Cverko's hold in the end zone not only nullified what the hometown Cowboys fans thought was a 99-yard touchdown pass from Eddie LeBaron to Frank Clarke, it gave the Steelers two points besides. (Note that an official had spotted Clarke stepping out of bounds during his run, according to Daly and O'Donnell in *The Pro Football Chronicle*, taking a bit of edge off the swing of the pendulum.)

12 on 11

Of all the *too many men on the field* penalties that have occurred, one stands out. The Kansas Jayhawks were leading the Penn State Nittany Lions late in the 1969 Orange Bowl. Rick Abernethy was part of Kansas's Nickel 40 defense, putting him on the field protecting a 14-7 lead. Penn State drove inside the KU 5-yard line, causing Kansas to bring in its goal-line defense—a defense that did not include Abernethy. But he remained in; substitute Orville Turgeon had not notified him to leave the game.

So it was that Kansas played goal-line defense with 12 defenders, easily the toughest defense that Penn State had faced all year: On first down, the Nittany Lions were stopped cold. On second down, nothing. On third down, Penn State mustered its best effort and overcame the numbers game to score a touchdown, bringing them within 14-13. They went for two and the win against the 12-man Jayhawks defense, but Abernethy disrupted the play. Incomplete, Kansas victory—except that the officials finally remembered to count the KU defenders on the two-point conversion. They came up with one Jayhawk too many. "Abernethy, who was defending the pass, remembers getting up and seeing the referee twirling, not throwing, a flag," wrote Tully Corcoran for the *Topeka Capital-Journal* in a January 2, 2008, retrospective. 'What's the flag for?' he asked." He was soon told, and Penn State was informed that it had one more chance. Given another play, the Nittany Lions took advantage, scored, and won the game, 15-14. "In the locker room after the game, Abernethy was crushed. 'It's all my fault,' he told his teammates. 'Blame me.' " (A postscript of the game, discovered by Corcoran: "It was Abernethy's wedding day, and [Joe] Paterno felt he needed to do something for a man who had done so much for him. So, the longtime Penn State coach penned a letter to Abernethy, dated Aug. 5, 1972: 'I hope your day is as good as you made our day. Best of luck, Joe Paterno.' ")

Too Loud

- *Excessive crowd noise* is highly encouraged in contemporary football—and can be awesome, as felt by the seismic activity generated by Seattle's jubilant Qwest Field rooters during a Marshawn Lynch playoff victory-clinching touchdown run in January 2011—but it was

controversially frowned upon two decades earlier.
Crowd noise penalties were introduced entering the
1989 season (passed in a 21-7 vote by the NFL's owners), costing the home team a timeout with each ruled
violation.

penalty flag

n. beanbag, cloth, flag, handkerchief, hankie/hanky, laundry (on
the field), linen, marker, penalty marker, rag

*"I always disliked the fish horn signal, figured it was a nuisance, irritat-
ing to the ears."—Dwight Beede*

call a penalty

v. assess, flag, indicate, mark off (yardage), signal, spot a foul, step
off (yardage); detect a penalty, spot a foul; throw a flag, toss a flag

History

- 1930s football was a bit different than the present-day
  game. "Only the referee had a whistle," wrote Daly and
  O'Donnell. "There were no penalty flags. When an
  official spotted a foul, he blew a small horn worn
  around his wrist. Hand signals, invented by college
  referee Ellwood Geiges in the late '20s, were used to
  inform the fans (and press box) of infractions. Most
  were the same as they are today. One exception was the
  signal for unnecessary roughness. Until 1955, it was a
  military salute." The story of the birth of the penalty flag
  derives from the college ranks, and it may be found on
  Youngstown State's athletics website, *YSUsports.com*:

  > It was created by former Youngstown State University
  > coach, Dwight Dike Beede on Oct. 17, 1941. The flag
  > was first used in a game against Oklahoma City Uni-
  > versity at Youngstown's Rayen Stadium.…

  > Before the introduction of the penalty flag, the officials

used horns and whistles to signal a penalty. This made it difficult for fans and the media to know that there was an infraction on the field because they could not hear the signal.

Beede came up with [the] idea of the flag and had his wife sew it together. His wife, Irma Beede, later became known as the "Betsy Ross of Football" because she sewed the first flags together. He asked her to make a flag that had a bright color (red) with white stripes. The flags were put together using pieces of the Beede's daughter's old Halloween costume for the red part of the flag and an old sheet for the white part. She used some lead sinkers from Beede's fishing tackle box to weight it down. It was 16 inches square with the weight all at one end of the flag. The flag has been modified over the years and today it is yellow cloth that has sand in it to weigh it down.….

The flag was officially introduced at the 1948 American Football Coaches rules session.

[Game official Jack] McPhee carried the original flag for many contests including games of Princeton-Yale and various Ohio State games until it faded. He made his way to the Rose Bowl, where the flag was tossed in front of 100,000 fans.

- It was in 1948 that the penalty flag also made its way to the NFL, replacing the horn. It was white. The current yellow flag arrived in 1965. (The reason for the change: bright yellow is easier to spot than white.)
- Officials used to throw their flags directly at the source of the penalty, but the case of Cleveland Browns offensive lineman Orlando Brown changed matters. On December 19, 1999, referee Jeff Triplette's thrown flag caught Brown in the right eye. The injury cost him the 2000 season in total, and he did not return to the NFL until 2003.

play

n. chance, down, pattern, snap; SPECIFIC passing play, running play; big play, botched play, bread-and-butter play, broken play, quick-hitter, slow-developing play, well-executed play; see **trick play**

"Players have to study off the field in order to be champions."—George Allen, "Inside Football"

"There is very little in a playbook that could help one team against another in a given game. Better you should have a quarterback who can throw the ball."—Paul Brown, quoted by Tex Maule

Terms and Jargon

- From Bill Connelly in *Study Hall*, "Football is, by nature, a sport based on bursts. Only the craziest, oddest plays are going to last more than about 15 seconds, and when the play is over, you'll get at least about 20-30 seconds to recover from it. Boom, lull, boom, lull."
- When counting up the number of plays in the game for a team, only the amount of snaps on the offensive side of the ball are included. The percentage of clock used while the team is on offense accounts for its time of possession (TOP).
- A *drive, possession,* or *offensive series* describes in total a team's series of offensive plays, from the time it takes over the ball to the team to the time it gives the ball to the other team, with the possession ending after punting, scoring points, turning the ball over on downs, giving the ball up on a turnover, or reaching the end of a half. A *defensive series* refers to the other side of the field, the defense's perspective on an offensive series from start to finish.
- A *drive* in particular refers to a longer offensive series, picking up first downs.
- The offense's goal is to *finish* the drive, with emphasis, concluding the series with a touchdown.
- If a team's drive looks promising before getting

suddenly halted, whether by incompletions or minimal pickups or negative plays, the drive *stalls*.

- A team's *bread-and-butter play* refers to that team's favorite, most reliable, most trusted play for a certain situation.
- A *broken play* goes wrong due to poor execution by the offense early in the play, whether due to a faulty snap or a miscommunication between players.
- A defender can *detect a play* or *sniff a play out* by figuring out the offense's intentions and snuffing their design. At its height, the defender *blows up* the play.
- A quick-hitter is a play, whether running or passing, that is executed in a hurry. The opposite of a quick-hitter is a *slow-developing play*. (This is often given as a criticism: "That play was too slow in developing.")
- The *spot* refers to where the official places the football following a play's conclusion. A "good," "great," or "fortunate" spot argues that the official gave the ball carrier as much forward momentum as he deserved—"He got a good spot"—and very possibly even a little bit more than he deserved. Calling the spot "poor" indicates that is believed the official did not credit the ball carrier with the forward progress he deserved.

Chalk Talk

"An often repeated locker room scenario looks something like this: A coach diagrams a system with X's and O's that shows how it works, let's a say a seven-step drop-back pass to complete a post pattern to a wideout. But at the end of his spiel, the coach circles one of the defensive X's and says, 'This play should work, but if that X is Dick Butkus, it's a different story. Dick Butkus is too good an X.'"—Tim Layden, Blood, Sweat and Chalk

- Plays are diagrammed in *X's* and *O's*, with O's used to represent offensive players and the X's representing the defenders. With these diagrams made on coaches' blackboards for the benefit of teaching the players, the lessons (*blackboard sessions*, *skull drills*, or *skull sessions*)

became known as *chalk talk*. "X's and O's" and "chalk talk" have since become catch-alls to describe inside-football discussion and analysis, breaking down and analyzing plays, players, and schemes.

- A team's collection of plays are kept in a playbook, which also includes team policies and other important information. In essence, the playbook is a player's football bible, and is often nicknamed as such.
- A *play-call* is the decided-upon play that a team runs, both on offense and defense. This play-call may come from the head coach, the offensive or defensive coordinator, or the quarterback himself. (The defensive equivalent is the middle linebacker, the "quarterback of the defense." Plays may be sent in via messenger, radio communication, or signal from the sideline.
- The opposite of 'conservative' in politics may be 'liberal,' but the opposite of a conservative (low-risk) play-call in football is a *gamble*.
- *Tendencies* describe a team's most-often used plays based on formation and situation. Knowing the opposition's tendencies puts a team in position to prepare for the likeliest play-call.

play (against)

v. battle, challenge, clash with, combat, come up against, compete against, confront, duel, encounter, face, hook up with, match up with, meet, take on, tangle with, test

play at home

v. entertain, host, play host to, welcome

play on the road

v. call on, head to, pay a visit to, stop by, travel to, visit

pocket

n. cup; SPECIFIC cauldron of fire, clean pocket, collapsed pocket, moving pocket, muddied pocket

- The *pocket* is the space provided a quarterback by a pass-blocking offensive line, allowing him to see the field and pass the ball (likely through a *passing lane*) with comfort and freedom.
- The offense can move the pocket to the left or the right off the snap with designed rollouts, throwing a curve ball at a tough pass rush and easing life for a quarterback under heavy pressure.
- The defense seeks to *collapse* the pocket around the quarterback.
- A quarterback with a *clean pocket* receives excellent protection without any defensive pressure to worry about, and consequently has "plenty of time" or "all day" to throw the ball.
- An uncomfortable pocket with pressing defenders is *muddied*. If things get really hairy, the pocket becomes a *cauldron of fire* for the harassed quarterback.

punt

n. SPECIFIC boomer, booming punt, coffin-corner punt, dancer, directional punt, drive punt, drop punt, end-over-end punt, flutterer, knuckleball, knuckler, pooch punt, quick kick, rugby kick, running rugby kick, sand wedge, short-field punt, sky punt, spiraling punt, surprise punt
v. boom, boot, bring the rain down, chip, drill, drive, elevate, fade, get it away, get off, hoist, kick, knock, launch, lift, loft, put in the air, put the leg to, put the toe to, strike, swing the leg through, tee up, toe, toe up; SPECIFIC boomer, pooch punt, quick kick; see **kick**

"When in doubt, punt."—Knute Rockne

Terms and Jargon

see also "Specific Terms: Punting, Offense" under **special teams**

- Many a punt is judged on its *hang-time*, measured in seconds of the ball in the air. The longer the ball hangs in the air, the greater the opportunity for the coverage team to surround the punt-returner, snuffing the potential of long return. (At one point, television broadcasts placed a hang-time clock on the screen to educate viewers on how well the punter had performed.)

- A punter who *outkicks his coverage* boots the ball so far that the punt-coverage unit does not have the opportunity to reach the returner by the time the ball comes down, allowing returner to put together a sizable return. (In modern parlance, this phrase has been extended to describe a relationship in which one-half of the couple is far more attractive than the other.)

- A *coffin-corner punt*, as defined by Rick Sang and punting great Ray Guy in "Techniques vary for punting a football" (*HumanKinetics.com*), "is a controlled drive punt normally driven at a lower trajectory out of bounds with the intent to pin the opponent deep in its own territory. The punter tends to hold the football on his approach slightly lower and longer before the drop heads out of bounds (or rolls to a stop) inside the ten-yard line, sometimes specified to inside the five-yard line."

- A *directional punt* is used against a dangerous punt returner, angling toward the sideline so that the defense can hem him in.

- A *pooch punt*, also called a sky kick or a short-field punt, is used when an offense faces a short field—a fourth down just outside of field goal range. If the punter gives the ball his usual strong boot, he'll crush it out of the end zone. Instead, he "pooches" it, kicking the ball with less strength, in hopes that the ball will "die" (stop rolling) or be downed by a teammate inside the other team's 20-yard line. An ideal pooch punt is fair-caught or downed inside the 10. Note that a pooch punt, almost by definition, does not go out of bounds. A pooch punt is a common sight for a place-kicker from a field goal formation, similar to a quarterback's quick kick. Speaking of...

- A *quick kick*, also termed a *surprise punt*, is exactly that: a punt that comes at an unexpected time—before fourth down, out of a field goal formation, from the quarterback, or from a similarly unexpected moment or player. From Brian Kilmeade's *The Games Do Count*, President Gerald Ford reminisces on his University of Michigan playing days under Fielding Yost: "We used the 'punt, pass, and prayer' style of playing. The theory was that if you had a good punter, a good passer, and a strong defense, you would always win. If you won the coin toss, you always kicked off and gave the other team the ball. You counted on your defense to force them into mistakes. Inside your own 40-yard line, you always punted on second or third down. If you were near your own goal line, you punted on first down. If your punter did his job, you could pick up 10 or 15 yards on every exchange. Then, if your quarterback connected on his passes, you could score and score again."

- Wrote Judy Battista for *The New York Times*, October 10, 2009, "The end-over-end kick—it's called the rugby kick, because that's what it resembles—is much easier to develop [than the coffin-corner kick]. It gives a punter better control of distance because it requires less calibration of how hard to boot the ball. It emerged about a dozen years ago and is now the preferred punt around the league. But there is no agreement about who introduced it to the NFL. [Jeff] Feagles said he thinks it was San Diego punter Darren Bennett, who brought it with him from his home country, Australia, in 1995. The kick requires a punter to hold the ball's nose down and kick the bottom of the ball, so it spins back toward the kicking team. It has a long hang time, which allows the coverage team to get down the field. Because the ball spins backward, no matter how hard a punter kicks it, the ball will probably not travel farther than 40 yards. When the ball is hit squarely and lands, it rolls very little and is supposed to move toward the kicking team—or away from the end zone and the touchback. Mike Westhoff, the Jets' special-teams coach, compared the action a golfer putting backspin on a chip so that when it hits a green, it spins backward."

- At the college ranks, punters are beginning to add a different part of rugby's style, running before kicking the ball away. Upon receiving the snap, the punter rolls to one side of the field. If there is room to run (and reasonable yardage needed to be gained), he does so. If not, he boots a line drive down the side of the field, making it difficult to return, and designed to roll forward. The running punt has deep roots. In *The National Forgotten League*, Dan Daly tells of Lafayette's Walt Doleschal, who played from 1959 to 1961: "On one pet play of Lafayette's, he'd fake an end sweep to draw up the safetymen and quick kick the ball, end over end, over their heads. The ball would roll forever."

- A *sand wedge* (or *sand-wedge ball*), like the golf shot, sees the punter drop in a high, short punt for the specific purpose of pinning the opposition close to its own goal line.

- A *tight punt situation* sees the punting team forced to snap the ball from inside the 5-yard line, backing the punter up into his own end zone without much room to maneuver. Worse, without room to his back, the punter is forced to be much closer to the line of scrimmage.

Flight of the Ball

- When *ESPN.com*'s Paul Kuharsky attempted to field punts in September 2010, seeing how difficult it would be, he received the following pieces of advice on judging the ball in the air:

  Said [running back Maurice] Jones-Drew: "If the nose of the ball stays up, it's going to be short. But if that nose turns over, you've got to get back because that ball is going to sail a bit."

Said Houston punter Matt Turk: "It really depends on the height of the ball. If it's turning over, and it's a low ball, you should be backing up. If it's turning over and it's a good hang-time ball, it might fall away from you."

Said [Indianapolis punter Pat] McAfee: "If the ball turns over, it's going to be straight; if the nose stays up, it's going to go right for a right-footed punter."

Said [Houston returner Jacoby] Jones: "With a right-footed punter, if it's a tight spiral, the ball will dive to your left. If it's a wobbly spiral, it dives to your right."

Furthermore

- Times sure have changed. Advice from the back of one of the National Chicle Company's 1935 football cards: "Don't wait until fourth down to punt, as a general rule, punt on third down. Then if the kick is blocked and recovered you will have another chance, instead of losing the ball on downs inside your territory."
- From *Rites of Autumn*: "In a 1925 game against Navy at Farragut Field in Annapolis, Maryland, on an exceptionally blustery afternoon, [Marquette's] quarterback, Bob Demoling, took the snap on his own 20-yard line. He boomed one all the way to Navy's 19, where it bounced, was picked up by the gusting wind, and was carried not just into the end zone but 30 yards beyond it where it plopped into Chesapeake Bay and was swept out to sea. Total yardage has never been precisely determined."
- And now, the longest legitimate punt in football history: The New York Jets snapped the ball from their own 1-yard line, and—on September 21, 1969—Steve O'Neal punted that ball as far as he could. "I just hit it well," said O'Neal in an October 2010 interview with *NewYorkJets.com*, "but of course back then the goal posts were on the goal line and they were to my right. So I had less than 10 yards to kick the ball, in a real tight situation. It went about 75 yards in the air, it went over

the returner's head, and when it hit the ground, it just took off like a ground ball." When at last the ball was downed, it was at the opposite 1-yard line, giving O'Neal a record-setting 98-yard boot.

punter

n. P; SPECIFIC left-footed punter, right-footed punter, rugby-style punter; see kicker

"It's a shankless job."—*Bryan Wagner*

- A punter *flips the field* when he swings field position, taking his own team from a disadvantaged spot and pinning the other team back toward their own goal line.

punt returner

n. PR, returner, return man

Q

Washington Redskins quarterback Sammy Baugh in 1947. (Pro Football Hall of Fame.)

quarter

n. chucker, period, session, stanza

- The first quarter, the *opening quarter*, "raises the curtain."
- The first and second quarters comprise the *first half*, the third and fourth quarters make the *second half*.
- *Halftime* is held between the second and third quarter.
- The fourth and final quarter is the *money quarter*. At the conclusion of the third quarter, it's a common collegiate

sight for the players to raise four fingers in the air, readying themselves for the final period.

quarterback

n. arm, ball-handler, coach on the field, cover boy, creator, distributor, engineer of the offense, field general, game manager, general, gunslinger, man under center, man who runs the show, man with the golden arm, operator, passer, pilot, QB, ringleader, ringmaster, sheriff, signal-caller, slinger, thrower; SPECIFIC #2 quarterback, #3 quarterback, backup quarterback, bomb-thrower, camp arm, dual-threat quarterback, dynamic quarterback, elite quarterback, emergency quarterback, entrenched quarterback, freelancer, franchise quarterback, good hand, hybrid quarterback, mobile quarterback, option quarterback, pistol quarterback, pocket passer, pretty passer, pro-style quarterback, pure passer, running quarterback, shotgun quarterback, statue, T quarterback, triple-option quarterback, wildcat quarterback

quarterback (the offense)

v. command, create, engineer, guide, lead, manage, navigate, operate, run the show, stand in the spotlight; DOMINATE THE DEFENSE blister, bomb, bombard, burn, carve up, dazzle, dismantle, (surgically) dissect, pick apart, play with, shred, toast, torch, toy with, work over

"A good coach needs three things: a patient wife, a loyal dog, and a great quarterback—not necessarily in that order."—Bud Grant

Types of Quarterbacks

- A *camp arm*, as described Stefan Fatsis in *A Few Seconds of Panic*, is brought in solely for preseason, "needed to help execute the voluminous passes and handoffs required during the summer but who has little chance of making the team."
- A *dual-threat quarterback* presents trouble to the defense

with both his arm and his legs, able to pass and run with equal effectiveness.

- An *emergency quarterback* is a player forced into the quarterbacking role from his normal position due to injury.
- A *freelancer* is more comfortable improvising, flying by the seat of his pants, than executing the designed play.
- A quarterback who requires a strong offensive line and backfield in order to succeed is merely considered a "function of the team around him." When surrounded by limited talent, his team's chances are thus also limited.
- A *game manager* is asked to take care of the football and take few risks, with little chance of turnovers. In a sense, there is the chance that being labeled a game manager is disparaging, since it assumes that the quarterback has to depend on his defense to win and cannot win the game on his own. On the other hand, a game manager is by definition a trustworthy sort, with the wherewithal to make the right decision and either throw a pass away or check down to a nearby target if a play breaks down.
- A solid quarterback is a *good hand*, with *hand* used in the same fashion as a ranch hand on a cattle ranch. From the *Arkansas Leader*, September 27, 2006: "But [Cabot High School Coach Mike] Malham expects a lot of LaNorris Dukes. 'They're getting back to running it more than anything else,' Malham said. 'The Dukes kid is good, and that quarterback is a good hand.'"
- A *gunslinger* is prone to *taking risks with the football* and prefers deeper passes to safer, short throws. As a result, the gunslinger typically has a higher-than-average interception rate, but a good gunslinger will also throw a lot of successful deep passes.
- A *pocket passer* works well from inside a well-blocked pocket, although they are reticent to leave the comfort of their blockers and are not as effective in operating the offense when forced outside of the pocket. The opposite of the pocket passer is considered the *mobile quarterback* or *running quarterback*, also called a *scrambler*, who is able

to use his feet to create plays when the pocket breaks down (though he is may be downgraded for poorer operating skills within the pocket).

- A *pro-style quarterback* is a high school or college quarterback who is deemed well-suited to play at the professional ranks, both because of his personal skills and the offense he has been groomed in.
- A *statue* is a quarterback with little foot speed and elusiveness, making him helpless to evade a pass rush.
- The *wildcat*, called the *Wild Hog* when it was introduced in 2007 at the University of Arkansas (and given similarly evocative names wherever it was also used, though its name hints at its origin with the Kansas State Wildcats), sees the quarterback spread to one side of the formation with a running back in the backfield in the quarterback's stead. Off the snap, the back can hand the ball off, run with it himself, or run an even more inventive gadget play involving the quarterback. It was instituted to great effect by the 2008 Miami Dolphins, using Ronnie Brown as the Wildcat quarterback. (As the formation spread, its names grew: the "Wild Horses" with the Denver Broncos, the "Wild Knight" at Central Florida, the "Wild Rebel" at Ole Miss, and the "Wild Turkey" in Virginia Tech.)

Other Terms and Jargon

- According to a classic wag: "There's no one more popular in a football town than the backup quarterback."
- John Madden's favorite quarterback axiom: "When you have two quarterbacks, you have no quarterbacks."
- A quarterback who is locked in, connecting on pass after pass, has a *hot hand*.
- In the metaphor of driving a car, the quarterback has the *keys to the offense*. (If a head coach gives a player "the keys," he names that player his starting QB.)
- A *pump-fake* is a fake pass, a gesture with the pumping of the throwing arm as if the quarterback is going to let a pass fly. Instead, he keeps a tight hold of it, hoping to

freeze the defense (or draw a defender to a particular receiver) and create the potential for a big play.

- A quarterback with *slow eyes*, as described by NFL Films' Greg Cosell in analyzing Geno Smith in 2013, has a "lack of anticipation" and "takes just a beat too long to deliver throws that are there and open."

- A quarterback *telegraphs* his pass when he lets the defense know where he intends to throw the football by staring down a receiver, looking at him the entire time (also termed *bird dogging*, *locking in*, or *zeroing in* on a receiver).

- To combat the defense, particularly the watchful safeties, he can *look off* the safety or "move the defense with his eyes" by looking toward one receiver before turning and firing to a different target. (A defensive back caught *looking into the backfield* pays too much attention to the quarterback's eyes and not enough to the movement around—and maybe behind—him.)

A Quarterback's Checklist

- Receive the play call from the sideline and deliver the play to his teammates, either in the huddle or the no-huddle offense. (see **huddle**)
- After delivering the play call to his teammates, approach the line and go through his *pre-snap reads*, finding the middle linebacker and the safeties and diagnosing the defense's pass-rushers and coverage.

get the snap from center

v. accept the snap, get the snap, receive the snap, take, take the snap; see **snap**

- Robert W. Peterson credits Chicago Bears coach Ralph Jones for coming up with the under-center snap setup for the quarterback in 1930: "Jones placed the quarterback behind and in direct contact with the center, as is common today. The quarterback took a handoff from the center, who found himself for the first time able to look ahead at the opposing linemen instead of having to look back between his straddled legs to center the ball."

- When a quarterback gets the snap, he can be *under center* (sometimes called *over center*, oddly), *in the pistol*, or *in the shotgun* (also called "the gun"). A quarterback under center stands directly behind his offensive line, with the ball placed directly into his hands. Both the pistol and the shotgun require the quarterback to stand away from the line of scrimmage, allowing him to see the field better. While the quarterback may stand closer to the line in the pistol, the major difference between the two lies in the positioning of the running back(s). In the pistol formation, a running back stands behind the quarterback, hiding him from the defense; in the shotgun, the quarterback is either alone in the backfield or has a running back (or two), termed the sidecar, standing at his side.

- The origin of the shotgun, from Edward J. Rielly's *Football: An Encyclopedia of Popular Culture*:

> Positioning the quarterback 5 to 7 yards behind the center gives the passer a clearer vision of the field and more time to locate his receivers as well as the enemy rushers and defenders. "Shotgun" refers to the quarterback's wide field of vision before he lets the pass fly, paralleling the wider target area that a shotgun shell hits.

> Although the shotgun owes something to earlier tactics, including the short-punt formation, the modern version appeared in 1960. Red Hickey, coach of the San Francisco 49ers, devised it to counter the rugged pass rush of the Baltimore Colts and used it against them on November 27, 1960. John Brodie, filling in for the injured Y.A. Tittle, was himself injured early in the contest and was replaced by the third-string quarterback Bob Waters. Waters worked the shotgun effectively against the surprised Colts, with San Francisco winning 30-22.

"San Francisco zipped off to a 4-1 record," added Bob Carroll, "scoring at least 35 points in each win. But just when it looked like the shotgun was the wave of the future, the Bears unloaded it, stopping the 49ers cold, 31-0. Once Chicago showed how to solve the shotgun, the rest of the league followed suit. The 49ers went back to a normal T and their normal disappointing season." The shotgun's best days were still decades away.

- By the 2000s, the shotgun formation was enabling the *air raid*, *fun 'n' gun* and *spread offenses* at the college level. In 2005, Nevada head coach Chris Ault added the *pistol formation* to that list. If the shotgun placed the quarterback 5 to 7 yards behind the line, the pistol placed him only 3 or 4 yards back. The running back set up directly behind him, about 7 to 10 yards behind the center. It made for a quicker snap, obscured the running back from the defense's view, and delivered key strengths from taking the snap under center (allowing play-action and bootlegs) and taking the snap in the shotgun (allowing the quarterback to survey the defense with the space to get off a quick pass in a hurry).

Play-Action (PA)

- In *play-action*, also called a *play-fake* or a *play pattern*, the quarterback fakes a handoff, thereby drawing (sucking in) the attention of the linebackers and safeties, before executing a pass. One of the best at this was Eddie LeBaron, who, it is said, learned that he had to make sure to warn the officials of an impending play-fake, otherwise they would blow the play dead, thinking his running back had been tackled—while Eddie kept the ball himself and located an open receiver down field.
- There are two types of play-action: the *empty-hand fake*, where the quarterback presents a bare hand to the runner with the ball in his other hand (or after already getting rid of the ball), and the *ball-fake*, where the quarterback presents the ball to the runner, sometimes

even putting it in his belly, before withdrawing it and surprising the defense with a throw.

- The description of the 1947 AAFC San Francisco 49ers in *Pro Football: The Early Years* featured this analogy: "Although the 49ers could not challenge the Browns for first place, quarterback Frankie Albert kept fans and players buzzing with his magical ball-handling and unpredictable play-calling. Little Frankie dealt out fakes in the backfield like the girl next door by sending defenders in hot pursuit of runners who didn't even have the ball." (David S. Neft and Richard M. Cohen write two sentences later that Albert's passes "wobbled like a crippled pigeon.")

dropping back to pass
types of drops: three-step, five-step, seven-step; five and a hitch, rhythm seven; short drop, quick drop, intermediate drop, deep drop; straight drop

- Once a quarterback has taken the snap from under center on a designed passing play, he drops back into the pocket to pass. (see **pocket**) "Whatever the drop is," wrote John Madden in *One Knee Equals Two Feet*, "it requires an odd number of steps—three, five, seven. When a right-handed quarterback takes the snap, his first step is with his right foot, his second is a crossover step with his left foot. No way he can throw on that crossover second step. In order to plant his right foot to throw, he's got to take that third step. Or that fifth step. Or that seventh step. Translated into yards, a three-step drop would be about 4 yards, a five-step drop would be about 7 yards, a seven-step drop would be about 10 yards."
- A *short* or *quick drop* is equal to a three-step drop, leading to a quick pass. On the other side, a *deep drop* is synonymous with a seven-step drop and likely sets up a deep passing attempt.
- In *Inside Football*, George Allen wrote, "The passer must get back to the pocket as quickly as possible…. As a yardstick, for the seven-step drop-back, we have our

quarterbacks strive for 1.75 seconds in getting back. For the five-step, it is 1.3 seconds."

going through progressions

- Once a quarterback finishes his drop, he *surveys the field* and *goes through his progressions*—deciding which receiver to throw to.
- Those progressions, the sequence of a quarterback's vision, from receiver to receiver, travel from *primary receiver* to *secondary receiver* to, perhaps, *tertiary receiver*.
- With regard to area of the field, quarterbacks are taught to look *deep to short*, focusing on the deepest options first before progressing to the shallower targets.
- If the quarterback's top options are covered, with time running out and defensive pressure about to arrive, he *checks down*, dropping off a pass to an underneath receiver (a *safety valve*).
- A quarterback who misses an open receiver is accused of "not seeing the field."

prepare to pass
cock, crank, load, wind up

- A long windup / long release is less than ideal for a quarterback, allowing the defense time to react to an upcoming pass. The opposite, a strength for any passer, is a *quick release*, getting the ball out of the hand quickly ("get it out").
- A quarterback *bailing out* throws a pass too early, worrying about potential pressure.
- If the quarterback sees that no good can come of a play, with the pass rush shortly arriving, he can *throw the ball away*. In order to avoid an intentional grounding, 1) while outside the *tackle box*—designated as the invisible area between the left and the right tackle at the snap—he must get the throw back to the line of scrimmage, or 2) while inside the tackle box, he must throw the ball in the nearby vicinity of a receiver.
- The opposite of throwing the ball away: A quarterback

who "throws it up for grabs," heaving a panicked blind pass down the field and hoping for the best.

activity in/outside of the pocket
backpedal, boot, bootleg, break contain, break the pocket, drift, drop back, go through progressions, hitch, look, roll, roll out, scramble, set up, shuffle, slide, sprint, stand tall, step up, survey the field, waggle

- A quarterback *rolling out* or *sprinting out* leaves the pocket away from the flow of the line, finding freedom to make a clean throw or *pull down the ball* and run with it himself. Rolling out is related to the *bootleg, boot,* or *waggle,* though the bootleg is accompanied by a play-action fake, drawing the defense toward the appearance of a run. Some forms of the rollout see the quarterback roll to the same side of the field that his team just faked the rush. A *naked bootleg* sees the quarterback execute the boot without any blockers to protect him in case of trouble.
- A quarterback with *pocket presence* is aware of defensive pressure, as though he can "feel the rush," knowing just when to step up in the pocket. When the opposite occurs, and the quarterback feels pressure even when it isn't there, he *hears footsteps.*
- Put a quarterback behind a deficient line, and he'll be *running for his life* or *under siege.* Defensive pressure that forces the quarterback to leave the pocket is said to flush him from the pocket. (See **pocket**)
- Improvising isn't just for jazz musicians and the fellows on *Whose Line is it Anyway?*—if the play breaks down, it's up to the quarterback to make something happen. (In this case, receivers running shallow routes are told to run deep, while receivers running deeper routes are told to "come back to the football.")
- A quarterback scrambling around, escaping the rush, but staying behind the line of scrimmage in order to retain the ability to throw a pass is said to *buy time* and *extend the play.*
- A quarterback who *breaks contain* gets around the

outside of a defense assigned to prevent him from reaching the corner.

- When the quarterback finally does decide that he must forgo a pass and take off, he *tucks the ball in* and takes off.

Slingin' Sammy

- From Shirley Povich's profile of Sammy Baugh in *Redskins: A History of Washington's Team*:

  The defining anecdote about Baugh through the years has been the story of how, when he first reported to the Redskins, he was told by coach Ray Flaherty, "Sammy, you're with the pros now, and they want the football where they can catch it. Hit 'em in the eye." Whereupon rookie Baugh said, "Which eye?"

  Of course, the tale was widely taken as a bit of hyperbole, a way to underline Baugh's passing perfection. But, whaddayaknow, it turns out to be true. Sammy confirmed it 60 years later on the phone from Texas. "Yep, ah said it," he acknowledged. "First and last time in my life ah was cocky."

Automatic Otto

"As a youngster growing up in Waukegan, Illinois," wrote Dave Anderson, "Otto Graham had not appeared likely to develop into a six-foot, one-inch, 195-pound quarterback. He played the piano, the violin, the cornet, and the French horn. He also played basketball better than he played football." But Graham was diverted to the gridiron by Northwestern football coach Lynn Waldorf, where he impressed Ohio State coach Paul Brown. After graduating, he joined the Navy in the pilot training program. "He later was transferred to the Glenview, Illinois, Naval Air Station," Anderson continued, "where Paul Brown visited him. 'When the War is over,' Brown said, 'I'm going to coach the Cleveland team in a new pro football league. I want you to be my T-formation quarterback.' " Gra-

ham demurred, having no experience in the T-formation, but Paul Brown was persuasive.

In 1946, Otto Graham joined the Cleveland Browns.
His rookie season also happened to be Cleveland's first
season as a franchise, an expansion team in the All-
American Football Conference (AAFC). That rookie
season ended in a championship victory over the New
York Yankees; Graham was the starting quarterback in
that championship, throwing for 213 yards and game-
winning fourth-quarter touchdown, in addition to
intercepting an Ace Parker pass and serving on punt-
return duty. The Browns won all four AAFC championships they played, 1946-1949, before joining the
NFL as an upstart in 1950 and proceeded to win the
NFL championship, too, thanks to a last-minute Graham drive culminating in a Lou Groza field goal. ("This
was the greatest game I ever saw," said Commissioner
Bert Bell.) No, life wasn't all roses for Cleveland: Graham and the Browns lost in the championship in 1951,
1952, and 1953—before recovering to top the league
again in 1954 and 1955.

And then musician, basketball player, and quarterback
Otto Graham, who had gone 7-3 in championship
games during a ten-year career, retired.

R

The Four Horsemen of Notre Dame: Jim Crowley, Elmer Layden, Don Miller, and Harry Stuhldreher. (Courtesy Library of Congress.)

receiver

n. handler of the receiving chore, option, pass-catcher, pass-catching option, pass receiver, target, weapon, wide, wideout, wide receiver, WR; POSITIONS end (E), flanker (FL), slot receiver (W), split end (SE), tight end (TE), U (second tight end), X receiver (weak-side receiver), Y receiver (slot receiver/tight end), Z receiver (strong-side receiver); SPECIFIC blocker-receiver, deep threat, far flanker, finesse receiver, glue-fingered receiver, home run hitter, home run threat, intended receiver, lonely end, lonesome end, open receiver, outlet, physical receiver, possession man, possession receiver, primary option, primary receiver, safety valve, secondary receiver, second option, slotback, solo receiver, spread end, sticky-fingered receiver, sure-handed receiver, tackle-eligible receiver, third down wide receiver, vertical receiver, vertical threat, wide flanker; INSULTING the prima donnas of the team; PLURAL collection, crew, crop, fleet, posse

"The first of the great receivers was Don Hutson, who went from Alabama to the Green Bay Packers. Certainly, I'll never forget my introduction to the fleet and elusive Mr. Hutson in our 1935 opening game at Green Bay. On the first play of the game Hutson streaked downfield from his seventeen-yard line. Beattie Feathers was in the safety position for us, and well past midfield he allowed Hutson to get past him. Arnie Herber left fly with a tremendous pass. Hutson made an over-the-shoulder catch without breaking stride and raced to a touchdown. That was the only score of the ball game!"—*"Papa Bear" George Halas,* Saturday Evening Post, *December 7, 1957*

Terms and Jargon

- A "gun-shy" receiver has *alligator arms* or *T-rex arms*, keeping his hands close to his body (not reaching out for the ball) due to wariness of an approaching defender and the possibility of a punishing hit. He may also be said to have "heard footsteps" (of a nearing defender).
- A receiver's *ball skills* judge his ability to make a play on a ball in the air. If his ball skills are excellent, he's a *ball athlete* and can "go up and get it."
- A *decoy* is a receiver who is sent out to distract the defense, freeing up a teammate.
- Receivers are taught to catch the ball with their hands, rather than letting the ball get to their chest. A receiver with *great hands*, *soft hands*, or *sure hands* is skilled at catching the ball, even when the pass is inaccurate. In this sense, he might be described as *glue-fingered* or *sticky-fingered*, since the ball "sticks" to his hands. This has a literal derivation; from the 1940s until its prohibition in 1981, receivers were applying Stickum to their hands to assist in catching passes. (A particular

receiver here or there preferred thumbtacks.) Stickum, by the way, is a spray-on adhesive particularly popular with receivers in the 1960s and 1970s. It was designed to help baseball players and weighlifters keep a better grip on their equipment.

- As Dan Daly wrote, Stickum had unusual consequences: "[In] Super Bowl [XII] the Cowboys called a halfback pass that Robert Newhouse wasn't quite expecting. 'I had Stickum all over my hands,' he said. 'I started wiping it off on my pants and started licking my fingers. I've never eaten so much Stickum in my life.' He then launched a 29-yard touchdown throw to Golden Richards for the clinching score in a 27-10 Dallas win."

- More recently, San Francisco 49ers legend Jerry Rice, considered the greatest wide receiver in NFL history, confessed to giving his gloves a little added assistance in catching passes. On January 17, 2015, Rice said in an ESPN interview, "I know this might be a little illegal, guys, but you put a little spray, a little Stickum on them, to make sure that texture is a little sticky."

- A receiver with *hard hands* or *stone hands* is just the opposite and drops many an accurate pass. A receiver—or a receiving crew—that drops a lot of passes has come down with a case of "butterfingers" or "the dropsies." (A common insult: "It hit him in the wrong place. The hands.")

- A receiver with dangerous speed, able to threaten the defense deep, is termed a *deep threat, home run hitter, home run threat, vertical receiver,* and *vertical threat.* (In the same vein, he is *vertically explosive* and *can threaten the other team deep.*)

- The *long man* is the receiver whose route takes him the deepest; the opposite is the *short man,* who runs the shortest pass route.

- A receiver *makes himself available* by finding the quarterback and getting his hands ready to catch the pass, no matter how hard it arrives.

- The *release* describes how a receiver gets off the line of scrimmage. If he is untouched, or fights through bump-

and-run coverage with ease, it's a *clean release*, allowing him to go into his pass route without trouble.

- An *inside release* sees the receiver step to the inside; an outside release brings the receiver's initial steps to the outside of the formation.
- It can get a lot more complicated than that: "We also use what we call the single head and step fake," wrote George Allen, "in which the end fakes with the head and a step to the outside and then releases inside. Conversely, he can head and step fake to the inside and release outside. Another release would be the double fake, where he fakes to the outside, fakes to the inside, and then comes back to the outside." Other release ideas from Allen:

> "Our tight ends also have used to good success a release whereby they actually fake as if they are going to hook the linebacker. The end simply starts out as if he is going to hook the linebacker who is responsible for containment. When the linebacker starts to defend himself, trying not to be hooked, the tight end is able to slip through on the inside."

> "The *low* release has proven a quick and effective way to release. The receiver should drop to all fours, scramble along the ground, get up and then resume his pattern."

> "The *inside arm* swing is another successful release….As the tight end drives, either to his inside or his outside of the linebacker, he takes his inside arm and makes a great sweeping motion over the top. As the linebackers try to grab hold, the end has a terrific lever which rips their hands off him."

- When faced with tight man-to-man coverage, particularly bump-and-run and hand-fighting at the line of scrimmage, it's up to the receiver to fight his way into his pass pattern. This he can do by smacking the defender's hands aside; swimming through, using his arms to work past the defender with an overhand strokes; or utilizing the *dip and rip*, getting underneath the defender and uppercutting past with an upward swing. ("This move," wrote Czarnecki and Long, "was a favorite of Hall-of-Famer Jerry Rice.")

- A receiver seeks *separation*, creating distance between himself and the defender covering him ("freeing himself up") in order to easily receive a pass. The less separation there is, the tougher his task becomes.
- Facing a zone defense, receivers are often taught to find holes (*pockets* or *voids*) in the zone—areas without defenders—and *sit down* (stop running) to make themselves available to the quarterback.
- When the quarterback is in trouble, scrambling outside the pocket, receivers are taught to enter the *scramble drill*: practiced routes for when the quarterback needs assistance.
- A *tackle-eligible* receiver is an offensive tackle who reports to the referee to declare himself an eligible receiver, often in a short-yardage situation. In his formation on the offensive line, he adds bulk and blocking to one side—but without any wide receiver to his side, he becomes eligible to catch a pass. Inevitably, he'll sneak away from the line and find himself wide open.

Locations for a Receiver to Set Up
bunched left, bunched right, far left, far right, flexed left, flexed right, near left, near right, near side left, near side right, slot left, slot right, split to the left, split to the right, split wide, stacked left, stacked right, staggered left, staggered right, in tight, tight, topside, to the top, wide left, wide right, wing left, wing right

- A *bunch* places receivers close together, though only one is on the line of scrimmage.
- A *flexed* receiver, usually a tight end being used as an *h-back*, is brought back into the shallow backfield to set up behind an offensive tackle.

- A receiver in the *slot* sets up near halfway between the offensive line and a receiver spread wide.
- A *split* receiver lines up several yards off the end of the line.
- *Stacked* receivers are stationed in a vertical line toward the line of scrimmage, one behind the other.
- *Staggered* receivers are placed alongside one another at varying distances from the line of scrimmage; the first is on the line, the second is a yard or two away and a yard or two behind the line of scrimmage, and a potential third would set up in the same way, a yard or two from his closest teammate and yard or two farther back from the line.
- A receiver *in tight*, usually a tight end, is placed on the end of the offensive line.
- A *wide* receiver puts the greatest distance between himself and the offensive line, setting up closer to the sideline than his nearest offensive tackle.

Receiver Alignments and Sets
bunch, doubles, multiple, quads, quints, stack, tandem, trey, trips, twins

- In specifically describing the receivers, count how many receivers are to each side. A 3×1 (or 3-by-1) set features three receivers on one side of the formation and one receiver on the other side. Two receivers on each side: 2×2.
- Two receivers together are *twins* or *doubles*.
- Three receivers together are *trips* or *trey*.
- Four receivers together are *quads*.
- Five receivers together are *quints*.

X, Y, and Z... and Friends

- The *Z receiver* (the *flanker* or the *#1 receiver*) lines up on the same side as the tight end and is often pulled back 1-3 yards from the line of scrimmage.
- The *Y receiver* is either the tight end or—in formations without a tight end—the slot receiver/#3 receiver.

- The *X receiver* (the *split end* or *#2 receiver*), lines up on the weak side of the formation, away from the tight end.
- The *W receiver* (*#3 receiver*) is a slot receiver used on plays including the tight end.
- The *U receiver* is a second tight end.
- *H* is used to designate another wide receiver or tight end in the event of a five-receiver formation.

All Alone

- The "Lonely End" was Army All-America receiver Bill Carpenter, in a 1958 innovation devised by head coach Earl "Red" Blaik. (The position was later called the "Lonesome End" by scribe Stanley Woodward, and it is that designation that has stuck in many memories.) Blaik decided to save Carpenter's energy for running routes and making plays, specifically instructing him to remain in the flank instead of returning to the huddles. There he stood throughout the Army offensive possessions: a lone figure split away from his huddling teammates, as if under the mandate of quarantine. Carpenter responded to the tactic with a school record-tying 22 catches, amassing 453 yards.

Notable Named Receiving Corps

- *The Smurfs*, Washington Redskins, 1982-1983: 5-10 Charlie Brown, 5-7 Alvin Garrett, and 5-8 Virgil Seay, working in tandem with quarterback Joe Theismann. The Smurfs, named for their diminutive heights, were a part of The Fun Bunch, a larger crew of receivers that included tight ends Rick Walker and Don Warren. After each receiving touchdown, the Fun Bunch would circle about and leap for a group high-five, paying tribute to injured teammate Art Monk.
- *The Marks Brothers*, Miami Dolphins, 1984-1992: Mark Clayton and Mark Duper, the favorite targets of Dan Marino. Clayton was named to the Pro Bowl in 1984, 1985, 1988, and 1991, leading the NFL in touchdown

receptions in 1984 and 1988; Duper was a Pro Bowler in 1983, 1984, and 1986.

- *The Three Amigos*, Denver Broncos, 1987-1988: The Broncos selected Vance Johnson, Mark Jackson, and Ricky Nattiel in consecutive seasons to provide John Elway capable targets. In 1988, the trio totaled 160 catches. In 1989, though, Nattiel fell off to only ten catches, reducing the amigos' numbers to two. (The name was based on the 1986 comedy starring Chevy Chase, Steve Martin, and Martin Short.)
- *The Posse*, Washington Redskins, 1988-1992: reliable Art Monk, tough Gary Clark, and deep threat Ricky Sanders gave running-oriented Washington a formidable passing crew, helping first Doug Williams and later Mark Rypien reach the highest levels of NFL success.

referee

n. see official

retire

v. call it a career, call it quits, hang up the cleats, hang up the pads

return

n. runback; SPECIFIC free kick return (following a safety), fumble return, interception return, kick return, kickoff return, punt return

"I felt like a deer with a hundred hunters after me."—Deion Sanders

Re: Returns

- From Howie Long and John Czarnecki: "Jimmy Johnson, who coached the Dallas Cowboys and the Miami Dolphins, called positive return yards hidden yardage. For example, Johnson equated a 50-yard advantage in punt/kick return yards to five first downs."

- Gale Sayers may have been the best return man ever, and if not him, then the electrifying Devin Hester. Also worth remembering: "The King," Hugh McElhenny, the first superstar the San Francisco 49ers ever knew. From Mickey Herskowitz in *The King*:

> Against the Bears, in his rookie season of 1952, he fielded a punt at his own 6 and rocked on his feet for a split-second or two—a McElhenny habit that enabled him to see how the field was spread. Two Chicago ends thought they had him trapped. As they closed in, McElhenny zipped straight ahead and the two ends collided, bumping heads, a moment of fine burlesque. He changed pace and a tackler appeared on his right. In two steps he was in overdrive again. He swerved to his left and the leaping Bear landed two yards behind him. He straightened up and went through the rest of the Bears as though it were some kind of barn dance. The run covered 94 yards, not including the mileage he traveled sideways.

> "That," said George Halas, never a man to mince words, "was the damnedest run I've ever seen in football."

> Later, McElhenny said, casually, "I thought I had caught the punt at about our twenty-six. If I had known it was the six-yard line, I would have let it go."

rout

n. see "overwhelming victory" under **win**
v. see **defeat**

route

n. see **pass route**

running back

n. back, ball carrier, football mover, ground gainer, offensive back, RB, riveter, runner, rusher, toter; POSITIONS flanker back (FB), fullback (FB), halfback (HB), h-back, I back (IB), tailback (TB), upback (U), wing back (WB); SPECIFIC all-purpose back, all-purpose guy, all-purpose runner, bell cow, big back, blocking back, breakaway back, broken-field runner, bruiser, bus, change-of-pace back, choice runner, climax back, dive back, dodger and dancer, do-everything back, downhill runner, every-down back, fancy dan, feature back, flanker-back, foundation back, freight train, half, heavy-duty runner, home run hitter, home run threat, hummingbird, hybrid back, I-back, in back, jackrabbit, left half, load, near back, north-south runner, offset back, plodder, "pour it in there" guy, power back, rabbit, right half, running machine, salmon, scatback, scooter, set back, setback, short-yardage back, sidecar, single wing back, slasher, sniffer back, three-down back, third-down back, top back, triple-threat back, versatile back, whoa back, workhorse

"An arm tackle is no soap; he runs right through you. The only way I've found to stop him is to hit him right at the ankles with your shoulder.... Otherwise, it's like tackling a locomotive."—Glenn Holzman, *Los Angeles Rams, regarding Jim Brown*

Types of Running Backs

- The *change-of-pace back* provides a different speed and running style than the man he replaces in the backfield. If the team's top back, for instance, is a bruising, physical type of runner, when he comes out for a breather, the ideal substituted change-of-pace back is quick and slippery.
- The *feature back*, or *foundation back*, is a team's #1 running back, who receives the football on the majority of running plays and provides a significant portion of the offense's potency. The feature back "carries the mail."
- *H-back* is short for hybrid back, who fills the dual responsibility of both a fullback and tight end, lining up

both in the backfield and along the line of scrimmage.
(Dropping the tight end back a yard, toward the
backfield, is *flexing* him.) Washington Redskins head
coach Joe Gibbs created the H-back role.

- The *home run hitter*, a *breakaway back*, presents speed and
  elusiveness, able on any play to take the ball all the way
  to the end zone.
- The *in back*, defined by Steve Belichick: "Any back that is
  aligned in his normal T formation position."
- A powerful back, tough to tackle, is a *load*.
- The *near back* or *up back* refers to the nearest running
  back to the play. If a play is run to the right, for instance,
  the back closest to the right at the start of the play is the
  near back. The *far back* is the opposite back, set farther
  back from the line.
- A *north-south runner* takes the ball straight ahead,
  vertically, with little to no lateral movement. A *downhill
  runner* builds up excellent vertical momentum, making
  him tough to bring down. The opposite, albeit related, is
  a *salmon*, who is forced to "swim upstream" in order to
  gain positive yardage.
- The *"pour it in there" guy* is inserted into the game in
  order to score a touchdown from in close.
- The use of *riveter* to describe a rusher is archaic but fun.
  From the *Moorhead Daily News*, November 18, 1932:
  "Purdue's three riveters, Horstmann, Purvis and Hecker,
  are the three best backs on any team in this
  section....Horstmann has averaged 4.3 yards every time
  he's carried the ball this season, Hecker 4.78 and Purvis
  6.06....which is some high-class galloping in any league."
- On *Monday Night Football* on September 22, 2014, Jon
  Gruden described New York Jets running back Chris
  Ivory as a "rolling ball of butcher knives, all knees and
  elbows."
- The *scatback* (a *hummingbird*, *jackrabbit*, *rabbit*, or *scooter*)
  is small, quick, and elusive.
- The *set back* describes any running back who remains in
  his position before the snap, rather than being sent in
  motion.

- The *sidecar* stands beside the quarterback in a shotgun formation, a reference to a motorcycle and its sidecar. The term is a favorite of broadcaster Gene Deckerhoff, voice of the Tampa Bay Buccaneers and Florida State Seminoles.
- The *sniffer back* lines up directly behind the quarterback in a three-point stance (one hand down) or a four-point stance (two hands down), and you can probably guess how the term came into being.
- A *third-down back* comes in for the starting running back on third downs, often to run draws, receive screen passes and swing passes, and pick up blitzes. (If the starting back remains in the game, he's a *three-down back* or an *every-down back*.)
- The *triple-threat back* dates back to the days when the same star player would pass, run, and punt the ball for his team.
- The *whoa back*, defined in *The Encyclopedia of Sports Talk*: "Now archaic, the whoa back was Amos Alonzo Stagg's term for a back who delayed and sort of reared up like a horse before starting to run on the old spinner play."
- The *wing back* sets up a yard outside of the end of the offensive line on either side.
- A heavily used running back is a *workhorse*, and is said to "carry the load" and "put the team on his back."

The Running Game

- The act of a team rushing the football, the counterpart to the passing attack, is the *ground attack*, *ground game*, *power game*, or *running game*.
- A team *chewing up*, *eating up*, or *grinding out* yardage gets its yards on the ground, a few at a time. It's an inexorable forward advance, a *grind-it-out*, *ball-control* offense, keeping the clock moving and the opponent's offense on the sideline. This is the offensive philosophy of "three yards and a cloud of dust" (the stated philosophy of Woody Hayes's Ohio State Buckeyes). The opposite of *grinding* the ball is *finessing*.
- A power running game plan in which the offense runs

the ball directly at the defense with no deception, daring the opposition to toughen up and stop them, is *smashmouth football*.

- It's *tough sledding* for a running back unable to find any holes in the defense.

- When a team *feeds* or *rides* a running back, it relies heavily on the back for the majority of its offensive plays. For the Washington Redskins in the early 1980s, this was the Riggo Drill, giving the ball to John Riggins play after play and watching the "Diesel" continually chug forward. (As Riggins told head coach Joe Gibbs in 1982, "Load the wagon. I'm going to carry it.") The Pittsburgh Steelers of the 1990s rode "The Bus," Jerome Bettis, while the Michigan Wolverines of the late 1990s rode "The A-Train," Anthony Thomas.

- Note that only four men are allowed in the offensive backfield, due to the mandatory number of seven men on the offensive line. The *fifth man in the backfield* describes any noteworthy defender who has himself a fabulous day, breaking through the line play after play to tackle the ball carrier for a loss.

- Running backs are taught to *press the hole*. Green Bay back Ryan Grant defined the term for the *Milwaukee Journal Sentinel*, September 9, 2010: "That means I am running in that direction as long as possible before I make a decision on my line. You've heard people say he makes a cut at the heels of his linemen. That's pressing the hole. It brings the linebackers whatever direction you're running, which helps the linemen because it engages them. It brings the linebackers up."

In the Backfield

- See "Notable Offensive Formations" under **Formation** for the diamond, the I formation, the wishbone, and more.

- According to Mickey Herskowitz and Steve Perkins in *Everything You Always Wanted to Know About Sports (and didn't know where to ask)*, the nickname Fearsome Foursome "is a longtime football cliché, once used in referring to various college backfields." See **defensive line** for football's most famous Fearsome Foursome.

- From Hollander and Zimmerman's *Football Lingo*, "The Los Angeles Rams of the early 1950s had a 'Bull Elephant' backfield of Dick Hoerner, Tank Younger, and Dan Towler, each of whom weighed between 220 and 230 pounds. In the late 1950s, Green Bay popularized the Two-Big-Back offense, using a halfback and fullback of great size and strength, complemented by the recently created flanker-back whose job was to catch passes rather than to run the ball."

- A team using a *pony backfield* features a crew of smaller running backs; this specifically described the 1953 Michigan State University backfield of LeRoy Bolden, Evan Slonac, Billy Wells, and Tom Yewcic.

Notable Offensive Backfields

- *The Four Horsemen of Notre Dame*, quarterback Harry Stuhldreher, right halfback Don Miller, left halfback Jim Crowley, and fullback Elmer Layden. "Outlined against a blue-gray October sky," wrote Grantland Rice, October 19, 1924, "the Four Horsemen rode again. In dramatic lore they are known as Famine, Pestilence, Destruction and Death. These are only aliases. Their real names are Stuhldrehler, Miller, Crowley and Layden." George Strickler, Notre Dame's student publicity director for head coach Knute Rockne, takes credit for inspiring Rice's famed lede and, thus, one of football's iconic nicknames. A subsequent photograph featuring the four-man Fighting Irish backfield seated atop horses made the moniker stick.

- *The Dream Backfield*, University of Pittsburgh, 1937-1938, with Dick Cassiano, John Chickerneo, Marshall "Biggie" Goldberg, and Curly Stebbins. The Dream Backfield ran Jock Sutherland's feared double-wing, the Sutherland Scythe. Goldberg later played for the Chicago Cardinals in the NFL, who also had a four-man offensive backfield nicknamed "The Dream

Backfield," alternately known as the "Million Dollar Backfield."

- *Mr. Inside and Mr. Outside*, Army, featuring tough fullback Felix "Doc" Blanchard and elusive halfback Glenn Davis. The *New York Sun*'s George Trevor came up with the nickname, and it fit the two star backs perfectly. With Blanchard running inside and Davis running outside, Army dominated the mid-1940s. Doc Blanchard paced the entire nation in scoring in 1945, capturing the Heisman Trophy. Davis finished second for the honor in '45, his second consecutive finishing second—and then captured the Heisman himself in 1946. "So famous did the duo become, and so representative of their country," wrote Edward J. Rielly, "that American soldiers began to identify enemy Germans posing as Americans by whispering 'Blanchard' and waiting to see if they heard 'Davis' in response."

- *The Pony Express*, Southern Methodist University, 1979-1982, starring quarterback Lance McIlhenny and running backs Eric Dickerson and Craig James. Two of the top prep running backs in the country, class of '79, were Texans: Sealy's Eric Dickerson and Houston's Craig James. Both of them decided to play for the Mustangs. Wrote Jeff Miller for *ESPNDallas.com*, November 1, 2011: "In 1979, [head coach Ron] Meyer often played James and Dickerson together in a primarily passing offense…. Meyer shifted to an option formation midway through the 1980 season, when strong-armed senior quarterback Mike Ford struggled coming back from a knee injury. Meyer promoted the run-oriented McIlhenny and began alternating Dickerson and James at tailback." This became the Pony Express, coined by sports information director Bob Condron. In 1980, Dickerson rushed for 928 yards and five touchdowns while James carried for 896 yards and six touchdowns. In 1981, those numbers increased to 1,428 yards and 19 TDs for the dominant Dickerson, with 1,147 yards and nine TDs from James. In 1982, their senior year, Dickerson totaled 1,617 yards and 17 touchdowns on the ground, with James adding 938 yards and four touchdowns. They both went to the NFL, with Eric Dickerson getting drafted 2nd overall by the Rams and distinguishing himself in a 12-year career, and Craig James going in the 7th round to the Patriots and lasting five seasons, posting a 1,000+ yard season in 1985.

- *DVD*, Atlanta Falcons, 2004. The Falcons compiled a team-record 2,672 rushing yards thanks to their backfield, starring shifty running back Warrick Dunn, quarterback Michael Vick, and bruising back T.J. Duckett. Wrote Jay Hart of *The Morning Call*, "In T.J. Duckett and Warrick Dunn, Atlanta seems to have revived the 'Mr. Inside' and 'Mr. Outside' combination….The Falcons' running attack starts with Dunn, a 180-pound Mighty Mouse who uses a combination of speed and power to stretch opposing defenses to the point of breaking. It ends with Duckett, a 254-pound bowling ball who had one carry for negative yardage all season." It was a fun run for Atlanta, but DVD peaked with a January 23, 2005, conference championship loss to Philadelphia.

rush

n. attempt, carry, jaunt, keep on the ground, line plunge, line smash, line thrust, run, scramble, tote, try; SPECIFIC belly, blast, counter, counter trey, delay, dive, double reverse, draw, end-around, end run, gut, iso, isolation, lead, line buck, misdirection, off-tackle, pass-action run, pitch, plunge, power, reverse, slant, smash, stretch, sweep, trap, veer, wedge, windback, zone read *v.* attempt, belly, blast, buck, carry, counter, delay, dive, jaunt, plunge, power, scramble, smash, sweep, test, thrust, tote, try; note that specific rushing plays can be turned into verbs, especially when shouted out during a game; see also **move about the field**

Notable Rushing Plays

- Near football's inception there were two basic run plays, *a line smash* (also called a *line buck* or *line plunge*), in which the back powered directly into the line, and an *end run*, in which the back carried it with speed around the end of the line. Running plays also became termed *bucks*; Yale's John Reed Kilpatrick wrote of his team's three plays in 1909, the *straight buck*, the *cross buck*, and, naturally, the *end run*.

- From here, things have grown slightly more complex, though running backs and offensive lines are still judged by how well they run *between the tackles* (interior/inside runs) and *outside the tackles* (exterior/outside runs).

- The *belly* sees a pair of running backs approach two different holes at the line of scrimmage, with the quarterback reading the defense's reaction and offering a fake handoff to one of the backs before or after giving to the other. Wrote John T. Reed, "in Vince Lombardi's Green Bay Packer offense, it was a fake fullback dive right, halfback dive left with the halfback taking a jab step to the right before running to the left A or B gap bubble depending upon the movement of the defensive tackle."

- The *blast*, also called the *lead* or the *iso/isolation play*, brings the running back inside behind the fullback, who is isolated on the middle linebacker. A good block blasts open a hole for the ball carrier.

- The *counter* is a misdirection run, seeming to flow in one direction before the running back plants his foot and cuts back the other way. (The running back's initial step in a counter is a *jab step*, a deliberate step in the wrong direction to get defenders moving the wrong way.)

- The Washington Redskins' famed Hogs offensive line delighted in running the Counter Trey. As defined by Chris Landry, "the running back takes three steps in one direction, then reverses field before receiving the handoff. The guard and tackle from the fake side pull to block for the ball carrier, picking off defenders who think they are pursuing the play from behind."

- The *delay* is a run, related to the draw, where there is a slight bit of deliberate hesitation before the quarterback presents the running back with the ball.

- The *dive*, also called a *quick opener*, occurs in a hurry, a quick rushing play without a lead blocker that is designed to go right up the middle, between the center and either the left or right guard.
- The *draw* sees the quarterback drop back, as if to pass, "drawing" the defenders forward—before slipping the ball to the running back. If the quarterback fakes a pass first before executing the handoff, the play is *pass-action*. (This is also called the pump-fake draw.) A *shotgun draw* is handled out of the shotgun formation. The origin of the draw play, from Paul Brown's autobiography, quoted in Robert W. Peterson's *Pigskin*:

> During a 1946 game [fullback Marion] Motley and [quarterback Otto] Graham collided trying to run a trap play on a muddy field. The collision created a broken play, and Otto, in desperation, seeing the linemen charging in on him, just handed the ball next to Marion as they stood next to each other. The opposing linemen simply ran past Marion, and he took off for a big gain. We didn't think much of it at the time, but looking at the game films, Otto said, "I think that could become a play," so we developed the blocking assignments and the techniques which went with it. At first we called it a pick, but since that word was also part of the passing terminology, I changed the name to draw, because we wanted our offensive linemen to visualize it as drawing in the pass rushers.

- The *gut* is another name for an interior running play, similar to the dive, going right up the "gut" of the defense.
- In an *end-around*, a receiver is given the ball in a bit of deception/misdirection and asked to use his speed to race around the corner before the defense can react. This is often confused with a reverse. But:
- In a *reverse*, the ball carrier on an end-around hands off

or flips the ball to a teammate sprinting in the opposite direction, catching the late-reacting defense on its heels.

- In a *double reverse*, the ball is transferred *again*, given to a receiver heading the opposite way.
- In a *reverse flea-flicker* or a *double reverse flea-flicker*, the ball is flipped finally to the waiting quarterback who finishes the play off with a pass.
- Care for a *triple reverse*? It was Grambling State head coach Eddie Robinson's "ultimate punishment" when his player displeased him in practice, according to *Breaking the Line*. The play was "called the 'merry-go-round,' which involved a triple reverse and a pass." Then there was this play, described by the inimitable Chris Schenkel:

> I remember one beautiful series of fakes in a Browns-Giants game during the 1962 season. Rich Kreitling, Cleveland's 6-foot-2 offensive end, was split wide to the left. Ray Renfro was a flanker right. Quarterback Jim Ninowski took the snap from center and quickly pitched out to his fullback, Jimmy Brown, who started a wide sweep. Renfro moved ahead as if to form a blocking pattern for Brown. But he suddenly stopped, reversed his field, and took a handoff from Brown while heading for the opposite side. Renfro then handed the ball back to Ninowski, who rifled a long clothesline to Kreitling, who had drifted down and across into the end zone while the triple reverse was in progress. The Giants' defense was numbed and embarrassed.

- The *off-tackle* is directed just to the outside of the line, requiring both the offensive tackle and the tight end to seal the corner and allow a lane for the ball carrier.
- The *pitch* is delivered with a flip rather than a handoff. Similarly, the toss is delivered with an underhand spiral rather than a handoff; see **handoff**
- The *power* is prevalent when the offense solely needs short-yardage, using a pulling lineman to serve as the lead blocker on an inside run.

- The *slant* describes the running back's angled route on an inside rush, receiving the ball on one side of the line from the quarterback and slanting to the other side behind his guard.
- The *stretch*, which sees the runner head diagonally along the line of scrimmage before choosing to *cram it*, bulling forward into a planned gap; *cut it*, slashing back inside to take advantage of overrunning defenders; or *kick it*, continuing (bouncing) to the outside and looking for room near the sideline.
- The *sweep* is named for the motion of a broom, describing the ball carrier darting around one side of the line. A *toss sweep* is differentiated by the quarterback's underhand delivery rather than handoff to get the play started.
- The classic call for a college sweep: *Student Body Right*. (Or, alternately, "Student Body Left.") Upon handing the ball, the entire offense heads as a unit to one side, with a mass of blockers wiping out the outnumbered defense. The Student Body Right sweep made John McKay's mid-'60s Southern Cal Trojans feared.
- Perhaps even more famous (and one of the most well-known designed plays ever) was Vince Lombardi's *Packer sweep* (also seen as the *Packers' sweep*, *Lombardi sweep*, and *Green Bay sweep*). "Run to daylight," advised Lombardi to running backs Paul Hornung and Jim Taylor. Behind crushing blocks, they did.
- Chris B. Brown traced the Packers' sweep back to the Wing-T "buck-sweep" on *SmartFootball.com*: "the concept is very similar, down blocking on the playside with the guards pulling to create an alley for the runner. The main difference between the bucksweep and the Lombardi sweep is the bucksweep has the added element of misdirection with the fullback up the middle." (The "bucksweep" has also picked up the modern name of "truck sweep," with the offensive blockers trucking the defenders.)
- Dan Daly and Bob O'Donnell, on the origins of the Packers' sweep: "It was an updated version of the old

single-wing power plays. In fact [Lombardi] used the same pulling guard techniques Jock Sutherland taught at Pitt in the '20s and '30s."

- The *crack sweep* sees the receiver come up to give a crackback block on the defensive end while the pulling linemen take care of any defenders on the outside.

- The *fly sweep* is credited to Bob Stitt of the Colorado School of Mines, though the play originated in a Steve Spurrier rushing design at the University of Florida. Wrote Dan Wolken for *USA Today*, October 30, 2012: "[In the Florida play] a receiver would come in motion at full speed and take a handoff from the quarterback almost as the ball was snapped. At Mines, Stitt found the precise timing of that play almost impossible to pull off until one day on the practice field it hit him: Have the quarterback shovel pass the ball, which meant that even if the timing got completely screwed up, it would be considered an incomplete pass." The play technically then does not belong in this section; it's a pass play through and through. The Ohio State Buckeyes call the same pattern a "pop pass." When the ball is handed off rather than flipped forward, it has been termed a "speed sweep" or a *jet sweep*, with the receiver coming in motion utilizing "jet motion."

- The *orbit sweep* or *rocket sweep* sees the ball given to a motioning player taking a wide circuit around the back of the quarterback.

- The *trap* brings the defenders into the backfield, trapping them there as an inside rush skirts through the now open defensive front. A related version is the "sucker play," which suckers a defender into the backfield before sending the ball carrier through his now open gap in the line.

- The *veer*, as described by Long and Czarnecki: "A quick-hitting run in which the ball is handed to either running back, who routes are determined by the slant or charge of the defensive linemen." From Chris B. Brown, "The traditional veer involves having the running back run inside while the quarterback reads a down lineman.... If the defender the quarterback is reading tries to tackle the running back, the quarterback pulls the ball from him and steps around (sometimes with an additional pitch read for a full triple option)."

- The *windback* sees the running back change field and wind his way back behind a zone-blocking line in a misdirection rush. More specifically, from Chris Landry: "The ball carrier begins by running a stretch course, then reverse[s] field and attack[s] the back side of the play. Defenders riding blocks one way usually cannot change direction in time."

- The *zone read* sees the quarterback place the ball in the running back's belly (this is the *mesh point*) while watching the defensive end. If the end comes inside to chase the running back, the quarterback takes the football away and keeps it on a run through the defensive end's vacated side. If the end keys on the quarterback, the running back is kept in possession, taking the ball through the line. In the *lead zone*, the running back serves as the quarterback's lead blocker.

Quarterback (QB) Designed Rushes
dash, draw, keeper, power, sneak, sweep, zone read (see previous entry)

- The term *quarterback keeper* may be used with a broad brush, describing any designed runs for the quarterback.

- The *quarterback dash* sees the quarterback drop back as if to pass before suddenly turning on the speed and racing around one side in a designed end run.

- The *quarterback draw* is similar: the quarterback drops back as if to pass, and then rushes straight forward, through a hole opened up by the line and an aggressive pass rush.

- The *quarterback power* features less disguise and more outright strength, with a fullback leading the way for a strong quarterback to drive forward on an interior rush.

- The *quarterback sneak* is used on short-yardage plays, particularly a 3rd and 1 or a 4th and 1 (and most definitely on a 4th and inches). The quarterback takes the snap and either leaps, leans, pushes, or wedges forward, hoping to pick up the first down. (It is incumbent upon the defensive line to stack up the offensive line at the snap and not allow any give.)

- The *quarterback sweep* is a rush around the end, often with blockers leading the way for a speedy quarterback.

S

Deacon Jones of the Los Angeles Rams, applying pressure to the quarterback. (AP.)

sack

n. SK; SPECIFIC coverage sack, Maggie Simpson sack, strip sack

"A sack is when you run up behind somebody who's not watching, he doesn't see you, and you really put your helmet into him. The ball goes fluttering everywhere and the coach comes out and asks the quarterback, 'Are you all right?' That's a sack."—Lawrence Taylor

Terms and Jargon

- A *sack* describes a tackle of the quarterback behind the

line of scrimmage. Though Lawrence Taylor might think he has the definition, the term itself was coined by his kindred spirit, defensive end Deacon Jones (1961-1974), the "Secretary of Defense." Deacon's own definition, as quoted by NFL Films, "I developed a term that is used in the game right now called sacking a quarterback. Sacking a quarterback is just like you devastate a city or you cream a multitude of people. I mean it's just like you put all the offensive players in one bag and I just take a baseball bat and beat on the bag."

- A *coverage sack* is caused by excellent pass coverage, forcing the quarterback to hold the ball until the pass rush arrives.
- When a quarterback realizes he is about to be sacked, he can choose to *eat the ball*, securing it close to him and perhaps even going to the ground before the defender arrives.
- A defender sacking the quarterback *gets home*.
- A top pass rusher goes *hunting* (for a quarterback).
- A *hurry* isn't the same thing as a sack, but it still can work out for a defense. Coined by Minnesota Vikings head coach Bud Grant, a hurry describes a play in which a rushing defender forced the quarterback to throw the ball sooner than he wanted, thereby avoiding a sack at the expense of attempting to make something out of the play.
- A *Maggie Simpson sack*, used on October 12, 2014, by the NFL RedZone's Scott Hanson to describe a Peyton Manning misplay, refers to a quarterback going down on his own. Imagine the animated baby wearing her onesie, left to crawl around on the ground, and you can picture the quarterback's misfortune.
- A *sack artist*, *sack kick*, or sack master is a defender noted for his ability to amass sacks.
- A *strip sack* sees the defender relieve the quarterback of the ball at the same time he finishes the sack.

safety (play)

n. end-zone tackle, two-pointer, two-point play

- A safety—awarding two points—can be recorded several different ways: a ball carrier is tackled in his own end zone; the ball leaves the offense's possession and goes out of bounds through its own end zone; or an offensive penalty is committed in its own end zone.
- Following a safety, the team that scored the two points receives a free kick. (This kick may be punted or booted off a tee, based on the kicker's discretion.)

safety (position)

n. S, safetyman; POSITION free safety (FS, F/S), left safety (LS), right safety (RS), strong safety (SS, S/S); SPECIFIC ballhawk, bandit, center fielder, floater, monster man, rat in the hole, robber, rover, tight safety, weak safety; also see **defensive back**, **defensive backfield**, **free safety**, and **strong safety**

"It's not important to be known as someone who hits hard. It's important to be known as someone who gives his all."—Ronnie Lott

Terms and Jargon

- The *free safety* is the faster of the two safeties, in addition to being the better coverage man, and is used on the weak-side and in deep zone coverage. The *strong safety* is used closer to the line of scrimmage, on the strong-side, covers the tight end, and assists the linemen and linebackers in stopping the run. (George Allen's Rams nicknamed the strong safety Sam, a name used by strong-side linebackers now, and the free/weak-side safety Jill.)
- The *bandit, floater, monster man, rat in the hole, robber,* and *rover* are all names used to describe a combination linebacker/safety who sneaks about the defense during specific schemes, watching the quarterback and causing trouble.

score

n. count, totals
v. break through, put on the board, record, tack on, tally, touch up the scoreboard

leading
n. above, atop, coasting past, cruising past, in front of, on the right side, over, up

tied with
n. all square, deadlocked, even, even up, knotted up, level

trailing
n. back of, behind, down, needing to play catch-up, on the short end, on the wrong side, yielding

Ways to Score in Football
field goal, PAT, safety, touchdown

- Kicking a field goal (or drop-goal, via drop-kick), worth three points. See **field goal**
- Recording a safety, worth two points. See **safety (play)**
- Scoring a touchdown, worth six points, immediately followed by the choice between kicking the PAT ("point after touchdown—1 point) or attempting a two-point conversion. See **PAT**, or **touchdown**
- In the college ranks, the defensive team can return a thwarted extra-point or two-point conversion to the end zone, earning themselves two points.
- There is a strange rules quirk in college football allowing teams to record one point on a safety during an extra point. From *QuirkyResearch.blogspot.com*: "Before the 1988 season, the NCAA made a rule change, awarding college football teams two points for returning a failed extra point or two point conversation. This happens occasionally (nine times in I-A football in 2005). This rule change brought in play a truly obscure rule: the one-point safety. If a defensive player retreats into his own end zone following an interception,

fumble, or blocked kick on a conversion attempt and is tackled there, the tackling team is awarded 1 point. (Similarly, if the converting team retreats into its own end zone and is tackled there, the defense is awarded 1 point, but that end zone is 97 yards away, so this is extremely unlikely.)"

secondary

n. see **defensive backfield**

sideline

n. boundary, boundary line, chalk, chalk line, line, out of bounds line, paint, stripe, white, white line, white stripe

"If you were to put me in the middle of a room, and in one corner was Albert Einstein, in another corner was Abraham Lincoln, in another corner was Plato, in another corner was William Shakespeare, and in another corner (this room is a pentagon) was a TV set showing a football game between teams that have no connection whatsoever with my life, such as the Green Bay Packers and the Indianapolis Colts, I would ignore the greatest minds in Western thought, gravitate toward the TV, and become far more concerned about the game than I am about my child's education. And so would the other guys. I guarantee it. Within minutes Plato would be pounding Lincoln on the shoulder and shouting in ancient Greek that the receiver did not have both feet in bounds."—Dave Barry

History and Jargon

- According to the NFL rulebook, the sideline is marked by "a solid white border a minimum of six feet wide along the end lines. This line, however, may be diminished to a minimum of four inches in "special circumstances"—such as if the field is also being used for baseball. Because of this, the general sight is of a four-inch wide sideline and end line bounding the field and then a six-feet wide additional border outside of the sideline and end line.

- "Offenses of the 1920s and early 1930s considered the sidelines the enemy," wrote Dan Daly and Bob O'Donnell. "There were no hashmarks in those days, so a play began where the previous one ended. If a runner was knocked out of bounds, the ball was spotted one yard in from the line."

- In the professional ranks, a player must get both of his feet in bounds in order to have his catch be recorded—although, as John Madden loved to say (and even titled his book on football), "one knee equals two feet." In the lower levels, only one foot need be in bounds. A player catching the pass near the boundary may well engage in sideline *toe-dragging*, *toe-tapping*, or *tiptoeing* in order to receive credit. There are toe-tapping drills in order to improve a receiver's sideline awareness.

snap

n. center-quarterback exchange, exchange, handoff to the quarterback, hike, snap-back; SPECIFIC aborted snap, bad snap, direct snap, high snap, long snap, low snap, pistol snap, quick snap, short snap, shotgun snap, snap from center
v. center, hand off, hike; see **get the snap from center** under **quarterback**

"We have the center bring the ball up in a quarter snap or turn of the ball... [B]y turning it a quarter, it allows the quarterback to get a good portion of the ball. If he allows the center to snap it naturally, the ball... will hit his hand with the laces against his fingertips. It should hit his hand hard, with a good 'pop.' "—George Allen, "Inside Football"

History, Terms, and Jargon

- "At Buchtel [College]," wrote Jack Wilkinson for the *Atlanta Journal-Constitution*, "[John Heisman] conceived the center snap. At that time, the center rolled the ball on the ground to the quarterback. That was cumbersome for Buchtel's 6-4 quarterback, so Heisman had his center snap the ball through his legs and through the air." The word hike also comes from Heisman, who had the center snap the ball when the quarterback barked out the word. (The quarterback also used the vocal signal of "Hep!")

- A *direct snap* is commonly used to refer to the center hiking the football directly to a player other than a quarterback, such as the running back standing to the quarterback's side. It was innovated by Pop Warner.
- The snap is delivered on the *snap count* from the quarterback, who barks out pre-snap signals, first, to deliver a *live* or *dummy audible* (see **audible**); second, to point out blocking responsibilities to the offensive line; and, third, to indicate to the center when to snap the football (and alert the rest of the offense when to move).
- The quarterback's pre-snap signal-calling is his *cadence*.
- A *hard count* is used by a quarterback to deceive the defense into thinking he's calling for the snap; instead, the offense knows not to move while the defense jumps offside and hands the offense an easy five yards on the penalty.
- From Michael David Smith at *ProFootballTalk.com*, January 13, 2014:

  > Peyton Manning didn't only use his arm to beat the Chargers on Sunday. He also used his voice.
  >
  > Manning's hard count so frustrated the Chargers that they were flagged for neutral zone infractions a whopping five times. That was very unlike the Chargers: According to *NFLPenalties.com*, the Chargers had only three neutral zone infraction penalties in their previous 17 games.
  >
  > But the hard count wasn't the aspect of Manning's cadence that had people talking during the Chargers-Broncos game. What really got everyone's attention was the way Manning yelled "Omaha" dozens of times during the game.

We don't know what exactly "Omaha" means in the Broncos' offense, but "Omaha" has long been a part of the football lexicon. Tom Brady has used it in the past as part of the Patriots' signal-calling, and NBC's Cris Collinsworth noted during a 2009 game that Peyton's brother, Eli Manning, seemed to be tipping the Cowboys off to the Giants' snap count because whenever Eli yelled "Omaha," the next word out of his mouth was the signal for the center to snap the ball.

- A *quick count* is used to hike the ball and start a play before the defense is ready.
- When dealing with overwhelming crowd noise that can drown out the quarterback's cadence, the offense uses a *silent count*. In one variant, an offensive guard checks in with the quarterback, then lets the center know when the quarterback is ready. The center gives a bob of his head, and everyone on offense begins counting to a preplanned number. The ball is then hiked after a silent count of one, two, or four.

special teams (ST)

n. special forces, specialists, specialty teams, special unit; SPECIFIC PLAYERS ace, deep blocker, designated catcher, end man, gunner, holder, jammer, kickoff specialist, kick returner, long snapper, place-kicker, punter, punt protector, punt returner, return man, safety, short blocker, special teamer, sprinter, upback, wiggler; SPECIFIC UNITS bomb squad, coverage team, extra point, extra-point block, field-goal block, field goal team / field goal unit, flying wedge, hammer team, hands team, kamikaze squad, kickoff unit / kickoff coverage, kickoff return unit, punting unit / punt coverage, punt-return unit, suicide squad

Origins

- The first coach credited with paying extra attention to special teams was Cleveland's iconic Paul Brown (1946-1962 with the Browns, 1968-1975 with the Cincinnati Bengals).

- As head coach of the Baltimore Colts, Don Shula named Alex Hawkins (1959-1968) as his special-teams captain, making the Colts the first team to have three captains: Hall of Fame quarterback Johnny Unitas heading the offense, Hall of Fame defensive lineman Gino Marchetti, heading the defense, and Hawkins leading the special-teams unit.

- Head coach George Allen (1966-1970 with the Rams, 1971-1977 with the Redskins) created the position of special teams coach, hiring Dick Vermeil away from Stanford for his Los Angeles Rams in 1969. Allen also wrote a book on the subject, *George Allen's Guide to Special Teams*. Vermeil supplied the foreword. In that book, as Dan Daly relates, "The last straw for Allen—what made him finally see the light—was when his Rams got knocked out of playoff contention in the next-to-last game of 1968. One of the key plays in the 17-16 loss was an 88-yard kickoff return by the Bears' Clarence Childs….Allen blamed the return on a missed tackle by reserve running back Vilnis Ezerins, an error George attributed to Ezerins's 'lack of tackling fundamentals.' 'We never should have placed him in that position; he was not the right man for the job,' Allen wrote. 'It was then that I decided a special teams coordinator was needed!' "

Specific Terms–Kicking Off

- The *hands team* is sent out to the field by the receiving team in anticipation of an onside kick; it includes the players with the best hands on the team, usually wide receivers, with the express directive to recover the onside kick. The *designated catcher* is the player specifically trusted to field the kick. See **kickoff** for more.

The Suicide Squad vs. The Flying Wedge

- The *suicide squad*, synonymous with the *bomb squad* and the *kamikaze squad*, was formed to combat the *flying wedge*, first introduced in 1892. From Robert W. Peterson in *Pigskin*:

> The flying wedge was the brainchild of Lorin F. Deland, a Boston businessman who had never played football. He suggested the play to Harvard's captain, and it was first used in the big game against Yale.

> To start the second half of a scoreless game, Harvard prepared for the kickoff by sending nine of its players back about 25 yards in a V shape. The kicker stood over the ball. The eleventh Harvard man was behind him. On the signal, both legs of the V began running at full tilt toward the kicker. Just as the V reached him, the kicker tapped the ball, picked it up, and lateraled it to the runner behind him, who was enclosed by the onrushing V. The play is said to have gained about 20 yards before Yale broke the wedge and made the tackle. Within months, the flying wedge was a staple in the offense of most teams.

> Facing such a weapon, the opposition resorted to sacrificial mania. (In one notable show of violence, historian J. Thomas Jable discovered a *Chronicle-Telegraph* report relating how the immortal Pudge Hefflefinger "ran and jumped at [the wedge] with full speed, bring his knees against the mass.") Over the passing decades, the players assigned to run at full force into the wedge, thereby busting its resolve, became known as wedge-busters as well as the more colorful titles of suicide and kamikaze squad. This was not a job for the weak of heart, although it certainly weakened the body in a hurry.

- On October 24, 1954, the NFL witnessed a gruesome play ripped out of the nineteenth century's tactics. From Dan Daly's *The National Forgotten League*: "Early in the second quarter, the Lions' Gil Mains ran downfield to bust up the wedge and—in a moment of temporary insanity—flew *feet-first* into it. One of his cleats plunged into the thigh of the Niners' Hardy Brown, who needed fifteen stitches to repair the damage. 'His cleats raked Hardy along the chest and arm,' the *Oakland Tribune* reported, 'and then one ripped through his pants to inflict the deep cut. However, with the wound closed by stitches, Brown came back to play the entire second half on defense.' "

- In Jerry Kramer's 1967 Green Bay Packers diary, *Instant Replay*, he reported the same thing happening to him, getting drop-kicked by a New York Giant during a kickoff. "His cleats tore my jersey and brushed my helmet," wrote Kramer, but there was no damage otherwise and it never happened again.

Specific Terms—Punting, Offense

- In a punting formation, the long snapper delivers the football to the *punter*, who stands about 14-15 yards back from the line of scrimmage.
- There is a recent rising momentum in college football toward *spread punts* rather than *tight punts*. This refers not to the kick itself, but rather to the distance between offensive linemen. In the spread, the offensive linemen are placed further apart.
- In the event of a spread punt, the punter may receive a *shield* personnel grouping in front of him, comprising (usually) three players prepared to protect him. There are spread punt formations, too, with zero upbacks used. Instead, *slots* are placed to the sides, providing greater speed in the ensuing punt-return coverage.
- The *gunners* are lined up to the outside and are thus also known as the *outside men* or *ends*. It is their job to dash down the field as the first players to reach the prospective returner, forcing either a fair catch, a minimal return, or perhaps even a turnover. These gunners are defended by *jammers*, who are assigned to prevent them from reaching punt-returner cleanly and quickly. A *single press* formation sees one jammer per gunner; a *double press* sees two jammers per gunner.
- The *wings* stand on each side of the line, ready to block

the speedy outside rush while also containing middle pressure.

- Any backs stationed behind the line during the punt are called *blocking backs*. The closest blocking backs behind the line are the *short blockers*.
- The deepest blocking back is the *deep blocker*, a hugely important position. Also known as the *upback (U)* or *personal protector*—Vince Lombardi's term was "personal interferer"—he is stationed anywhere from one to three yards behind the offensive line, ready to block against a strong rush... and equally ready to carry out a fake, should the opportunity present itself. It is the upback who signals for the snap from center.

Specific Terms and Schemes—Punting, Defense

- The *six-man center stack* refers to six rushers on the defensive line, awaiting a punt. The more rushers, the larger the center stack.
- On a *punt-block*, the special teams defenders come after the punter with everything they've got. The *hammer team* is the punt-block unit, and a fiery unit they are. A September 11, 2004, article by Todd Jacobson for *The Gazette* (Colorado Springs) profiled the Air Force Academy's successful punt-block team, one of the top collegiate units in the nation, "dubbed the Hammer Team by coaches more than a decade ago." From Jacobson's piece:

> "A blocked kick will demoralize your football team quicker than anything else and will have an impact on the game more than anything else," coach Fisher DeBerry said....

> Rarely does the Hammer Team line up the same way from game to game. When the team lines up to block a punt, it's impossible to know which players are coming after the punt, and which ones could be bluffing, or there to divert blockers.

The rest is up to the Hammer Team, whose members have names straight out of a cartoon.

Jammers often take care of blocking wide receivers but sometimes are sent after punts from the flanks.

Wigglers line up in the middle and try to squirm through blockers on their way to the punt.

Sprinters have one goal: get to the ball.

- The opposite of a punt-block is a *punt-safe*, often used in the suspicion of a possible fake punt, where the defenders fall back and let the punter boot the ball away in comfort.

The Ace

- One of the highest compliments that can be given to a special-teams player is calling him a special-teams *ace*. A special-teams ace may not ably affect his team offensively or defensively, but his special teams performance—particularly during kickoff and punt coverage—is impactful and eye-catching. In all likelihood, he is the team leader in special teams tackles. (Second behind ace: either a special teams *specialist* or a special teams *core player*.)

stadium

n. arena, bowl, center, coliseum, complex, dome, field, palace, park; see **football field**

Enter the Cyclodrome

- Football players are equated with gladiators; therefore, football stadiums are equated with arenas and coliseums. Then there was the unforgettable Providence Steam Roller. From *The Pro Football Chronicle*: "The Providence Steam Roller played in a 10,000-seat stadium built for bicycle racing called the Cyclodrome.

The field was surrounded by a banked, four-lane track that cut five yards off the corners of one end zone. Temporary bleachers were set up on the track, putting fans right next to the action. It wasn't unusual for players to crash-land among them."

Added Robert W. Peterson, "The Cyclodrome was a cozy place for both players and fans. It was not, however, the scene of the NFL's first night game, which was played in Providence on November 6, 1929. That game, between the Steam Roller and the Chicago Cardinals, was played at Kinsley Park, Providence's minor league baseball stadium. Ernie Nevers, the former Duluth Eskimo, was in his first year with the Cardinals, and naturally he was the star of the game. He ran for one touchdown, passed for another, and kicked a field goal as the Cardinals shut out the Steam Roller, 16 to 0. The lights were floodlights about 20 feet above field level. The game ball was painted white and, said the Providence Journal, 'looked just like a huge egg.' "

Providence stood atop the NFL as champions in 1928 but was one of three teams to fold during or after the 1931 season, as economic struggles threw the league for a loss.

Notable Stadium Nicknames

- *The Autzen Zoo*: University of Oregon
- *Between the Hedges*: University of Georgia
- *The Big House*: University of Michigan
- *The Cock Pit* (or *Cockpit*): University of South Carolina
- *The Dawg Pound*: Cleveland Browns
- *Death Valley*: Clemson University
- *Death Valley*: Louisiana State University
- *The Farm*: Stanford University
- *The Furnace*: Purdue University
- *The Grand Old Lady*: University of Southern California
- *The Horseshoe* or *The Shoe*: Ohio State University

- *The House That (Knute) Rockne Built*: University of Notre Dame
- *The Swamp*: University of Florida

strong safety

n. S, SS, safetyman, safety man, small linebacker, tight safety; see **safety**

- The *strong safety* originally earned his name because he was the "strong-side safety," lining up on the same side as the offense's tight end.
- Because the strong safety lines up closer to the ball than the free safety, he is able to provide *run support*, assisting his teammates on the defensive line and the linebacking crew in stopping the run.
- With defenses often featuring a 4-3 or 3-4 look, with the total number of defensive linemen and linebackers equaling seven (the *front seven*), if the strong safety comes up and joins them, *walking up to the line*, he becomes the "eighth man in the box," creating a *loaded front* or *loading the box*. The alignment is utilized specifically to stop the run and disrespecting the pass. Offensive units are expected to run the ball against seven men in the box, but pass the ball against eight. (The "box" in this context is the *tackle box*, stretching from left to right tackle along the offensive line.)

Super Bowl

n. The Big Game, the big one, championship, final game, title game

"Once again it is time for Americans of all races and religions to set aside their petty differences and spend half a day drinking beer and watching large persons injure each other's knees. You guessed it: it's Super Bowl time."—Dave Barry

History and Jargon

- From the Kansas City Chiefs' media notes:

  After the AFL-NFL merger was announced in June of 1966, Commissioner Pete Rozelle appointed a committee consisting of himself, Lamar Hunt (Kansas City), Tex Schramm (Dallas) and two other owners from each league (AFL & NFL) to firm up the details of the merger agreement.

  At one of those initial merger meetings, there was a discussion about the date of the game. As the committee discussed the championship game (which ultimately became referenced as the Super Bowl), there was some confusion on whether the parties were discussing the respective AFL and NFL title games or the game between the two leagues. It was then that Hunt first recalled saying, "You know, the last game, the final game… the Super Bowl."

  The "inspiration" for Hunt's whimsical suggestion was the high bouncing "Super Ball" produced by the Wham-O company. Lamar's wife, Norma, had previously purchased one for each of the Hunt children (Lamar, Jr., Clark and Sharron) and the toy had become somewhat of a craze in the Hunt household and many other homes across the country.

  Hunt was later quoted as saying, "Nobody ever said let's make that the name of the game. Far from it, we all agreed it was far too corny to be the name of the new title game."

  Because of that perceived corniness, the first two Super Bowls, each won by the Green Bay Packers, were officially named the AFL-NFL World Championship Games. It was only in approaching the third championship between the two leagues that the AFL and NFL bowed to the constant usage of Super Bowl in the press, by the networks, and amongst the fans. When

272 JESSE GOLDBERG-STRASSLER

the New York Jets met the Baltimore Colts in January 1969, the game officially became the Super Bowl.

- The winner of the Super Bowl receives the Vince Lombardi Trophy.
- The Sunday of the Super Bowl is "Super Sunday."
- The true test of quarterback's talent, according to many a pundit and critic: Can he win the big one? (There is no need to specify what the 'big one' refers to; it is unanimously understood.)
- Approaching the Super Bowl each year, the reminder is sent out that the NFL has trademarked the game's title. Thus, in the words of the legal language officially directed to any parties concerned: "The words "Super Bowl" or "Superbowl" or its logo/logotype cannot appear in ads at all, unless it is in an officially sponsored event. However, you are permitted to make written reference to " The Big Game," "Super Football," "The Big Bowl Game," "Super Sunday," etc."
- With this in mind, on January 27, 2014, host Stephen Colbert introduced his own euphemism for the NFL's championship game on Comedy Central's *The Colbert Report*: The Superb Owl.

T

Cleveland Browns coach Paul Brown, Sept. 26, 1947. (AP.)

tackle (play)

n. collar, halt, stop; ILLEGAL clothesline, horse collar tackle, necktie tackle; SPECIFIC ankle tackle, arm tackle, assisted tackle, block tackle, flying tackle, form tackle, gang tackle, grass/turf monster tackle; head-on tackle, high sideline tackle, missed tackle, open-field tackle, shoestring tackle, shoetop tackle, shoulder block tackle, side tackle, solo tackle, tackle for loss, touchdown-saving tackle, unassisted tackle

v. arrest, bring down, bring to a halt, collar, corral, cut down, drag down, drive down, drop, halt, flag down, halt, hog tie, knock down, lasso, mow down, ride down (or out of bounds), rip down, sideswipe, smother, snag, snow under, spill, spin down, stack up, stand up, stone, stop, subdue. submarine, take down, throw (for a loss), throw down, topple, torpedo, track down, trip, trip up, tug down, twist down, upend, uproot, wrap up, wrestle down, yank down

"I just gather 'em all up and peel 'em off one by one till I find the one with the ball."—Gene "Big Daddy" Lipscomb

Terms and Jargon

- Groups of tacklers are described in a variety of ways, some more colorful than others: an *avalanche* of tacklers ("snowing under" the ball carrier), a *gang*, a *host*, a *mob*, a *plethora*, and onward.
- A *block tackle* or *shoulder block tackle* sees the tackler throw his shoulder into the ball carrier rather than use his arms. A *form tackle* describes a properly made tackle, with great form. In *Take Your Eye off the Ball*, Pat Kirwan wrote, "No matter what base defense a team runs, playing defense will eventually come down to one thing—tackling the guy with the football. That most fundamental skill for a defensive player is really becoming a big issue in today's NFL. Ironically, you could probably trace the decline of tackling skills back to Ronnie Lott—one of the greatest players of all time. In his 14 seasons with the 49ers, the Raiders, and the Jets, Lott was a great form tackler but preferred putting his shoulder into ball carriers. Fans loved that kind of physicality, and *SportsCenter* and other highlight shows fed their appetite by featuring hits like those each and every Sunday evening. Young players would watch Lott and wanted to emulate him—only they didn't have his speed or ability to recognize a developing play. When those young players want to throw a 'Ronnie Lott tackle,' they'd miss their guy."
- A tackler who faces down the ball carrier at point-blank range has him *dead to rights*.

- A *gang tackle* is executed by multiple players, massing around the ball carrier; the opposite is a solo or unassisted tackle.
- A ball carrier is *in the grasp* and the play is whistled dead when he is wrapped up with his forward progress stopped, even though he has not yet been brought down to the ground.
- In early football, there was no such thing as forward progress. Henderson Van Surdam played from 1902 to 1905 at Wesleyan. He reminisced, "In those days if you happened to be tackled in a mass play and were being pushed back, you yelled 'Down' at the top of your voice to save losing yardage by being pushed back. The ball was dead where you yelled 'Down.' "
- Even without defenders around, the grass monster can still bring down the most confident ball carrier. Don't be frightened, just be embarrassed. A player running free who loses his footing and stumbles to the ground was felled by the *grass monster* (on a natural surface) or a *turf monster* (on an artificial surface).
- In a *horse-collar tackle*, the ball carrier is grabbed by the back of his collar and yanked dangerously backward to the ground. This will generate a yellow flag.
- In a *necktie tackle*, a favorite of Dick "Night Train" Lane, often equated to the clothesline, the ball carrier is grabbed around the neck and pulled down.
- An *open-field tackle* occurs as a one-on-one tackle in space, away from the rest of the players on the field.
- A defender who *stands up* or *stacks up* a ball carrier halts that ball carrier's momentum and holds him in place.

break a tackle
v. bully past/through, dart free, escape, extricate from, get away, pull away, shake off, shed, slip, step out of a tackle

Wahoo!

- A Bob Carroll story: "Linebacker 'Wahoo' McDaniel was the Jets' first star, albeit a manufactured one. A fair defender, he had that great nickname. The Jets' PA man began asking the crowd, 'Who made that last tackle?' and the crowd would answer back, 'Wahoo!' Soon tackles were being credited to Wahoo when McDaniel was 20 feet away from the play." He was easy to spot on this field—it was WAHOO on his jersey, not McDaniel—and he certainly had a flair for the dramatic, transitioning easily from the gridiron to a second career as a high-profile professional wrestler.

tackle (player)

n. T; DEFENSE see **defensive line, defensive tackle, nose tackle**; OFFENSE see **offensive line, offensive tackle**

team

n. aggregation, brigade, cast, club, competitor, contender, contingent, eleven, gang, outfit, phalanx, platoon, side, squad, squadron, unit; SPECIFIC bench mafia, bench mob, cab squad, champions, college team, contender, cupcake, dynasty, elite team, first team, goon squad, junior varsity (J.V.), practice squad, professional team, scout team, second team, spoiler, standard bearers, taxi squad, top-ranked team, varsity; POWERFUL goliath, juggernaut, powerhouse, steamroller; LESS THAN FAVORED Cinderella, David, dark horse, long shot, underdog, upstart

"This is a team game and you want to win as a team. It's not about me, it's about winning."—Oakland Raiders linebacker Khalil Mack

home team
n. fan favorites, hometown squad, hosts, occupants, residents

road team
n. guests, visitors

Terms and Jargon

- The *roster* lists a team's players.
- The *depth chart* places the team's roster in the perspective of starters and reserves. The *two-deep* lists all

starters (first-string / first team) and their immediate backups (second-string / second team); the *three-deep* lists the starters and the next two players waiting in line.

- The *bench mafia* or *bench mob* refers to a proud crew of second- and third-stringers (nonstarters). See **football player, nonstarter**.

- The *practice squad*, *taxi squad*, or *cab squad* is a ten-man unit (increased from eight in August 2014) of young pro football players under contract who are allowed to practice with their team but not play for them. Should a member of the team's regular roster go down with an injury, a member of the practice squad is often signed to the roster in his place.

- A team placed on the practice squad is *stashed* or *smuggled* there.

- A team that signs a player from another team's practice squad *poaches* him.

- The *taxi squad* name has a literal origin. Cleveland Browns head coach Paul Brown had more players he wanted to keep around than he was allowed to hang onto in the 1940s, with rosters limited to 33 players. To retain those extra players in Cleveland, they were "employed" by Browns owner Arthur McBride's Zone/Yellow Cab company.

- The *scout team*, sometimes used synonymously with the practice squad, serves the role of playing like the upcoming opposition in practice, thus preparing the team for the coming game.

- A *spoiler* is a team that deals an unexpected defeat to an opponent that needed (and maybe even expected) to win, whether to clinch a postseason berth or near a milestone.

tight end

n. TE; SPECIFIC blocking tight end, bruising tight end, complete tight end, F, flex tight end, in-line tight end, joker, receiving tight end, traditional tight end, Y

"People say, 'Since you got rich and famous, you've become insufferable.'
I say, 'That's not true. I've always been insufferable.' "— Shannon Sharpe

Terms and Jargon

- A tight end ideally combines the skills of a lineman and a wide receiver, and sets up either in the backfield, *tight* (next to the tackle along the line of scrimmage), or *wide* (spread out from the line as a receiver).
- A *complete tight end* is equally adept at blocking and receiving.
- The *joker* can run any pass pattern out of any formation, credited first to Kellen Winslow, Sr., and personified by the record-setting Tony Gonzalez.
- From "Why did the Patriots embrace tight ends?" Greg A. Bedard's article for the *Boston Globe*, September 5, 2012, "The Patriots have always had two classes of tight ends. There is the traditional 'Y,' who job requirements read: 6 feet 5 inches or taller, at least 255 pounds, can run but absolutely must be a standout blocker. He has to be a viable receiver, but not a great one. The 'F' or flex tight end is 6-3 or taller, around 235 pounds, must be able to run and be an excellent pass receiver. Does not need to be a good blocker." After watching the Patriots utilizing their tight ends in 2012, Atlanta Falcons head coach Mike Smith declared, "They're like queens on the chessboard."

timeout / time-out
n. stoppage, time, TO / T-O; SPECIFIC charged timeout, official timeout

use a timeout
v. ask for, burn, call, call for, consume, eat, get, request, take, waste

Terms and Jargon

- AP Style holds that the word is written as "timeout." Chicago Style holds fast to a "time-out" spelling.
- Each team receives three timeouts per half.

- A *charged timeout* is either taken by a team or specifically charged to them as penalty for challenging a play to be replayed and having that play upheld.
- An *official timeout* occurs due to injury (except in the final two minutes of the half), penalty, measurement, end of quarter, conference (with fellow officials or with a head coach), or replay review.
- The privilege of calling a timeouts used to be restricted to team captains. (This was difficult on rugged lineman Bob St. Claire, who was voted captain but soon learned "if the quarterback needed a quick time-out, the referee couldn't be looking for me because I'd be off somewhere with my face in the mud.") Soon any player on the field was given the ability to call a timeout. In today's NFL, the head coach is now included among those who can ask for a TO.
- Mike Shanahan is credited as being the first coach to call a timeout in the split-second before the ball was snapped for an opposition field goal attempt. This tactic is known as *icing* the kicker.
- Time management is one of the biggest keys to any football game—how a coach uses his play-calling and timeouts to best serve his team and deny the opponent. Poor time management sees a coach uses his timeouts too soon, costing his team late, or fail to utilize them at all. As one axiom goes: You can't take the timeouts with you; either use them or lose them.

Joe Schmidt Loses His Mind

- "I should think you could lose your mind out there," said George Plimpton to Detroit Lions quarterbacks Milt Plum and Earl Morrall. That led Plum and Morrall to tell Plimpton the following tale, as related in *Paper Lion*:

  Apparently, Joe Schmidt once was sent into a preseason exhibition game in the terrible late summer heat of Texas with only a few seconds to go. Detroit was leading. The Philadelphia Eagles had the ball in Detroit territory, but all their timeouts had expired. Schmidt ordered a rush on Van Brocklin, the Eagle quarterback, and dropped him as he was trying to get off a long, last pass. The second hand on the clock swept around and the onlookers stood up to begin filing out of the park. Whereupon Joe Schmidt called: "Time out!"

The referee looked at him blankly for a second or so. His eyebrows then arched up, and he blew his whistle to stop the clock with five seconds to go. The players all stared at Schmidt. Some of them had started off the field, expecting to hear the final gun before they reached the sidelines. Schmidt himself couldn't think then, or ever, why he had shouted for a timeout. He said, "Maybe I just wanted a drink out of one of those little paper cups. The heat was horrible out there." The time-out gave Van Brocklin another chance to throw the football, which he did with success—connecting for a touchdown.

touchdown

n. counter, house call, payoff, score, six, tally, TD, touch, tug; SPECIFIC fat guy touchdown, game-tying touchdown, go-ahead touchdown, kick-return touchdown, passing touchdown, punt-return touchdown, receiving touchdown, return touchdown, rushing touchdown, scoring pass, scoring run, tie-breaking touchdown

score a touchdown
v. find the end zone, get in, get into the end zone, go all the way, go the distance, make a house call, ring the bell, strike pay dirt, take it the distance, take to the house

score a touchdown from in close
v. carry across, go over, plunge in, plunge over, pour it in, punch in, punch it

History, Terms, and Jargon

- The term *touchdown* comes from football's parent sport,

rugby. In rugby, in order for a player to score a "try," he must bring the ball across the white stripe signifying the in-goal zone of the opposition, whereupon he has to touch the ball down to the ground, "grounding" it. The idea of breaking the white line retained meaning, as did the idea of an after-touchdown/after-try kick for bonus points, but there's no need for a football player to do anything at the goal line except retain possession to score a touchdown. (After a touchdown is another matter: handing the ball to the referee, spiking the ball, dancing, and vaulting into the stands in Green Bay on a "Lambeau Leap" are all legal.)

- For much of football's first three decades, a touchdown was worth four points. It was adjusted to five points in 1898 and to six points in 1912.
- A ball carrier on his way to scoring a touchdown is "Gone!" sometimes heard with a lead-in of "He could go!" or a "There he goes!" ESPN's Chris Berman's staccato turn of phrase: "He – could – go – all – the – way!"
- The *fat guy touchdown* is a recent cult favorite, and it describes exactly what you'd think: one of the largest players on the field throwing for a touchdown (highest marks), catching a touchdown, rushing for a touchdown, or picking up a loose ball and lumbering for a touchdown.
- While *house call*, *touch*, and *tug* are more recent slang terms for touchdown, payoff dates back quite a while. Consider Ted Papes's description in the *Michigan Daily*, October 6, 1951: "Titan Bob Lippe hoisted a punt from his own 31 to Billy Barrett who fielded the ball on the Notre Dame 27, then slipped it to Petitbon who flashed down the chalk line again for a 73-yard payoff."
- *Six the other way* refers to a fumble or interception return for a touchdown. If a quarterback narrowly misses throwing an interception in the flat, with only daylight ahead of the prospective defender, an announcer might be heard to gasp, "That could've been six the other way!"

- If a player scores a touchdown easily, without getting touched by the defense, it's a *walk* (or *stroll*) in the park.

Furthermore

- Pennsylvania high schooler Joe Sobucki had himself one heck of a moment on October 8, 2010. WR/RB Sobucki received a shotgun snap in the Wildcat formation, and then, Cameron Smith wrote for *Yahoo.com*, "he tossed a 2-yard screen to teammate Anthony Stuart, then made a beeline to Stuart's side of the field. As Stuart was going down he saw Sobucki running alongside and pitched it back to his quarterback in a classic hook-and-ladder maneuver, with Sobucki bursting through the gap and flying down the sideline the remaining 86 yards to the end zone. 'We just call that "Oop-de-oop," Sobucki told the [*Erie*] *Times-News*." Summing up: an 82-yard touchdown pass for Joe Sobucki—and an 86-yard touchdown gallop to help his own cause.
- From an article by Lindsay H. Jones in *USA Today*, September 24, 2013: "[Ronnie] Hillman, unseated as the starter at the end of the preseason, averaged 7.3 yards per carry on his nine attempts and carried the Broncos on a drive all the way to the 1-yard line early in the fourth quarter. As the officials deliberated if Hillman had crossed the goal line after a 13-yard gain, Hillman, [Knowshon] Moreno and [Montee] Ball decided to play rock-paper-scissors for which running back would get the goal-line carry if the score was overturned. Hillman said Moreno threw down a rock one beat too early and was disqualified, and Hillman's scissors trumped Ball's paper. So on the next play, it was Hillman's touchdown."

trick play

n. dipsy doo, gadget, gadget play, gadgetry, gamble, garbage play, gimmick play, gimmickry, hipper dipper play, hocus pocus, razzle-dazzle, razzle dazzle, schoolyard play, trickeration, trick up one's sleeve; SPECIFIC The Annexation of Puerto Rico, bounce pass, bounce rooski, Clock Play, double pass, double reverse, fake field goal, fake knee, fake punt, fake spike, flea-flicker, fumblerooski, halfback option, halfback pass, hidden ball, hideout, trick, Holy Roller, hook and ladder / hook and lateral, jump pass, Little Giants, misdirection punt return, Music City Miracle, onside kick, Puntrooskie, reverse, reverse flea-flicker, sleeper play, Statue of Liberty, swinging gate, throwback pass, wide receiver option, The Wrong Ball

- A coach who calls for a trick play *reaches up his sleeve* (like a magician) or *rolls the dice* (like a gambler).
- A *garbage play* seems a rather nasty designation for a trick play, doesn't it? As described in Hollander and Zimmerman's *Football Lingo*, garbage plays describe "[p]lays in which the spacing is so wide, the alignment so weird, the execution so tricky in concept that they are considered to be outside the realm of normal football—in other words, garbage. They often have spectacular results. The San Francisco 49ers had one favorite garbage play in which Y.A. Tittle, the quarterback, rolled out to one side, wheeled, and fired completely cross field to Hugh McElhenny, his great running back, who had sneakily drifted out there with a couple of linemen for support. The play usually lost 5 yards or gained 50."
- Louisiana State head coach Les Miles received the nickname "The Mad Hatter" in part due to his perpetual LSU baseball cap and in part due to his risky decisions and tendency toward razzle-dazzle. For this latter trait, Miles is often compared to the riverboat gambler of lore.

Specific Plays

- In the *bounce rooski*, also known as the *bounce pass*, the quarterback purposely bounces a wide receiver screen pass behind the line of scrimmage. The receiver grabs the pass on a hop while feigning disappointment at the failed play… and then quickly fires downfield to an open teammate. The key: the original pass must be thrown backward, keeping the ball live. Colorado State's 1966 one-hop bounce pass against #10 Wyoming, leading to a Rams upset victory, is perhaps the most famed play in CSU school history.

- The *fake spike* (also called the *Clock Play*) was unveiled by Miami Dolphins quarterback Dan Marino on November 27, 1994. Rushing to the line with 30 seconds remaining, his Dolphins trailing the New York Jets 24-21, Marino (shouting "Clock! Clock!") faked a spike to stop the clock and found Mark Ingram for a game-winning touchdown. When the Green Bay Packers' Aaron Rodgers repeated the feat in Miami on October 12, 2014, indicating that he would spike the ball before suddenly zipping a pass to Davante Adams with seven seconds left to set up the Packers' eventual winning score, he was described as "pulling a Marino."

- The *flea-flicker* was devised by Illinois offensive wizard Bob Zuppke who named it, according to Hollander and Zimmerman's *Football Lingo*, after "the quick, flicking action of a dog getting rid of fleas." In the flea-flicker, the running back takes a handoff and starts toward the line before quickly turning and pitching the ball back to the quarterback. With the defense pressing for the line on a prospective running play, a wide receiver heads deep and the quarterback lets it fly. A *reverse flea-flicker* sees the offense run a reverse before flipping the ball back to the quarterback for a designed pass.

- The *fumblerooski*, credited to John Heisman, sees the football left immediately on the ground after the snap; with the offense all flowing in one direction, a lineman slips behind the play, picks up the ball, and rumbles into the open field. The play was most famously pulled off by Nebraska in the 1984 Orange Bowl against Miami, and then replicated on the silver screen in 1994's *Little Giants* as "The Annexation of Puerto Rico." ("Fumblerooski!" hollers opposing head coach Kevin O'Shea, spotting the deception.) The play has now been legislated against at both the college and professional levels. Michigan State University pulled off its own

"Little Giants" play on September 18, 2010, though it was no fumblerooski. The Spartans executed a fake field goal in overtime, with holder Aaron Bates lofting a game-winning touchdown pass to tight end Charles Grantt. ("We always name our trick plays after movies," said MSU head coach Mark Dantonio.)

- *The Golden Stairs* was an effective trick play in which the New York Giants' Eddie Price received a handoff and leveraged his way off the backs of his offensive linemates, climbing a stairway of bodies before vaulting over the lines and into the end zone. The Cleveland Browns were ready in the 1950 postseason, however. As Price pushed up his offensive-linemen-turned-stairs, standout defender Bill Willis climbed up an answering defensive-linemen-turned-stairway, met Price at the acme, and firmly halted his efforts.

- The *halfback option/pass* and *wide receiver option/pass* each place the ball in the hands of an offensive player unlikely to throw the ball—which makes it all the more unexpected when they suddenly let fly downfield.

- The now-illegal *hidden ball play* was used to great effect by Pop Warner's Carlisle Indians around the turn of the twentieth century. It saw a player grab the football, put it underneath his shirt, let his teammates scatter (many of whom are doubled over, pretending they have the ball), and then head nonchalantly for the end zone, has long since faded from memory. "Percy Haughton, the old Harvard coach, had an ingenious way of testing a trick play in practice," wrote Zander Hollander. "He would scent a ball and let Pooch, his wife's cocker spaniel, smell it. At practice if the ball was hidden so well that Pooch would chase a player without the ball, Haughton knew he had a play that would work."

- The *Holy Roller* was dropped, bounced, hopped, and batted into infamy by the Oakland Raiders, September 10, 1978. Down 20-14 to San Diego in the dying seconds, Raiders quarterback Ken Stabler was wrapped up from behind in a seeming sack. With desperation, he fumbled the ball forward. Running back Pete Banaszak was next on the scene, reaching the pigskin and flinging it forward. Tight end Dave Casper helped the ball the rest of the way, herding it into the end zone, where he fell upon it for a touchdown. With Errol Mann's extra point, the Raiders had won and the Chargers were furious. It is now prohibited for any offensive player aside from the fumbler to recover and advance a loose ball on a fourth down or in the final two minutes of a half.

- The *hook and lateral* (often pronounced, in corrupted slang, as the *hook and ladder*) has a receiver run a hook pattern, take in a pass from the quarterback, and deftly lateral the ball to a galloping teammate cutting around them. Facing a 4th and 18, the upstart Boise State Broncos forced overtime against Oklahoma in the 2007 Fiesta Bowl with a well-timed hook and lateral, nicknamed "Circus" in the team's playbook.

- The *jump pass* sees the ball carrier, whether quarterback or running back, approach the line on a seeming rush before leaping upward and tossing over the line to an open receiver. The play was a favorite of the Florida Gators and quarterback Tim Tebow from 2007-2009.

- The *misdirection (fake) punt return* was introduced to the NFL by the Chicago Bears on September 25, 2011. Down by 10 to the Green Bay Packers in crunch time, the Bears sent punt returner Devin Hester to one side of the field, seemingly waiting underneath a Packer punt, while Johnny Knox sneaked to the other side of the field and the ball's true destination. The play resulted in a Knox 88-yard touchdown return, but it was called back by a holding penalty. Credit the St. Louis Rams for paying attention. On October 19, 2014, the Rams executed the fake perfectly; Stedman Bailey fielded a Jon Ryan punt on the right side of the field while his teammates deked the Seattle Seahawks into pursuing left. Bailey's ensuing touchdown led the Rams to an upset win over the eventual NFC champions. Seahawks head coach Pete Carroll was a gracious loser; his description of the special-teams trickery: "unbelievably cool."

- The *Puntrooskie* (shortened sometimes to *The 'Rooskie*) was pulled out of a hat by the Florida State Seminoles, who relish its legacy every year when the play's anniversary rolls around. On September 18, 1988, the Seminoles and Clemson Tigers were tied at 21-21 with 90 seconds remaining. Punting from their own 21-yard-line, the snap was received by up-back Dayne Williams, who handed it through the legs of the fellow up-back LeRoy Butler. The Tigers searched madly for the ball while Butler took off for the sideline, eventually knocked out of bounds at the Clemson 1 to set up an FSU game-winning field goal. "The greatest play since My Fair Lady," said ESPN analyst Beano Cook.
- The *sleeper play*, sometimes called the *hideout*, tests the defense's alertness. Ten members of the offense line up around the ball, but the eleventh sneakily hides near the bench (a sleeper agent, of sorts).
- After the hook and lateral brought Boise State to OT in the 2007 Fiesta Bowl, the *Statue of Liberty* (playcall: "Statue") won the game for the BSU Broncos. The titular role is played by the quarterback, who reaches Lady Liberty's pose with one hand high and the other low by pumpfaking with an empty hand while simultaneously holding the ball behind his back. From this position, a passing running back or receiver is free to take a no-look handoff and skirt his way past a confused defense. The Statue of Liberty was first utilized by Amos Alonzo Stagg, with his University of Chicago superstar Clarence Herschberger taking full advantage.
- The *swinging gate* puts the offensive line save for the center set up on one side of the field, with the quarterback and a running back behind the center. In this formation, a quick toss to a receiver behind the line allows the gate (line) to swing forward and pick up easy yardage.
- Following misdirection toward one side of the field, the *throwback* is passed to the opposite side of the field,

sometimes to a tight end, sometimes to a wide receiver, and sometimes even to a quarterback handing off to a back and sneaking away down the sideline. The most famous throwback was the "Music City Miracle," executed by the Tennessee Titans on a kickoff return to grab a shocking win in their Wild Card playoff contest against the Buffalo Bills. A Steve Christie field goal had given the Bills a 16-15 lead with 16 seconds left; the ensuing kick was taken in by Lorenzo Neal, who handed the ball to Frank Wycheck heading toward the right side of the field. With the Bills angling toward him, Wycheck turned and fired back across the field to an open Kevin Dyson, who dashed his way behind a wall of blockers to a winning 75-yard score. The play was controversial: Was Wycheck's pass a true lateral, or did it travel illegally forward? The ruling stood, and the Titans advanced.

- "The Wrong Ball Trick" is a classic at youth levels. Once the official declares the ball fit to be snapped, the quarterback begins to complain. The offensive line remains still, but inconspicuous, as the quarterback tells everyone within earshot that the ball is wrong. In mock disgust, he asks for the center to give him the ball, which his helpful teammate snaps into his waiting hands. Now in possession with the play live, the quarterback marches the ball toward his sideline, asking for a different ball. Once he reaches the corner, freedom is his, and he makes a break for it. (In a variation, "The Fake Penalty Trick," the quarterback complains about an uncalled penalty, declares that he'll step off the yardage himself, demands the ball from the center, and starts marching forward through an unsuspecting defense.)

turnover

n. boo-boo, gift, no-no, TO, TRN, TURN; SPECIFIC fumble, giveaway, interception, muff, takeaway (TAK)

turn the ball over

v. gift, giftwrap, give away, give up, leave behind, lose, surrender, yield; SPECIFIC see **fumble**

Terms and Jargon

- A *turnover* changes possession of the football, turning the ball over to the other team to the other team's offense. See both **fumble** and **interception** for more.
- *Takeaways* refer to turnovers collected by one team, while *giveaways* are the turnovers collected by that team's opponent. The underlying meaning: If we get a turnover, we took it. (Full credit to us.) If they get a turnover, we gave it away. (Full blame to us.) In the same vein, teams both commit turnovers and force turnovers, and you can immediately tell the difference between the two: You "commit" a giveaway—but "force" a takeaway.
- *Ball security* refers to how well a team does at limiting its own turnovers. A team that commits many turnovers is "loose with the football." If a team has outstanding ball security, committing scant turnovers, it "takes care of the football."
- *Total turnovers* are judged in plus-minus ratio, comparing giveaways to takeaways. A team that forces three turnovers from its opponent while at the same time committing one turnover of its own is +2 in turnover ratio.

U

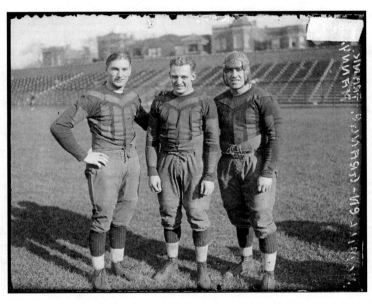

Harold "Red" Grange is flanked by two Chicago Bears teammates at the team's home field, Weeghman Field (later Wrigley Field), 1925.

undefeated

n. spotless, unbeaten, unblemished, unbowed, unconquered, without defeat

Notable Undefeated Teams...and the 2007 Patriots

- One of the most famous non-champions of their heyday, the Colgate Red Raiders finished the 1932 season without a loss—and also without a championship-game invite. Wrote John Kekis for the Associated Press, December 13, 1987, "all they did was finish the year undefeated, untied and unscored upon, beating their opponents by a combined 264-0. Until the last game of the season, no team got inside the Colgate 20-yard line. Ah, but that was also when only two teams got to a bowl—the Rose Bowl." The onus was placed on Southern Cal, champ of the west coast, to decide its opponent. The Trojans selected the Pittsburgh Panthers. Coach Andy Kerr and the Colgate Red Raiders were left in the cold.

- There has only been one undefeated season in the NFL's modern era, that of Don Shula's 1972 Miami Dolphins, who won the AFC East with a 14-0 record, downed the Cleveland Browns 20-14, stopped the Pittsburgh Steelers 21-17, and doubled up the Washington Redskins 14-7 to win Super Bowl VII.

- Thirty-five years later, the 2007 New England Patriots nearly bested the Dolphins' mark, winning all 16 of their regular-season games before eliminating first the Jacksonville Jaguars (31-20) and then the San Diego Chargers (21-12) to put themselves on the brink of glory. But Eli Manning and the New York Giants popped the Patriots' dream season with a 17-14 victory in Super Bowl XLII, leaving New England with a mere 18-1 overall record.

uniform

n. armor, attire, clothing, colors, duds, ensemble, garb, garment, gear, jersey, outfit, uni, wardrobe; see **jersey**

Cast Iron Pads and Colorful Pants

- The *uniform* more specifically refers to the total ensemble worn by a player: helmet, pads, jersey shirt, pants, cleats. (The short-lived Duluth Eskimos wore entirely white uniforms.)

- Types of football equipment pads and protection: athletic supporter (jock), gloves, elbow pads, hip pads, knee pads, mouth guard, rib pads, shoulder pads, tailbone pads, thigh pads.
- There has long been the tale that Jim Thorpe used sheet metal—cast iron, in some tellings—as his shoulder pads, or underneath his shoulder pads. "Of course, the insinuation was completely false," wrote William A. Cook in *Jim Thorpe: A Biography*. "The only metal in Thorpe's shoulder pads was just a small bit in the interior ribbing to hold the layers of felt padding in place. The pads were constructed of hard sole leather that was riveted together. In fact, Jack Cusack and Thorpe had plans to market the pads, but a manufacturer they approached was wary of them, concerned that they might be classed as illegal. So they abandoned the project."
- The World Football League's plans for color-coded pants was no myth. From the WFL's own press release, June 30, 1975:

  New York—In an attempt to increase the fan's understanding and enjoyment of pro football, the World Football League will experiment during the exhibition season with pants that will be color–coded to a player's position.

  All offensive linemen will wear purple pants, running backs green pants and receivers orange pants, while defensive lineman will be dressed in blue, linebackers in red and defensive backs in yellow. The various colors are emphasized by vertical striping. Quarterbacks and kickers will wear white.

  Chris Hemmeter, president of the World Football League, announced that the experiment will be tried in four games. They are Memphis at San Antonio and Southern California at Philadelphia on July 19, Hawaiians at Jacksonville on July 26 and Philadelphia at Portland on July 27.

The various colored pants are the idea of William B. Finneran, a New York management consultant, who devised the action point for last year's WFL.

Finneran refers to the pants idea as "color dynamics" which he defines as "the concept of implementing means whereby one's visual appreciation of dynamic movement is significantly increased."

Color coding will allow the fan to be constantly on top of what is happening on the playing field. Who is that player cutting across midfield that the quarterback is throwing to? Is it a receiver or is it a running back out of the backfield? Who is desperately trying to cover that receiver? Is it a defensive back? Or has the receiver been isolated on a linebacker?

The pants, which Finneran refers to as "color grids", will provide the answer as the action is taking place. And the term "red dog" which means a linebacker blitz of the quarterback will now have real relevance.

The idea was soon scrapped, and the color-coded pants were never worn during a WFL regular season game. On October 22, 1975, the league shut down.

W

Celebrating the win in 1960 NFL Championship Game: Philadelphia Eagles players center/linebacker Chuck Bednarik (60), quarterback Norm Van Brocklin (11) and fullback Ted Dean (35) congratulate head coach Buck Shaw. (AP Photo/NFL Photos.)

wide receiver (WR)

see **receiver**

win

n. success, triumph, victory, W; SPECIFIC easy win, statement

win, upset win
v. see **defeat**

"This is what's great about sports. This is what the greatest thing about sports is. You play to win the game. Hello? You play to win the game. You don't play it to just play it. That's the great thing about sports. You play to win. And I don't care if you don't have any wins. You go play to win. When you start telling me it doesn't matter, then retire. Get out. 'Cause it matters."—Herman Edwards, head coach of the New York Jets; October 30, 2002

overwhelming victory
annihilation, avalanche, battering, beating, blasting, blowout, bombardment, cakewalk, clobbering, decimation, destruction, demolition, devastation, dismantling, domination, drubbing, embarrassment, fiasco, flattening, humiliation, lambasting, laugher, licking, lopsided victory, mashing, massacre, mauling, obliteration, one-sided win, plastering, pounding, pummeling, ravaging, romp, rout, ruination, runaway, savaging, shellacking, shredding, slaughter, smackdown, smashing, spanking, squash, steamrolling, stomping, swamping, thrashing, throttling, thumping, trashing, trouncing, walkover, walloping, wasting, waxing, whipping, whomping, whupping

shutout victory
v. blanking, blanketing, quieting, silencing, skunking, whitewashing

Specific Terms

- You can find many a coach and quite a few players, too, who don't believe that there is a such thing as a *moral victory*. A moral victory, after all, can only come in a loss.
- A *statement win* is termed as such because it makes a powerful statement as to the quality of the victorious team, either to themselves, to their conference/league, or to the country.
- To *win out* means to win every remaining game left on the schedule.

"I don't think it's possible to be too intent on winning. If we played for any other reason, we would be dishonest. This country is built on winning and on that alone. Winning is still the most honorable thing a man can do."—Woody Hayes

222 to 0

- "The world immediately recognizes three sets of figures," wrote historian G. Frank Burns, "2001, December 7, and 222 to 0. The first is a movie, the second is a day that lives in infamy, and the third is indissolubly connected with Cumberland football, a veritable landmark of American sports." On October 7, 1916, John Heisman's Ramblin' Wreck from Georgia Tech wrecked poor Cumberland College by that score, the most lopsided rout in football annals. ("There was a worse defeat in prep school records," Burns noted, "but the 227 to 0 win by Dickinson over Haverford is suspect.") The photograph of the final scoreboard register speaks for itself: 63 points for Tech in both the first and second quarters, 54 more in the third, and an icing-applying 42 points in the final period. Lonely zeroes from Cumberland sit beneath. Historian Burns did his best to clear up myths surrounding the game, including noting, "Cumberland's longest gain was NOT a two-yard loss; there was one forward pass completed for a ten-yard gain. Unfortunately it was fourth and 22 at the time. The truth is bad enough. Neither team made a first down. Cumberland couldn't, and Tech scored every time it got the ball....Cumberland's total net yardage was minus 28. Except for touchdown runs, every play in the game was run by the Cumberland team. The second half was cut short, by fifteen minutes." It's fun to note that there was a bit of a pregame narrative to the beating. During the previous spring, Cumberland had routed Georgia Tech 22-0 on the baseball diamond. (The Cumberland baseball team was actually a "Nashville pro team masquerading as Cumberland College," according to Jack Wilkinson, in an article for the *Atlanta Journal-Constitution* reposted on

RamblinWreck.com.) In August 2014, the price of $40,388 was paid for a game ball from the memorable rout in an auction, with patent attorney Ryan Schneider, a Georgia Tech grad, returning the keepsake to his alma mater for safe keeping.

BIBLIOGRAPHY

Article

Burns, G. Frank, Cumberland College historian."The Story of the Game of the Century"

Books

Aaboe, Niels. *The Little Red Book of Football Wisdom*. New York, NY: Skyhorse Publishing, 2013.

Allen, George, with Weiskopf, Don. *Inside Football: Fundamentals, Strategy, and Tactics for Winning*. Boston, MA: Allyn and Bacon, Inc., 1970.

American Football Coaches Association. *Defensive Football Strategies*. Champaign, IL: Human Kinetics, 2000.

American Football Coaches Association. *Offensive Football Strategies*. Champaign, IL: Human Kinetics, 2000.

Arthur, Howard, and Ebeling, Alvin. *The Falcon Illustrated Football Dictionary*. New York, NY: Young Readers Press, Inc., 1971, 1972.

Barry, Dave. *Dave Barry's Bad Habits*. New York, NY: Henry Holt and Company, Inc., 1987.

Barry, Dave. *Dave Barry Talks Back*. New York, NY: Three Rivers Press, 1991.

Belichick, Steve. *Football Scouting Methods*. New York, NY: The

Ronald Press Company, 1962; reissued by Saratoga, CA: Liber Apertus Press, 2008.

Berghaus, Bob. *Black and Blue*. Cincinnati, OH: Clerisy Press, 2007.

Bradley, John P.; Daniels, Leo F.; and Jones, Thomas C.; compilers. *The International Dictionary of Thoughts*. United States: J.G. Ferguson Publishing Co., 1969.

Brown, Chris B. *The Essential Smart Football*. CreateSpace Independent Publishing Platform, 2012.

Carroll, Bob. *When the Grass was Real: Unitas, Brown, Lombardi, Sayers, Butkus, Namath, and All the Rest: The Best Ten Years of Pro Football*. New York, NY: Simon & Schuster, 1993.

Carroll, Bob; Palmer, Pete; and Thorn, John. *The Football Abstract*. New York, NY: Professional Ink, Inc., 1989.

Connelly, Bill. *Study Hall: College Football, its Stats and its Stories*. CreateSpace Independent Publishing Platform, 2013.

Conner, Floyd. *Football's Most Wanted: The Top 10 Book of the Great Game's Outrageous Characters, Fortunate Fumbles, and Other Oddities*. Washington, D.C.: Brassey's, 2000.

Cook, William A. *Jim Thorpe: A Biography*. Jefferson, NC: McFarland, 2011.

Daly, Dan. *The National Forgotten League: Entertaining Stories and Observations from Pro Football's First Fifty Years*. Omaha, NE: University of Nebraska Press, 2012.

Daly, Dan, and O'Donnell, Bob. *The Pro Football Chronicle*. New York, NY: Collier Books/MacMillan Publishing Company, 1990.

Danzig, Allison. *Oh, How They Played the Game: The Early Days of Football and the Heroes Who Made It Great*. New York, NY: The MacMillan Company, 1971.

Epstein, Noel, publisher and editor. *Redskins: A History of Washington's Team*. Washington, D.C.: Washington Post Books, 1997.

Fatsis, Stefan. *A Few Seconds of Panic*. New York, NY: The Penguin Press, 2008.

Feinstein, John. *Next Man Up: A Year Behind the Lines in Today's NFL*. New York, NY: Little, Brown, and Company: 2005.

Fortin, François. *Sports: The Complete Visual Reference*. Buffalo, NY: Firefly Books Inc., 2000.

Freedman, Samuel G. *Breaking the Line: The Season in Black College Football that Transformed the Sport and Changed the Course of Civil Rights*. New York, NY: Simon & Schuster, 2013.

Herskowitz, Mickey, and Perkins, Steve. *Everything You Wanted to Know About Sports* (*and didn't know where to ask)*. New York, NY: Signet, 1977.

Hollander, Zander. *The Encyclopedia of Sports Talk*. New York, NY: Corwin Books, 1976.

Hollander, Zander, and Zimmerman, Paul. *Football Lingo*. New York, NY: W.W. Norton & Company, 1967.

Holtzman, Jerome. *No Cheering in the Press Box*. New York, NY: Henry Holt and Company, 1995 (revised edition).

Horrigan, Joe, and Thorn, John, editors. *The Pro Football Hall of Fame 50th Anniversary Book: Where Greatness Lives*. New York, NY: Grand Central Publishing, 2012.

Jenkins, Dan. *You Call it Sports, but I Say It's a Jungle Out There*. New York, NY: Simon and Schuster, 1989.

Kilmeade, Brian. *The Games Do Count*. New York, NY: HarperCollins Publishers Inc., 2004.

Kirwan, Pat, with Seigerman, David. *Take Your Eye Off the Ball*. Chicago, IL: Triumph Books, 2010, 2011.

Kramer, Jerry, with Schaap, Dick, editor. *Instant Replay: The Green*

Bay Diary of Jerry Kramer. New York, NY: New American Library, 1968.

Layden, Tim. *Blood, Sweat and Chalk: The Ultimate Playbook.* New York, NY: Time Home Entertainment Inc., 2011.

Leuthner, Stuart. *Iron Men: Bucko, Crazylegs, and the Boys Recall the Golden Days of Professional Football.* New York, NY: Doubleday, 1988.

Lewin, Esther, and Lewin, Albert E. *The Thesaurus of Slang*: Revised and Expanded Edition. New York, NY: Facts on File, 1994.

Lewis, Michael. *The Blind Side.* New York, NY: W.W. Norton & Company, 2006.

Liebman, Glenn. *Football Shorts: 1,001 of the Game's Funniest One-Liners.* Lincolnwood (Chicago), IL: Contemporary Books, 1997.

Long, Howie, and Czarnecki, John. *Football For Dummies*, 4th Edition. Hoboken, NJ: John Wiley & Sons, Inc., 2011.

Madden, John. *One Knee Equals Two Feet.* New York, NY: Villard Books, 1986.

Michelson, Herb, and Newhouse, Dave. *Rose Bowl Football: since 1902.* Briarcliff Manor, NY: Stein and Day, 1977.

Nash, Bruce, and Zullo, Allan. *The Football Hall of Shame 2.* New York, NY: Pocket Books, 1990.

Neft, David S., and Cohen, Richard M. *Pro Football: The Early Years* (An Encyclopedic History, 1895-1959). Sports Products, Inc, 1979.

Paolantonio, Sal, with Frank, Reuben. *The Paolantonio Report.* Chicago, IL: Triumph Books, 2007.

Peterson, Robert W. *Pigskin: The Early Years of Pro Football.* New York, NY: Oxford University Press, 1997.

Piascik, Andy. *Gridiron Gauntlet: The Story of the Men Who Inte-*

grated Pro Football in Their Own Words. Lanham, MD: Taylor Trade Publishing, 2009.

Plimpton, George. *Paper Lion*. New York, NY: Harper & Row, 1965, 1966.

Porter, David L., editor. *Biographical Dictionary of American Sports: Football*. Westport, CT: Greenwood Press, Inc., 1987.

Rielly, Edward J. *Football: An Encyclopedia of Popular Culture*. Published by the Board of Regents of the University of Nebraska, 2009.

Roberts, Howard. *The Big Nine: the story of football in the Western Conference*. New York, NY: G.P. Putnam & Sons, 1948.

Sample, Johnny, with Hamilton, Fred J., and Schwartz, Sonny. *Confessions of a Dirty Ballplayer*. New York, NY: Dell Publishing Co., 1970.

Schenkel, Chris. *How to Watch Football on Television*. New York, NY: The Viking Press, 1964, revised in 1965.

Smith, Red, with Anderson, Dave, editor. *The Red Smith Reader*. New York, NY: Random House, 1982.

Thorn, John, with Ruether, David, editors. *The Armchair Quarterback*. New York, NY: Charles Scribner's Sons, 1982.

Whittingham, Richard. *Rites of Autumn: The Story of College Football*. New York, NY: The Free Press, 2001.

Newspapers and Wire Services

Ada (OH) *Herald*
Arkansas Leader
Associated Press
Boston Globe
Daily Herald Suburban Chicago
Las Vegas Review-Journal
Los Angeles Times
Mansfield (OH) *News–Journal*

Miami News
Miami Times
Milwaukee Journal Sentinel
Moorhead Daily News
The Morning Journal & The News-Herald
Newsday
New York Times
Pittsburgh Post-Gazette
Portsmouth (OH) Times
San Francisco Chronicle
The Sporting News
St. Petersburg Times
Syracuse Herald
The Telegraph
Topeka Capital-Journal
Tucson Daily Citizen
Washington Post

Magazines

Harvard Magazine
Sports Illustrated
Time

Websites

AggieTraditions.tamu.edu
APvsChicago.com
BearReport.com
BigCatCountry.com
Blog.DetroitAthletic.com
BuffaloRumblings.com
BuffaloWins.com
Chargers.com
Chicago.CBSlocal.com
Chi.Scout.com
CommercialAppeal.com
DenverPost.com
ElevenWarriors.com

ESPN.com
ETSN.fm
EvanBrennan.com
Football.about.com
FootballBabble.com
FootballOutsiders.com
Grantland.com
Heisman.com
JimLightFootball.com
JohnTReed.com/fbdictionary.html
LandryFootball.com
MaxwellFootballClub.org
Mcall.com
Minnesota.247sports.com
MMQB.SI.com
NationalFootballPost.com
NBCsports.com
NewspaperArchive.com
NFLfilms.nfl.com
NFLPenalties.com
NYTimes.com
Packerville.blogspot.com
ProFootballDaly.com
ProFootballHOF.com
Pro-Football-Reference.com
ProFootballResearchers.org
ProFootballTalk.NBCSports.com
QuirkyResearch.blogspot.com
Raiders.com
RamblinWreck.com
SBnation.com
Seahawks.com
ShakintheSouthland.com
SmithsonianMag.com
SNLtranscripts.jt.org
SportsAttic.com
Sports.Yahoo.com
TheOnlyColors.com
TheUConnBlog.com

WFL.charlottehornetswfl.com
Wilson.com
WinningYouthFootball.com
YSUsports.com

ABOUT THE AUTHOR

Jesse Goldberg-Strassler attended middle school just down the street from FedEx Field in Prince George's County, Maryland. A graduate of Ithaca College, he now resides in Lansing, Michigan, where he broadcasts Lansing Lugnuts baseball, Central Michigan women's basketball, and Mid Michigan high school football. This is his second book, following *The Baseball Thesaurus*.